MW01291639

Vietnam

–Triumphs and Tragedies

Our Mission Story

By Ralph and Gladys Burcham

Xulon
PRESS

Vietnam–Triumphs and Tragedies
by Ralph and Gladys Burcham

Printed in the United States of America

ISBN 978-1-60266-586-6

www.xulonpress.com

CONTENTS

Acknowledgments... ix

Vietnam—"Our Motivation for Going"....................................13

Early Adjustments to Vietnam 23

The American-Vietnamese International School 57

The Vietnamese People..69

New Challenges to Life in Saigon in 1967 107

The Vietnamese Orphans 131

The American Servicemen 157

Vietnam—"I Shall Not Die" (The Tet Offensive)......................169

Back to Vietnam in 1969...199

Vietnam—Here We Come Again—
      An Unbelievable Summer 223

The Tragedy of South Vietnam 277

The Triumph of Some South Vietnamese 299

After the Fall of Vietnam 309

Overcoming Tragedies with Triumphs—
      "Making the Best of Trying Circumstances" 323

Appendix A—Tribute to a Missionary Wife by
      Ona Belknap..335

Appendix B—Sam's Family 15 Years after the Fall....................341

Appendix C—"The Path that Leads to Eternal Life" 345

Endorsements

"Ralph and Gladys, thank you for letting us read the Vietnam book. Other than the Bible, I cannot think of a book that has had such a profound affect on us. Thank you for sharing what you were thinking and for all the stories of how God worked in the lives of so many people. This should be required reading for those planning to be missionaries. I'm making a list of applications (things I learned) so I will not forget. Love, Steve and Gail Brookman." Brookman serves as an elder of the Memorial Road Church of Christ in Oklahoma City.

"Ralph and Gladys, I was really moved as I read this account of your experiences in Vietnam. This story needs to be told to as many as possible. May God continue to bless this experience as others read about your Kingdom service. Thanks for allowing me this opportunity. Joe McCormack." McCormack is a retired English Professor from Oklahoma Christian University and an elder at the Memorial Road Church of Christ in Oklahoma City, Oklahoma.

Acknowledgments

First, I could like to express appreciation to Beth Brewer and Joe McCormack for reading this book in its rough form, correcting my grammar, and making significant suggestions.

It is impossible to acknowledge everyone who made our mission work possible. I am always fearful of leaving out someone who made a major contribution; if I do, please forgive me.

Two ministers impacted my life in a most profound way. Raymond Kelcy, who loved and nurtured us, is responsible for my being at Oklahoma Christian and taught and baptized Gladys. K. C. Moser gave me new insights into the cross and the grace that God extends to us through His Son Jesus Christ and, thus, gave me a message to share.

I must credit the students at Oklahoma Christian College in Oklahoma City for providing the opportunity to learn about missions by encouraging me to attend their World Mission Workshop in 1963. It was at this workshop that I was challenged by Maurice and Marie Hall to consider Vietnam as a place where I could serve. It was the Halls who recruited and nurtured us into the mission field.

My wife, Gladys, gave her full support and helped me by teaching and acknowledging mountains of letters. Our children, Roger and Kathy, loved and encouraged me during trying times and taught children's classes.

Churches, Bible school classes, friends and family–all provided financial and loving support. Three congregations–North Park in Rockford and Brookfield in Chicago both in Illinois; and Tenth and Rockford in Tulsa, Oklahoma–made it possible for us to go by providing financial support. Ansel Worley served as the correspondent and he kept the elders informed and helped build trust in my decisions, even though I was a virtual stranger to two of these churches. I will sing his praises to my own grave. When we lost the use of the Hall's car, a long-time friend, Ida Deming, sent the funds for us to buy a Volkswagen bus.

Special credit goes to the Village Church of Christ in Oklahoma City who sponsored the orphan program and to the College Church of Christ in Oklahoma City who sponsored scores of Vietnamese refugees during the fall of South Vietnam.

Much credit for making our efforts known to our brotherhood and other newspapers goes to Ona Belknap. She served as an unofficial press corps and got our story and our needs out to people all across the United States. *The Christian Chronicle, The Firm Foundation, The Gospel Advocate, White's Ferry Road's Radio News, The Christian Woman, Jimmy Lovell's Action, The Rocky Mountain Christian, and The Daily Oklahoman*–all contributed to the success of our work. It is through Ona Belknap and the Sweet Publishing Company that I got a Press Card with all the privileges associated with it.

Howard and Mildred Horton came at just the right time to our mission. Howard provided love, nurture, and wisdom; truly God empowered him to wade through problems and embrace people with the love of Jesus Christ. His positive outlook–from his plane crash in Hong Kong to helping us escape during the Tet Offensive–gave me a new perspective of how God works through His servants.

I received encouragement, inspiration, and love from the dedicated teachers in the American-Vietnamese International School. Curt and Evelyn Accord, Patti Alley, Leecia Bruce, Gladys Burcham, Linda Carpenter, Judy Colvin, Gene and Nancy Conner, Jim and Betty Casey, Dick and Jennifer DiNucci, Arlen Ewing, Diane Powell, and Paulette Wright–all supported me and the mission in every way possible; some served for various periods of time. Not only did they teach academic subjects, they taught the Scriptures and lived the Christian life before their students and parents. All developed relationships with several Vietnamese; many are Christians today because of their work.

Others serving on the mission team at various times include Fred Ayers, Leonard and Dona Blake, Wayne and Charlotte Briggs, Phil Carpenter, Ron and Jeanette Cotton, Ron Matthews, Jim Powell, Jim Ridgeway, Dennis and Toni Rush, Dan and Lutricia Skaggs, Florence Vinyard, Don Wright, and Lynn Yocum.

Many civilian workers provided tremendous support, such as Bob and Chau Fairless, Fred Givens, and Owen Thomas. However, before the collapse of South Vietnam, God used Bill Estep and Mac LeDoux to help many Vietnamese escape. These men are the true heroes.

Tremendous credit goes to service men and women; this mission effort could not have occurred without their help. From the servicemen who started the church in Vietnam to those who supported it, I am humbled by their dedicated service to our nation and to God. It is impossible to recognize all of their efforts, but here are talents they used in the Lord's work: they faithfully attended worship services, many preached and taught Bible classes, several served as my mentors and provided encouragement, others started congregations, and many helped our orphanage. Some stand out as always being there to help: Paul Cook and Ralph Nichols–who kept my typewriter busy many hours every day; Gary Simpson, Johnny Everett and Fred Hall–who served as our guardian angels during the Tet Offensive; Jim Reynolds–who preached; also, Jim Hopkins, Billy W. Williams, Captain Meinert; Bob Hague, Fred Wiggins, Gordon Stalcup, and Don Yelton.

I will be forever indebted for the unbelievable support that came from the servicemen at Cat Lai Camp, who built our orphanage at their expense, equipped it, gave the children a Christmas party that none will forget, and provided medical and dental care for the orphans. Much credit belongs to Captain Andrean, who used the orphanage to improve the morale of his men.

Of course, the success of the work goes to the Vietnamese. I am indebted to all the Vietnamese who worked for the success of the mission: Tran Van Can, Nguyen Dan Bao, Nguyen Van Khanh, Vo Thanh Duc, Nguyen Van Ming, Nguyen Van Thuong, Nguyen Dang

Minh, and Y-Kim, the Montagnard. Because some of these still live under communism in Vietnam, it is necessary to change their names for fear of reprisals.

The chapter on events leading up to the fall of Vietnam provide vivid descriptions through the correspondence, telephone calls, and reporting of Bill Estep, Tran Van Can, and Vo Thanh Duc. Only God could make the deliverance possible for some of the faithful Vietnamese Christians and He sustained those left behind.

Truly a remarkable effort was made to reach the lost of Vietnam; but the real credit belongs to God, who gave guidance through His Word and answered prayers on His terms, and to Jesus Christ, who is the only Savior for the lost.

Vietnam—"Our Motivation for Going"

"For Christ's love compels us, because we are convinced that one died for all . . . . And he died for all, that those who live should no longer live for themselves but for him who died for them and was raised again. So from now on we regard no one from a worldly point of view . . . All this is from God, who reconciled us to himself through Christ and gave us the ministry of reconciliation: that God was reconciling the world to himself in Christ, not counting men's sins against them. And has committed to us the message of reconciliation. We are therefore Christ's ambassadors, as though God were making his appeal through us.
(2 Corinthians 5:14-16a, 18-20a, NIV)"

All my life I have been an educator. First, I taught in the Tulsa Public Schools and at the University of Tulsa in Oklahoma. Then I taught at the University of California in Los Angeles while working on a doctorate. Next, I went to Oklahoma Christian College in Oklahoma City where I taught Secretarial Science, Business Communications, and Computers. Because OC was a small private university, in its early days I did much of the school printing.

How God led my family to Vietnam.

The students at Oklahoma Christian impacted my life by their spiritual fervor. The students planning the 1963 World Mission

Workshop came to me and asked for help in printing their advertising and program. They said, "We know this will require a lot of extra time on your part but we would really appreciate your help."

I agreed and over the next few months I became close friends with this group. When it came time for the workshop, they invited me to attend. Out of courtesy to the group, I attended which changed my life forever.

During this workshop, I met Maurice and Marie Hall. Maurice, one of the keynote speakers, told in graphic terms the plight of the Vietnamese people. He opened up for me what is often referred to as the Great Commission "to go into all the world." At this workshop, the Halls first approached us to consider mission work in Vietnam.

How the Church of Christ got its beginning in Vietnam.

At the workshop, Hall explained that one of the amazing ways in which Christianity is spread throughout the world is by our servicemen. Our Christian servicemen start congregations in the most difficult areas. After World War II, the Halls and the Otis Gatewoods started mission efforts in Germany and France.

This is also true for the work in Vietnam. In 1960, American troops began to arrive in South Vietnam in greater numbers. Among them are a number of members of the Stateside Churches of Christ: from Midland, Texas, Navy Lieutenant Joe Hale, who managed the Navy Commissary; from Bakersfield, California, Sergeant Ken Wilson, a Military Attaché to the U. S. Embassy.

Lieutenant Hale held Sunday worship at his home. In the beginning, Vietnamese in attendance included friends of Lieutenant Hale and Sergeant Wilson and some other Christian GIs. One of the Vietnamese Lieutenant Hale came to know is Tran Van Can, who later became my interpreter, translator, and close personal friend. Tran, a talented linguist, worked as a translator for the American government. Captain Hale invited Tran to these services. Here he translated Lieutenant Hale's sermons into Vietnamese for the local audience.

In 1962, Lieutenant Hale returned to the States. Sergeant Wilson moved the worship services to his home. Because of the turnover of servicemen, the Vietnamese wanted a missionary family to give stability to the work; therefore, they suggested to Sergeant Wilson that he seek help from the States to invite a missionary family to Saigon. Later that year, Maurice and Marie Hall accepted the challenge by making a survey trip to Vietnam; they taught at Michigan Christian College. By 1963, the number of Vietnamese converts exceeded 20 persons.

In February 1964, Maurice and Marie Hall with their son Ronnie arrived in Saigon from Michigan. Philip Carpenter, a graduate from Michigan Christian, accompanied them. They made up the first full-time missionaries of the churches of Christ in South Vietnam. From that time on, the Halls kept us informed through their newsletters and personal letters on their work and how we could serve.

The Halls possess charismatic personalities. While serving as missionaries in France after World War II, they came to speak fluent French; they brought to Vietnam a rich background of experience. Their French allowed them to move freely among the educated and professionals of Vietnam, since it had been a former French colony. Because of their experience and background, they possessed the natural qualities to serve in Vietnam. Again, Tran Van Can, who also spoke French, assisted the Halls as a translator.

The Halls made a return trip to the States in 1965 to seek funds and recruit additional workers. During this visit, we made our commitment. Maurice convinced me that I could and should be an "ambassador for Christ in Vietnam." But I realized this commitment involved our whole family—Gladys, my wife, and our two children, Roger and Kathy. This commitment started an adventure that affects our lives up to the present moment.

I can remember how we planned to tell our parents. We thought carefully about our strategy. It so happened that my parents and Gladys' mother planned to visit us on the same weekend. While our mothers visited in the living room, Kathy, our eight year old, came in and said, "We are going to Vietnam; what do you think about that?" What a bombshell and not a part of our strategy!

My mother said, "Oh my, we can't let them do that, now can we?" as she looked at my mother-in-law. But something in her tone indicated the news did not come as a surprise.

My mother-in-law said, "They are over 21; I believe they have made up their minds. I believe about all we can do is give them our blessing!"

I thought, "Thank God for my mother-in-law."

When one of the local papers heard of our plans for Vietnam, their reporter asked us about the dangers of Vietnam and reminded us that one or all of us might never return from the war. I replied, "We have to go; we do not have to return." Gladys simply said, "We've tried to tell our children the worst that can happen."

However, we had weighed many "pros" and "cons" and spent much time in prayer before making the decision to reach out and serve the Vietnamese people. Our biggest obstacle concerned a sponsoring congregation and finances. We felt if we did not get support, this would be God's answer for us not to go. The Tenth and Rockford congregation in Tulsa, where Gladys had been baptized, offered to help on our monthly support. Raymond Kelcy, our minister in Tulsa, taught Gladys and nurtured us in our Christian walk and eventually encouraged me to teach at Oklahoma Christian.

Again, Maurice Hall came to our rescue; he had visited many churches with appeals for the work. Two congregations indicated to Maurice their desire to sponsor a missionary. Therefore, he put me in contact with Churches of Christ in Brookfield, a suburb of Chicago, and North Park in Rockford, Illinois. After meeting with both congregations, they decided that each would provide half of our support, not provided by Tenth and Rockford, with North Park in Rockford providing our guidance and direction. The two congregations asked Ansel Worley to be our correspondent. What a wonderful answer to many prayers!

When the students at Oklahoma Christian learned of our plans to go to Vietnam, I received much encouragement from them. The students put out a little publication called, "Arise." They dedicated to me one of their issues in "Soldiers of Christ Arise," which touched me deeply.

They wrote: "What man can really know the value of a godly life? It shines into corners and crevices that the source itself never contacts. Even though never actually sitting in his classroom, nor contacting him directly, almost every student at Oklahoma Christian will, in some manner, be influenced by the Christian example of Ralph Burcham. His influence is felt in many spheres because of his many and varied activities on behalf of the Lord; for example, he is a deacon in the church, the director of a Christian camp, a worker in the poverty-stricken slums area of Oklahoma City, a sponsor on Mission Workshop trips, a counselor of young Christians, and a Bible class instructor.

"His refusal to allow Christianity to exist simply as a doctrine without making it a life has pointed the way for students and challenged them to a greater commitment to Christ. Christ on the cross has become real to him, so he strives to impart this spirit to his associates.

"In a recent giant step for the Father, Burcham committed himself to work in Saigon, Vietnam. Hardly a man would be more abundantly qualified to serve the Lord in such a difficult field. His example of dedication and love for the Master and for fellow men will be missed at OC, but his willingness to step forward on a working faith will be an influence for many hundreds of young people.

"To this man of God, we proudly dedicate this issue of Arise!" When the students presented this issue to me, I felt maybe God could use our experiences in Vietnam to further His purposes in Christian education.

Some of our friends and loved ones thought I had lost my mind to take a family into a war-torn country as American military dependents had been evacuated earlier in the summer. But the Maurice Halls' faith in Christ and their desire to share God's love with the lost in a war-torn country moved us to take seriously the command to go into all the world with the good news of a Savior.

Without a doubt, we believe God called us to share the Good News of Christ with a people who had struggled for so long for political freedom; yet, we believe the inner struggle for every person is for spiritual fulfillment. It is good that God allows us to live a day at a time without knowing what the future holds. Yet, we knew, without a doubt, who holds the future!

With OC granting a leave, funds raised, our house rented, shots taken, passports and visas obtained, we made our first overseas flight to Vietnam.

What a day, our family is introduced to Vietnam.

I remember that unforgettable day—August 21, 1966–when my family and I arrived in Saigon, Vietnam, about 12:30 noon on a hot August day, but then we soon learned that all days are hot in Saigon. Just one long hot spell—six months of those are very, very wet and the others very, very dry. Yet, in the high country of the north, the nights can be bitter cold in mile-high mountains. In the more temperate climate in central Vietnam in the Da Lat area, beautiful flowers and vegetables are grown commercially.

Thirteen of us arrived at the International Terminal in Saigon, which boosted the total to 32 missionaries. A host of people welcomed us with a large banner. Those welcoming us included several other missionaries and servicemen. Somehow the welcome from the servicemen made us feel secure in our decision to serve in this war-torn country.

As we left the air terminal and drove down Cong Ly, a main thoroughfare, the masses of people engulfed us riding motorcycles, pedicabs, cyclos, small taxies, bicycles, ox carts, small horse-drawn wagons, military vehicles of all sorts—all seemed to crowd in from every direction as we traveled from the airport to the place where we would stay the next few weeks.

In the heart of Saigon, I looked at the masses of people; some wore western wear, some looked charming in their national dress, and some wore military uniforms. Our curiosity teased us by the open markets, flower shops, sidewalk food vendors, and little stalls filled with all kinds of enticing merchandise. Many of these little merchants barely eked out a living. We saw people in every walk of life from beggars rummaging through garbage piles to orphans selling most anything for money while others had the appearance of material prosperity; but I felt all had to be searching for the real meaning of life. I prayed for God to use me in bringing hope and love to those seeking a better way of life.

Our initial culture shock came during our first worship service in Saigon.

Since we arrived on Sunday, we heard our first sermon interpreted into the Vietnamese language. Because of an early curfew, the service started at 4 p.m. Maurice Hall had invited many guests, and the assembly room overflowed with Vietnamese, servicemen, and American missionaries. Deeply moved by the beautiful singing, it reminded me of a tape we had received earlier with Vietnamese singing "I Surrender All." The haunting melody and words of this song made me ask, "Can I surrender all?"

Two in the audience would come to impact our mission efforts: an elder from the Halls' sponsoring congregation and with him a missionary from another country. The visiting missionary spoke at the service; as he spoke, it became evident he had an agenda. During the two-hour service, he criticized the housing arrangements the Halls had made for those of us who had just arrived. The Halls had obtained small apartments in one small building. With great emphasis, he said: "I know you Vietnamese would like to see these missionaries in your neighborhoods. As it is, they are all in one place. This is just like a pile of manure in the corner of the garden. As long as it is in a pile, it does nothing but stink, but spread it out over the garden and the whole garden benefits."

During this tirade, I glanced at Marie, who looked ashen and embarrassed. She had worked so hard in order to make our transition to Vietnam a good experience. My feelings: "What a terrible way to treat a gracious lady who worked so diligently for all of us who had just arrived."

When the speaker finished, I wanted to get on the next plane back to the U. S. After the service, Maurice introduced me to many of the guests, mainly professional people from Saigon. The guests made such a wonderful impression. But I wondered how all the guests felt about this service.

I made an appointment with the guest speaker for the next morning. At that time, I expressed my disappointment in his pronouncements. I said, "Some of your remarks could have been helpful in a private meeting with the missionary team."

He replied, "You're just a green bean on the mission field and don't know which way is up."

I agreed with his assessment of me, but I objected strongly to the appropriateness of the remarks to a general audience with many guests.

This attack on the Halls had a chilling effect on our mission because Maurice and Marie had recruited all. Most supported the Halls but a few sided with the visiting missionary. The events that followed put all of us under a great deal of stress.

Many evidences pointed to the war around us.

The soldiers on the streets and the military vehicles made us mindful of the war. This really came home to us during our first night—the padlocked gate and locks on the outside and inside doors to the house; the flares giving off an eerie light; and the sounds of shelling several kilometers outside the city.

The events of this first day made me wonder if I had made a mistake to bring my family into this situation; this thought kept cropping up in my thinking.

At night, the flat roof of our temporary residence often seemed to invite us to watch the flares as they illuminated the city. Occasionally, we saw planes strafing with machine gun fire and napalm some distance from the city. The released napalm left streaks of liquid fire. We knew the military to be trying to keep the VC (Vietnamese Communists or Viet Cong) from moving in closer. These constant reminders made the war very near.

Maurice and Marie Hall provide loving nurture in our adjustments.

Prior to our arrival, Marie Hall, along with some servicemen, worked diligently in getting together the essentials to set up housekeeping for each of the new missionary families. She worked tire-lessly in helping us adjust to Vietnam.

As a part of our orientation, the Halls took us for a ride out of Saigon. We crossed the huge bridge on the Bien Hoa highway. This area—never safe at night—but, oh, so beautiful during the day. We saw a long row of women setting out rice plants in water-filled paddies. They seemed to do this in cadence; their finished work had the appearance of being done by machine. As we looked toward the horizon, we could see rice paddies in the various stages of growth. From recent rains, everything looked so clean with a bright blue sky above. Flowers, too, took on brilliant colors. Everything seemed so peaceful.

About half way to Bien Hoa, we passed jeeps assembling for a convoy. The lead jeep loaded with American GI's flagged us down. Immediately your heart went out to them. They jumped out of their jeep, poked their heads in each window of the car and with unbe-lief said, "What are you doing out here?" Being the first American civilians they had seen in months, it seemed hard for them to accept that we came by choice. They explained they were on their way up country to be replacements in one of the battle zones.

One looked at our children and, with a catch in his breath, explained, "You are the first American children I have seen in eleven months. If I can make it just one more month, I'll be returning home." He seemed so overjoyed to see us he jokingly wanted to take us along. He told Kathy that she could ride on top of his jeep along-side his machine gun. He had been in several battles and seemed to be dreading the battle ahead. I felt sadness just thinking about what might happen to him.

When the convoy had fully assembled, the GIs headed north into the hills and battle. We had a good visit, but they warned us not to go farther; we turned around and went back to Saigon. For the moment, these men moved me deeply because they so wanted to bring peace to Vietnam at the risk of their lives.

Over time many of the GIs shared with us their personal strug-gles from being away from family and friends. But in spite of their personal struggles, all felt extremely loyal to our country, and they so wanted to see peace and freedom come to the Vietnamese.

The servicemen treated us royally and played a significant role in encouraging our work , particularly, when the war came into Saigon. What an example they set for me! Since they risked all for physical freedom, dare I not face risks to bring spiritual freedom?

The people of Vietnam possess many ethnic and religious backgrounds. The Vietnamese make up the largest segment of the population; though there are a large number of Chinese—in Saigon many are concentrated in a subdivision called Cholon. The religious backgrounds include Buddhists, Confucians, Muslims, Catholics, Taoists, Christian Protestants, and a religion called Cao Dai, which is composed of many of these. In the mountain areas, there are the Montagnards, who are known for their honesty. We would later come to love and appreciate a Montagnard, Y-Kim, one of the finest young men I have ever known.

Somehow I wanted to share Christ with those who had suffered oppression for so long. In following Christ's instructions in Matthew 28:19-20, I wanted to begin with teachings about Him. The Apostle Paul is my missionary hero; therefore, I will begin by following his example of preaching and teaching Christ ". . .not with words of human wisdom, lest the cross of Christ be emptied of its power. . . . For I resolved to know nothing while I was with you except Jesus Christ and him crucified. (I Corinthians 1:16; 2:2, NIV)"

As I looked into the faces of the Vietnamese, I knew God had a love for them and desired a relationship with each one; can He use me in being an ambassador, a reconciler? My prayer is that God will use me in touching lives with His Good News of life eternal in His Son, Jesus Christ. "And this is the testimony: God has given us eternal life, and this life is in his Son. He who has the Son has life; he who does not have the Son of God does not have life. (I John 5:11,12, NIV)" This provided the motivation for the challenges we faced.

Early Adjustments to Vietnam

"This is the day the Lord has made; let us rejoice and be glad in it."

Psalm 118:24, NIV

During the night of August 31, our first real feeling of fear griped us. Awakened by a racket in the street about 2 a.m., neither of us seemed interested in going out to look. We read in the paper the next morning that an American had been attacked and stabbed about a block from where we lived. He had not been hurt badly; it seemed this had to do with the unrest related to the coming election.

Adapting to cultural differences in Saigon required patience.

It takes time to fit into another culture. Life in Vietnam seemed to be filled with daily surprises. Having been reared in the open areas of Oklahoma, I missed the space. Because of the war, thousands of people sought refuge within the security area of Saigon, boosting the population to around three million. The scarce housing came at a premium. Thousands lived in small shacks built on stilts over water that flowed in and out from the ocean tide. These shacks attached to each other—back to back–and separated by a small board walk just wider than a bicycle so people could move freely and keep their bikes indoors. Also, land along the train tracks provided space for a shack. Squatters built small shacks wherever a place could be found.

Of course, those living above the river, or squatters, bathed in water carried in; often we saw children bathing at fire hydrants; many used the ocean water for their bathroom. As Roger put it, "God has blessed these people with a toilet that flushes each time the tide goes out."

As Gladys observed, "It's hard to get used to seeing mothers bathing their children on the sidewalk by the public street. And all those bare bottoms!" None of the babies or small ones wore diapers—just skirts or pants with a slit in the back. Even adults used the great outdoors for the restroom if the call came. It took some time before our children discovered that men standing next to a wall were not painting it. About this Gladys wrote,

> "The culture here is quite a shock,
> It'll knock you off your feet;
> They eat, and play, and urinate,
> And bathe out on the street."

When she wrote this, I said, "Is this something you want to write back home? Maybe use a 'word' not quite so blunt!" She replied with a footnote: "Ralph tried to think of a word less crude, but I told him that if we see it all the time, surely they can read about it!"

Then we read in the local newspaper about the police cracking down on those going to the restroom in public. Given cameras, the policemen made pictures of guilty parties; the article indicated anyone caught would be fined.

However, the policemen lost their cameras about as fast as they got the order. Investigation found only one public rest room in Saigon. And for three million people that helps very little. "It is *public*, too!" As Gladys viewed the situation, "I've walked downtown; and I always look straight ahead and walk fast past that public restroom. In fact, about two days after the police got the order, I could have taken a picture of a guilty policeman had I had my camera."

Cultural differences provide daily surprises. Most of the Vietnamese prepare their food in one corner of their kitchen, which they keep as clean as any cabinet counter. Sometimes they use a cutting board. They squat on the floor and chop their meat and vegetables there. One day Marie Hall came home to find her maid in the corner of the kitchen preparing food on the floor. She kindly told her the food should be prepared on the cabinet. When Marie came the next day, she found the maid, squatting on the cabinet preparing our food.

Time moves at a different pace in Saigon. Business endeavors and life come to a halt at noon. The people observed siesta time from twelve until two o'clock or so. Just after our arrival, we visited an office at noon. We saw one secretary curled around her desk sleeping peacefully. Others stretched out on chairs or on the floor enjoying a nap.

Life stops at siesta time. Gladys expressed her feelings: "Americans need to look into some of these customs." It took me some time to learn that you cannot schedule anything during siesta. But their siesta time made so much sense because the people start their day very early and take time off during the heat of the day to rest. Gladys said, "Perhaps this is a custom we need to adopt!"

In Oklahoma, we always start conversations about the weather. In Vietnam, we never heard anyone mention the temperature. We asked one day and a Vietnamese explained, "Most do not worry about the heat; they can take that; their concern is for their next meal."

Everywhere we turned we could hear people talking and the noise of busy streets. Beggars crowded us on every corner. Their pitiful look made us want to cry. The orphans, or young people separated from their parents by the war, seemed to be everywhere. Later, the constant reminder of the plight of these children moved me into action.

Sometimes I felt overwhelmed by the events of a single day. For example, one of our missionary friends, Lynn Yocum, invited me to go downtown in a borrowed car. The torrents of rain filled the streets. The fuel line on the car broke and the gas caught on fire. As the water swept under the car, the fire floated under it. We jumped out of the car and tried to push it out of fire's way. We succeeded; but we looked like a couple of drowned rats.

Bicycle and motorcycle accidents are quite common. Many of them are fatal. One morning on our way to school, we saw a dead man on the street and his body covered with newspapers. But, as Kathy said, "It takes all the joy out of you." Another time, we saw a motorcyclist try to cut in front of a large military truck; his motorcycle struck the side of the truck and threw him in the path of the back wheel. For someone, who had never witnessed a death, I found it awesome to see one on the street killed, which served as a reminder of the brevity of life and our limited time in bringing the lost to Christ. In all, we shall never forget the twelve or so we saw lose their lives.

What we did to meet our health needs.

Before leaving the States, our family doctor encouraged us to take all the shots suggested for our military. Therefore, we took shots for the plague, yellow fever, cholera, typhus, typhoid, diphtheria, and tetanus; Gladys's brother, who is a medical doctor, recommended Gamma Globulin shots which can give additional resistance while adjusting to a new country; these are given by weight. Being the heaviest, I got a shot in each hip and each shoulder. The family thought it amusing that I wanted to stand most of that first evening; these shots gave us such a boost that of the new arrivals only we did not get sick the first few days in Saigon. Some of the shots had to be repeated every six months. In addition, we took a malaria pill each week.

To avoid amoeba, Gladys boiled water each day for 45 minutes; then it had to drain through a charcoal filter system. It is amazing how much water it takes for drinking, cooking, and brushing teeth.

I felt sorry for Roger because he frequently suffered with a sty on his eye or eyes, probably caused from a polluted air virus. He faced these bravely and I tried to humor him at such times. But in spite of his eye problem, he frequently provided comic relief as he possessed the ability to imitate the speech of almost anyone.

Learning to shop required special finesse.

In order to set up housekeeping in a new location, everyone must learn where to buy food and household items. Marie Hall, who had been on the field for some time, took Gladys and Kathy for an orientation to the markets and the Vietnamese way of bargaining.

"Bargaining" is foreign to our Western way of doing things (except when buying a car!). There is an art to "bargaining" and it takes time to do it well. Marie introduced Gladys to some of the merchants she visited on a regular basis. Marie took Gladys to see a French lady, who raised chickens and sold eggs; she felt these safer than buying eggs at the market. Accustomed to buying eggs in a carton, we found it so different to see eggs stacked on each other in large baskets; in fact, we often saw someone on a bicycle with a basketful of eggs or chickens tied to the handlebars.

It soon became evident that Kathy fascinated the people. They wanted to touch, pinch, and feel this eight-year-old with light brown hair, blue-eyes, and a white complexion. Her features contrasted with the dark hair and eyes and beautiful, natural tan of the Vietnamese. Most all called her Number One. We soon learned that the Vietnamese rated people from Number One to Ten; ten being the worst.

The Vietnamese children amused us. When we walked down the street, most of them looked up and said, "Hello." Then we looked at them and said, "Oh, you speak very good English." They smiled and said, "Okay." That's probably the only two words they knew.

Since Vietnamese ready-made clothing did not fit us, Gladys found a tailor who made dresses for her and Kathy. Also, the tailor made a Vietnamese dress for Kathy. This dress is so becoming and is called an "Ao Dai." This outfit consists of silk trousers under a long-sleeve, ankle length dress with a slit on both sides from the waist to the shoes. While riding their bikes, a group of schoolgirls wearing the "Ao Dai" look like butterflies with their skirts fluttering in the wind. Many of the Ao Dais are silk with beautiful embroidery down the front.

The Central Market contained many surprises.

Since Gladys planned to teach in the school where our children would attend and while she made preparations for its opening, I took the children shopping. They loved every minute of it. Fascinated by the big Central Market, they enjoyed looking at the merchandise in each small stall. The vegetables looked so tasty; but the fruit stands with unfamiliar fruits seemed to be inviting us to give them a try.

The fresh pork, beef, water buffalo—hanging by hooks from a crossbeam above the stall or spread out on tables—introduced us to the world of un-refrigerated meat. Other sights caught our attention: dressed preserved ducks hanging grotesquely above the stalls; live chickens with legs tied; bushels of eggs; dried fish; stalls filled with beautiful fabrics and silks from all over the orient; beautiful hand embroidery and crochet; hardware; lacquered pictures with mother-of-pearl inlays; bronze artifacts for every occasion; and vases so artfully handcrafted by the Vietnamese.

Later, we discovered the fish market; the air reeked with unfamiliar odors; our Roger put it succinctly with "Dad, do you know what travels faster than the speed of sound?"

"No!"

"It is the smell of the fish market." We were not the only ones to cover our noses with a hanky!

Gladys put it this way: "It's something else to be in a traffic jam by the fish market, and this has happened to us several times. The odor is so strong; you want to move on as quickly as possible."

Not only did we hurry by the fish market, we rushed past the garbage heaps every few blocks. When you have three million people living in a small area, there are mountains of garbage, not in plastic bags; it is difficult for the city to remove this promptly, particularly if the dumpsite area is under attack by the Viet Cong. Of course, rats found a good food supply at these raw garbage heaps; once we even saw a man skinning a rat to be eaten.

Our children's greatest thrill came as we walked through the Pet Market. Here little shops and sidewalk vendors enticed our children with monkeys, guinea pigs, snakes, puppies, and yellow-orange kittens painted with black spots to look like baby leopards. Some of the snakes included huge boas crated to send to zoos all over the world; the boas could swallow a whole guinea pig or chicken in one gulp. However, Kathy found four pets "that I must have"; I knew this would soon require some fast-talking.

Both Kathy and Roger made me promise to return for the purchase of a pet as soon as we got our permanent residence. I felt this had to be a priority as the Hall's son, Ronnie, spent a lot of time playing with his pet monkey. Not knowing how destructive a monkey can be until we lived with Ronnie's, I promised our children a monkey. With a change of mind, I persuaded them for a different kind of pet.

A short time after our arrival, I started to realize how much our children had sacrificed in order for us to serve the Vietnamese people. Kathy loved her Chihuahua, named Frosty, who always slept with her. She left it back home with friends. When Kathy got lonesome for Frosty, the tears flowed. Gladys reminded me that we had to get her a puppy soon.

While looking for a place to buy Bibles, I found a Christian bookstore with beautifully illustrated children's books. Roger and Kathy spent a great deal of time reading.

Looking for a place to live;
a place became available in an unexpected way.

For the first several days in Saigon, we searched for a place to live. The landlord, where the Halls lived, increased the rent so much they, also, had to move. They found a place. A Vietnamese General owned the townhouse. On a dead end street, it seemed safe because of the high wall at the end.

We helped the Halls move. Being recalled by their supporting church in the States, the Halls started making plans to leave Vietnam. This unexpected turn of events served as a crushing emotional blow to a wonderful Christian lady. Our bedroom being next to the Halls, we could hear Marie lament what had happened. Eventually she required hospitalization.

Therefore, the Halls turned their place over to us with all of its furnishings including a gas stove, washer, and refrigerator. Included with the bargain was their large watch dog "Cindy." Also, they gave us the use of their car. Since they used their personal funds or raised the funds to purchase these items while in Vietnam, they felt they had the right to give or sell their possessions.

In front of the townhouse, the small, enclosed yard had a concrete wall with broken glass on top and rows of barbed wire above; we gained entrance to the yard and house by a large gate wide enough for a car; the tiled, paved driveway led into an attached garage. The walled back yard had a higher wall with broken glass embedded in the concrete with barbed wire on top. Concrete covered the small back yard, which had a drain for disposing of water from laundry or rains. It also contained a water storage tank. A pump carried the water to a storage tank on the roof and the water in the house moved through the lines by gravity.

Our children wanted to make a return visit to the Pet Market.

As soon as we settled in, I knew we had to revisit the pet market. I took Roger and Kathy for each to select a pet.

Kathy found a little brown dog about the size of her Frosty. The vendor told us it wouldn't get big, but time will tell. Honesty is not one of the known characteristics of the street vendors. However, Kathy made the purchase and named the dog "Henry."

It soon became evident that Henry liked Kathy the best of all. As Roger said, "Doesn't that just beat you!" Of course, Roger liked to tease! Henry would run towards Roger, who would spread his legs and Henry would slide on the tile floors trying to stop before hitting the wall.

Our watchdog, Cindy, blessed us with pups. Of course, Kathy wanted to keep them all; however, after weaning, we gave all but one away.

Roger decided on a pair of parrots and purchased a bamboo cage to keep them in. What a surprise! Roger named them Pete and Gladys. Soon after we got home, the parrots pealed the bamboo and got out. In trying to catch them, I grabbed one by the neck; it grabbed me by the finger. Its vice-like grip shot a terrible pain; I started choking the parrot to get it to turn loose while the kids screamed, "Don't kill it." He finally let go. I'm not a slow learner as I threw a towel over the second one to catch it.

I instructed Roger to take wire and weave it around the cage to hold those birds. Roger did a good job; however, in a day or two we heard the parrots squawking and flying against the wall. I sent Roger back to the pet market for a better cage. He got one with strong wire.

But the parrots soon learned they could pull the bars apart and get out. Roger again rewired the cage.

The parrots provided entertainment for a time. Then they got out again and started flying and hitting the ceiling. Soon Pete flew against the wall and it ended his escapes. Then Mom persuaded Roger that "Gladys" being so lonesome needed to be set free to return to the jungles. They had been so troublesome that Roger seemed glad to abide.

Gladys began a war on cockroaches and accepted the things she could not change.

Some things are difficult to accept. Cockroaches seemed to be in every nook and cranny of the kitchen, garage, and back yard. Not the little ones we had known but cockroaches big enough to spring a mouse trap. As Gladys wrote in her journal: "Ralph sets my mouse traps every night, and we have cleared out many mice. One morning I got up and found a lizard in one. That wasn't what I was aiming for. And almost every night, we catch a cockroach in one. I am not from Texas; but, I'm here to say, these cockroaches are big. Kathy's little dog, Henry, loved to catch one and then take him apart piece by piece." So Gladys declared war on the little critters; she sprayed, put everything in sealed jars, and kept the critters on the move. Each time she would go through her little routine–to stamp out the cockroaches–our maid simply smiled.

The agile rats harassed us from their home in the drain in the backyard. They seemed to dare us "catch us if you can." They multiply in spite of traps and poison.

Around the ceiling small lizards darted to and fro. The lizards' skin seemed transparent as you could see its bone structure. But we soon learned these are friends because they thrive by catching mosquitoes or other flying or crawling insects.

The townhouse had high ceilings with fans in most rooms. Screens, shutters, and bars covered our windows with no glass in them. We had fluorescent lights. The electricity could not be fully depended on in the evenings; therefore, we had to turn the lights on early to be sure the power to be strong enough to engage the starter switches.

Often we had no electricity. At such times, we used three kerosene lamps and candles. Gladys said, "Dinner by candlelight is *not* romantic!" This reminded us of our youth when we lived on farms without electricity. Gladys put it this way: "I'm not sentimental so the lamps don't do a thing for me." But we learned to live with lamps again; however, Roger and Kathy seem to enjoy them. Over time, we used a lot of kerosene.

Maurice Hall asked me to take on overwhelming responsibilities.

During the Halls' final days in Saigon, Maurice spent a great deal of time turning over much of the mission work to me. This involved a weekly radio program, arranging for the translation and printing of materials in the Vietnamese language, the administration of the school, and the teaching of many Bible students.

"Overwhelming" cannot begin to describe my struggles since the Halls recruited us, and we had come to work with them. I explained to Maurice how inadequate I felt to take on such responsibility. He encouraged me by saying "God will provide."

Needed help cane with a most capable maid.

When the Halls left, fortunately we got one of their maids. Chi Hai served us well. She served as a protector of our place during the day, helped with laundry, cleaned house, shopped at the market, and cooked.

Kathy had a fun time going to the market with Chi Hai, who showed her fondness for Kathy in so many ways; it soon became evident why certain foods always seemed to appear on our menu. Also, Chi Hai helped Kathy develop her bargaining skills.

Servicemen provided constant encouragement and advice.

The servicemen took a special interest in our children. Kathy loved to ride a cyclo, which is a motorized pedicab. The passengers ride in front, where the action is, with the driver behind. Somehow she could persuade the driver to go faster by pretending to be holding the throttle on the handlebars and making a roaring sound. Frequently, after a church service, she persuaded a serviceman to take her home on a cyclo; also, she enjoyed another bonus as they often stopped by the USO for ice cream.

The servicemen provided excellent advice, which I always tried to follow. However, early on, one serviceman came up to me and said, "You can't trust any Vietnamese. You need to exercise extreme caution around any Vietnamese." I replied, "This is good for the military. But as a missionary, I can't be suspicious of every one I meet. I believe this will create a barrier that will be easily detected. I will need to trust everyone unless their behavior proves otherwise."

But I came to appreciate what the serviceman said because the Viet Cong used women and children for suicide missions. Also, the VC tried to permeate every element of society.

I asked a Vietnamese: "How is it possible for the Viet Cong to recruit children for suicide missions?"

He replied, "Often these are recruited in small villages or rural areas. Many of these are uneducated and have never had any form of public recognition. When the Viet Cong are recruiting, they hold up the parents and honor them for their willingness to make a sacrifice for freedom and patriotism. They commend the family publicly and hold up the volunteer as a 'hero.'"

My response "Do they get any recruits for these suicide missions?"

He replied, "They get more volunteers than they are able to use."

Somehow I wanted to interject a different worldview into the hearts of the Vietnamese. I wanted them to know Jesus, be a spokesman for Him, and become living sacrifices in reaching their fellow countrymen with true peace. I kept searching their history for a better understanding of their cultural heritage.

Understanding the Vietnamese required me to delve into their historical background, which gave me an appreciation for the struggle going on for the minds of the Vietnamese.

Vietnam is an ancient country with a proud history and quaint traditions going back many centuries. After having been ruled by China for a thousand years, Vietnam gained its independence in 939 A.D. The Vietnamese lost their freedom when the French took over Indochina in the latter part of the 19th Century. The French captured Saigon in 1859. It became a part of the French empire by treaties signed in 1862 and 1874.

The French did not build up a system of public education for the masses but a system of private schools often owned and run by the French. It became advantageous to the French to keep the people backward and submissive; they exploited their natural resources.

However, the French developed Saigon into a beautiful resort area with tree-lined boulevards and parks. Beautiful villas looked out on the colorful parks and boulevards.

Then the Japanese occupied Vietnam in 1940 and used her resources in conquering most of Southeast Asia. Vietnam possessed great natural resources–large ports, miles of sandy beaches, the river delta's rich soil allowed the production of large quantities of rice and other agricultural fruits, and the rivers and ocean swarmed with all kinds of fish and exotic sea foods. But its greatest resource is an intelligent, gentle, polite people with all kinds of artistic talents.

The British and Americans recaptured Vietnam from the Japanese and returned the country to the French.

Strong Vietnamese leaders in the North expressed the feelings of many by saying "We are an ancient people and we should not be under the domination of any foreign power." Nationalism combined with communism, under the leadership of Ho Chi Minh, rejected the French rule. Therefore, their war with the French started in 1946 and ended in 1954 with the defeat of the French at Dien Bien Phu.

The Geneva Agreement divided the country at the Seventeenth Parallel, separating the communist North from the freedom-seeking people of the South. As the communists gained control of the armed forces in the North, peace was short lived. The communists outlawed religion, eliminated private ownership of property, and took over the family as everything belonged to the state.

In 1954, before the closing of the borders between north and south, the Vietnamese voted with their feet by going to the South. Many of those I came to know once lived in North Vietnam.

Refugees started fleeing the north by the hundreds of thousands to escape the communists, who would enslave their bodies, minds, and souls. Most left their possessions behind in the North as they could take with them only what they could hand carry. Over a million went South and it is estimated that another two to three million tried to escape. People living in the South had the privilege of going to the North; however, most stayed in the South. The war changed to guerrilla tactics as the communists moved to control all of Indochina.

The Wandering Souls' Day gave us our first glimpse into different holidays.

Not only is their history significant for understanding their mind set but also their holidays. Each holiday in Vietnam carries with it special traditions and many myths because these have been around for centuries. The first holiday after our arrival the Vietnamese recognize as "The day for all the departed to return to visit their ancestors." According to their traditions, both good and evil spirits make an annual return to earth. The good spirits belong to those who lived a good life; these spirits bring good fortune to their families. The evil spirits belong to those drowned, orphans, or prostitutes; they are responsible for accidents, disease, and all kinds of misfortune.

This holiday season begins on the last full moon of August and lasts until the middle of September. In each household, the women prepare special foods—roasted head of pig, sticks of sugar cane, sweet pork, bowls of rice, and rice alcohol. These foods are offered up to the spirits. On certain days, stores and offices are closed.

Our first medical scare provided insights on available help.

Many in our mission taught at the American-Vietnamese International School where our children attended and where Gladys taught. The school is in another chapter.

About a month after the opening of school, Gladys developed a sore thumb that kept her from sleeping. She went to school; but as the day wore on, the pain increased. When school turned out, she went over to the 17th Field Hospital.

The doctor indicated she had an abscess and blood poisoning; he lanced it; and said "This is something we treat regularly on soldiers who come in from the field; I think it is caused by some kind of an insect bite. You need to come back tomorrow and let me check it again." Gladys assured the good doctor that she had not been out in the field. However, this experience gave us some security in knowing we could go to the military hospital when needed.

Our first formal Chinese dinner introduced us to many professional leaders working in Vietnam.

One of the patrons, who had four daughters in the school, wanted to express their appreciation for our opening the school. The Paul Wongs invited all the teachers to their home for dinner. In addition to the teachers, the Wongs invited ambassadors and financial leaders.

They put me as guest of honor at one table and Gladys as the honoree at another. The settings on the tables included their finest crystal, silver, and china. Their Chinese dinner consisted of 12 to 14 courses; six of these were different meats. We ate the delicious food with chopsticks even though some of us seemed a bit clumsy. The dinner lasted for almost three hours.

What an occasion! The Wong's beautiful mansion with construction to withstand heavy shelling impressed all of us.

Challenging Bible classes provided excitement to our mission.

At the conclusion of our first worship service, Maurice Hall announced that I could be available to teach free Bible classes in English. The response amazed me as I found myself filling in my day-timer. I tried to schedule classes in the mornings while Gladys and the children attended school. However, I soon found it necessary to offer classes in the afternoons and evenings and sometimes on Saturdays.

Early in October, I advertised in newspapers—two Chinese and one Vietnamese–for free Bible classes to be taught in English. At first, I tried to schedule these studies for one-on-one teaching. However, each one invited friends and soon these studies grew from one student to twenty-five.

With the group and the one-on-one classes, I often studied with over 60 people in a day. I soon had so many students that I could not give the personal attention I thought each person needed. Therefore, I gave some of these studies to others of our missionary team or to servicemen. These studies are in another chapter.

Somehow I wanted each student to know that the God who gives life, loves each one, and is concerned about every person. Like the writer John, I wanted people to see the miracles as proof that Jesus is the Messiah, the Son of God; and those who put their faith and trust in Him will experience eternal life (John 20:30-31).

How God provided for our greatest needs!

At the request of the Halls, we packed their personal items and stored them in our garage. Not long after the Halls left, their sponsoring congregation asked us to turn the car, the refrigerator, washer, gas range, a fan, and a bed over to another of the missionaries they planned to sponsor. This left us without transportation and no place to cook and store food. It meant that Gladys and Chi Hai had to do the laundry by hand. Though disappointed, I asked the Lord for guidance, as the mission effort could not afford to get bogged down in petty things.

I wrote to the Halls' sponsoring congregation and offered to cooperate in any way I could. In return, I received a terse reply. I found it difficult to understand their hostile feelings. Their attacks directed toward me and the Halls became brotherhood knowledge because of their widely published newsletter, which had a large circulation. This required me to spend many hours in answering their charges with my sponsoring congregation. Also, many individuals and churches wrote me about their concern for the Halls and wanting to know what happened. Though I felt an obligation to answer all letters, I found myself resenting the wasted time which I felt could have been more profitably spent in visiting in homes, preparing sermons, classes, and materials for translation.

For our first few months in Vietnam, the personal attacks toward myself became more vicious. The Halls former supporting congregation sent a registered letter to be read before the congregation indicating I did not represent them in any way (this I had never claimed). I felt the devil to be having a "heyday" in keeping me from my main mission of reaching the lost.

As we dealt with these personal attacks, Ansel Worley, the correspondent for our sponsoring congregations, encouraged us regularly. He kept the elders informed on our work; made reports to the congregation; gave us sound advice; and managed our work funds and personal finances. No missionary ever had a better correspondent. Also, his wife, Gloria, encouraged us with meaningful expressions of their love for us and for the work. Two of the elders, Noel W. Cannon and Allen McCord, wrote personal letters encouraging us: "Brother Burcham, our prayers at North Park are with you at all times. I'm a strong believer in prayer and the strength of prayer. Keep up the good work and keep your spirits up. . . ."

Later the entire eldership of the Brookfield congregation wrote: "Words cannot express strongly enough the confidence and faith we have in you and in your ability for making right decisions. We have never had any doubts concerning you and every time we correspond our love for you grows stronger. We continually pray that you will be able to bear up under the hardships that have been placed in your path." The letter was signed by three elders: R. E. Albright, Will Wright, and J. N. Baker.

Truly, we felt the strength of prayers from Godly men.

Though I had many mature advisors among our servicemen, I still felt angry and betrayed. I needed divine assistance. Then I read: "In your anger do not sin. Do not let the sun go down while you are still angry, and do not give the devil a foothold . . . Get rid of all bitterness, rage and anger, brawling and slander, along with every form of malice. Be kind and compassionate to one another, forgiving each other, just as in Christ God forgave you. (Ephesians 4:26,27a, 31-32, NIV)"

Further, I continued to look to God's Word for guidance for our mission team. I immediately recalled Jesus' desire for His followers to be one. Later, I found another Scripture that helped me greatly and should be the theme passage for any mission team. "May the God who gives endurance and encouragement give you a spirit of unity among yourselves as you follow Christ Jesus so that with one heart and mouth you may glorify the God and Father of our Lord Jesus Christ. Accept one another, then, as Christ has accepted you, in order to bring praise to God . . . May the God of hope fill you with great joy and peace as you trust in him, so that you may overflow with hope by the power of the Holy Spirit. (Romans 15:5,6,7, and 13 NIV)" Paul wrote this to encourage the Church in Rome. Rome was the superpower that dominated much of the known world during Paul's time. In the preceding verse, Paul indicates that through this "endurance and the encouragement of the Scriptures we might have hope." God is the one who provides endurance and His Word provides the encouragement I need to keep my focus on our mission. Truly, I needed to be empowered by the Holy Spirit.

What an answer to my deepest need! God is the One who gives a spirit of unity to His followers in order for us to speak with one heart and mouth. I determined to be more compassionate remembering how much God had forgiven me through His Son and how God is so desirous of unity within His body. Though failing at times, I tried hard to be "kind and compassionate."

These events proved even more divisive within our mission team. One of the lessons God wanted me to learn is the power of prayer. I turned to God in prayer for our mission and asked for His wisdom because I knew there must be "peace" within our group in order for our mission to be successful in bringing Christ's peace to a war- torn country. With God's grace, we remained friends with the entire mission team and invited all to our home for planning sessions and special occasions, such as Christmas and Thanksgiving. In many areas of our mission work, we decided to work separately but cooperatively.

God provided Christian servicemen, who came to our rescue. One serviceman found and purchased for us a refrigerator and a propane gas range and gave these to us as a gift.

One of our friends in the States heard about our difficulties and sent us the funds to buy a used Volkswagen bus.

Since the Halls' congregation received most of the work funds, I soon began to feel limited on what I could do without more funds. Again, God provided. Mrs. Ona Belknap–a personal friend, a talented writer, and editor of *The Christian Woman*–took our newsletters and prepared articles for *The Christian Chronicle,* being published by her brother, Ralph Sweet. In addition, she sent articles to papers put out by our fellowship and to several other newspapers. I truly basked in having my own "press corps." As a result, funds started pouring in from all over the United States. I never cease to be amazed how God uses all our collective talents to further His purposes.

Through Ona Belknap's encouragement, she sent me the credentials to get a Press Card to represent *The Christian Chronicle.* This enabled me to attend military briefings. It also gave us APO, PX, and Commissary privileges, which provided an opportunity to do some shopping in familiar territory.

Maurice Hall had started the translation of a Bible correspondence course. Since we needed printed materials in Vietnamese, I began working with the translator on the BCC. Because we did not have funds for printing, I wrote to Jimmie Lovell, who published a paper called *Action*. Through this paper, Lovell raised funds for publishing Bible correspondence courses on the mission field.

Here is a quote from his editorial, "Ralph Burcham wrote me that they needed money to print lessons in Vietnamese and we sent $2,000 immediately of your Miss-A-Meal money, which was all we had in the fund as we try to keep it moving about as fast as we receive it . . . But in the same mail, mind you, was a check for $15? Not so–it was a check for one thousand dollars! Our keepers of orthodoxy call such as this 'accidents.' Well, I don't. I've come to the place in my life and in my work where I see too many of these 'accidents' . . . Whenever we start using our few little fishes and loaves to feed the multitudes of our world the gospel of Jesus Christ,

He will supply the balance needed just as He has always done and always will do."

When I received the check, I rushed to the printer, who invited me to watch those first lessons role off the press. How exciting to see this first Bible Correspondence Course printed in the Vietnamese language with corresponding pages in English. God truly works in mysterious ways that are beyond our comprehension.

The funds for our radio work came from the White's Ferry Road Church of Christ in West Monroe, Louisiana. They indicated their desire to continue their support of this effort.

Remembering Maurice's encouragement that "God will provide" made it possible for me to function under adverse circumstances. And God did provide. Our home became a rallying point for servicemen, Vietnamese Christians, and our mission team.

Our servicemen provided needed help!

The servicemen provided direction and encouragement. Many had a rich background in church work. God provided these servants who gave excellent advice and encouragement. Most offered to help in any way possible.

In the early days of our mission, Captain Jim Hopkins became my mentor and chief advisor. Often visitors stayed with us until late in the evening. I found it difficult to do my study in the evening so I started getting up between four and five each morning. We soon started feeling the fatigue of our work with the late nights, early mornings, the problems within our team, and full days.

When I felt overburdened and wondered how to get it all done, God provided Christian servicemen to help by using their time off. Ralph Nichols and Paul Cook spent hours answering correspondence and typing lesson materials. Don Yelton helped in teaching Bible classes.

The servicemen and a friend, who worked for the CIA, gave us advice on areas or events to avoid. We gladly honored their concern for our safety and well being.

Fred Wiggins, a serviceman, who came to our place frequently, missed being able to watch TV on his visits. When the PX got in some portable TVs, he purchased one and gave it to Roger and Kathy. From this time on, servicemen often came to watch TV with our kids.

If we did not turn the TV on early, the picture would be about the size of a postcard. Another serviceman gave us a transformer that helped stabilize the power. Bob Hague, a serviceman, spent many evenings with our children watching TV and offered free babysitting. When Bob left Vietnam, another serviceman, Fred Hall, who lived in a billet about two blocks from our place, often spent the evenings at our home watching TV with our children; later, he played a part in being our guardian angel when the war came into our area.

From the moment of our arrival, the focus seemed to be on Election Day, September 11. Daily the newspapers put out warnings for Americans to be careful. The papers carried stories of the Viet Cong (the Vietnamese Communists or VC) threats and terrorist activities. Each day you could sense the tension of the coming election.

The day before the election all American servicemen received orders to be confined to their base or quarters. Because of the many warnings, we stayed at home. Everyone around Saigon seemed tense. The Viet Cong did a good job of keeping everyone on edge.

The Election Day itself proved to be a quiet one. The day fell on Sunday so we went to church. The scare must have kept many out of sight because the streets had little traffic. None of the military came to church because of military restrictions; many were placed on alert. We marveled at the large number of Vietnamese that came to church and voted in their election in spite of all the threats of terrorist activity.

God provided me with a wonderful helper!

Most evenings we had visitors and Gladys always invited them for dinner. After a hard day at school, she spent much of the afternoon being a mother, preparing lessons, grading papers, answering correspondence, keeping our work fund books, serving as a counselor to young single and newly married missionary women, and baking.

When we gave up the washing machine, our wash had to be done by hand because we did not have funds for a washing machine and "help-your-self" laundries did not exist. But Kathy loved helping Chi Hai, our maid, do the wash. Kathy seemed very adept at linens and bed spreads. In our concrete back yard, she and Chi Hai filled a large pan, put in the wash soap, and started stomping them with their feet. They went round and round. When Gladys looked out at this weekly event, she made the comment "If I didn't know better, I'd have thought she was making wine."

Gladys found herself in a special role with the women missionaries. She tried to help the newly married ones understand normal adjustments to be different from difficult cultural adjustments–some confused these as being problems within the marriage. Gladys provided sage counsel for several.

Gladys always made our mealtime open to guests; therefore, servicemen and civilian workers frequently brought a sack of groceries; otherwise, our budget would have required us to limit guests only to those invited.

She gave me excellent counsel and loving support during times of crises, which reaffirmed Maurice Hall's statement "God will provide."

For several years, God had been preparing us for our present situation. I truly believe that God uses all of the trials and difficulties we experience to help us face even greater struggles. In our first year of marriage, we kept a German exchange student, Hildegard Eckhart. She came to live with us shortly after World War II; her home had been bombed; her father died during the war; and she had strong, negative feelings about America and all the hardships of her early life. Gladys worked so hard with her; on the day she arrived, they went shopping to get her new school clothes for her senior year in high school. As they walked through large department stores, Hildegard, looked at the shelves and racks full of beautiful merchandise with awe; she said, "Our stores are almost bare." As Gladys poured out her love, she blossomed before our very eyes into a confident young lady who fell in love with America and the students in one of America's largest high schools came to love her.

From the beginning of our married life, Gladys made the determination to use our home for Christ. Through the years, countless people lived with us from a day or two, to a few weeks, or even to two or more years. Probably one of our greatest challenges came through the foster care of three teenage boys. Each brought his problems and struggles that we attempted to help each one overcome. We constantly sought God's wisdom and help in all of these struggles.

Another time, Gladys offered to help a college student who suffered from a ruptured appendix. While he struggled in the hospital for life, his parents came from Michigan and lived with us until he got better. When he left the hospital, Gladys dressed his wound and ministered him back to health. Later, this same student married; then his wife had to have back surgery. We set up a hospital bed and Gladys took care of her for several weeks until she recovered.

For six summers, we directed a camp for children. Our last year at Camp Rock Creek, we had over 1,100 children attend.

Therefore, it is not surprising that many guests frequented our home for overnight stays. Gladys always made them feel welcome even though it required some of her valuable energy.

Everyone agreed Gladys to be an excellent cook. All remember her cinnamon rolls, doughnuts, cookies, pies, cakes, and bread. When Gladys was baking, the sweet aromas permeated our place. Her mouth-watering refreshments, made for our fellowship time after the Wednesday evening Bible study, proved to be very popular.

Gladys recognized a tremendous need for children's Bible literature. With another of our workers, Dona Blake, she started a series of Bible lessons for children. She received permission from the R. B. Sweet Company to translate stories from two of their series– *"Journeys through the Bible"* and *"Living Word."* From these, they adapted stories with picture illustrations that children could use to color. Not many of the Vietnamese children read English; therefore, Gladys felt it most important to provide them with literature in their language.

Also, she provided free English classes using the Bible; this became so popular that she had to limit the number she could handle.

She did not turn down a student but directed many of these to others of our missionary women.

Truly, God provided me with the greatest helper of all. I really do not know how she accomplished all she did. (Note. Appendix A has a tribute to Gladys written by Ona Belknap.)

Another great holiday introduced us to a special day for children—The Mid-Autumn Festival.

Not long after school started, we noticed brightly colored lanterns of various shapes dangling in the breeze in front of little shops. When we asked the meaning of these, we got various answers as there are many myths surrounding this holiday. This is a special day of rejoicing for children throughout Vietnam. The artistry of these lanterns is beyond description. The lanterns' frames took on the shape of fish, birds, animals, dragons, unicorns, fruits, stars, rockets, and jets. The Vietnamese stretched brightly colored cellophane over the frame. Then they placed a candle inside to provide light to shine through the many colors.

On the day of the festival, schools let out for a day. I took Roger and Kathy shopping for lanterns. Roger got a Japanese type; Kathy got a big parrot; and they got a butterfly for their mother.

At night, adults light the lanterns and hand them to children; then the excited children fall in behind the dragon dancers. This colorful event allowed all to see the children march down the streets carrying their lanterns. I watched in amazement at this beautiful, peaceful sight. There is something contagious when children are excited; somehow we wished we could capture the beauty of this festival and carry it home for our friends to enjoy. While the children participated in their march, adults enjoyed the moonlight by drinking a steaming cup of perfumed tea and plates full of sugar-coated lotus seeds.

Many of the Vietnamese worship the full moon to welcome in the fall. As Gladys wrote in her journal, "The fall is half over, and it is still summer. We'll have to get used to summer all year."

Security was a concern of daily life.

In early October, we went to worship with one of our missionary couples, Leonard and Dona Blake, out at Quang Trung, where they worked with a children's home sponsored by Churches of Christ.

As we left Saigon, the military, with my press ID in hand, allowed us to go through the base to reach Quang Trung. We always felt secure on the base.

The countryside always fascinated me with its green rice paddies. We saw a farmer plowing a new rice paddy with a water buffalo; the banana trees could be seen from the bloom stage to stalks of fruit; and the graceful palms, some with coconuts, tickling the clouds above–all reminded us that our Creator made such a beautiful world and gave us the ability to see and enjoy it. What a blessing!

As I witnessed the children at play at the orphanage, I realized again the marvels of God's creation. Each child possessed special qualities. God has a purpose for each. How wonderful to see such beautiful children worshiping God. What an enjoyable experience!

This pleasant experience at the orphanage made us want to return, which we did a few weeks later. We decided to go through the base as before. But my memory failed me when we got through the base and I chose the wrong road.

As we traveled along, I did not recognize some of the markers of our previous trip. I thought to myself: "What should I do now? I think I better turn around at the first place where I can do this safely because of the narrow road."

When I am uncertain about things, I get especially silent; Gladys noticed and said, "You're lost!"

About this time, we reached a dead end in an unknown village market; soon people surrounded us as they pressed in against the Volkswagen with curiosity written across their faces. Their noses pressed against the windows all around the bus. I wondered, "Are we among friend or foe? How am I going to communicate our dilemma?"

Out of the crowd a young man spoke in broken English and said, "Can I help you!" I have never heard more welcome words. He asked, "Where are you going?"

I replied, "We are on our way to Quang Trung and I must have made a wrong turn." He gave precise instructions on how to get there from that point. He shouted for everyone to move back from the bus and he started helping me back up– through the crowd of people–to the main road. When we got to the main road, he went over the directions again. We followed his directions and a little later arrived safely at the orphanage. From this experience, I determined to get specific directions before going anywhere even if I have been there.

Each day I took many of the teachers to and from school in our Volkswagen bus. On one such morning on our way to school, the police had blocked off a street we usually took. On down that street there had been an explosion in front of a military billet. A bicycle with a plastic bomb had gone off killing one American soldier and injuring seven others. Normally, we would have been there about that time, but we were running a little late.

Just a few days later, another explosion went off in Saigon. We heard the rumor that terrorism might be increasing from this time until Christmas or New Year. I found myself praying frequently throughout the day for the safety and well being of my family, our mission team, the Vietnamese, and our servicemen.

A short time later, the VC blew up an ammunition depot about 9 p.m. This caused us all to "jump."

An early Christmas present helped move our work forward.

When at home, I spent much of my time studying; preparing materials for translation; providing counsel for Vietnamese, servicemen, and young missionaries; and answering correspondence. It came as a real blow when I had to turn the Hall's typewriter over to another missionary.

Soon after, we decided to start our Christmas shopping. The whole family went downtown together and we had fun shopping for Christmas. To my surprise, Gladys took her first check for teaching and purchased me a typewriter. She said, "Santa is bringing you an early present." Better than anyone else, she knew my work required a typewriter.

During our shopping, we noticed that Kathy had learned to bargain. She bought some bouie, which are larger and more delicious than our grapefruit, and she got them at a real bargain. I think the merchants found it entertaining to bargain with this little white girl with light brown hair. It became evident she had learned a great deal from her trips with our maid to the market.

Kathy's bargaining ability really came home one day when we started to return from the church building. Of course, she wanted to take a cyclo instead of a taxi. I said, "All right. But I won't pay more than it costs to ride a taxi; the going rate being 50 piasters to our place."

The first one stopped wanted 100. The second wanted 100. I said, "50." He countered with "70." And Kathy said, "Oh, please, 50." To my surprise he said, "OK." As we crawled on, I could see a big smile on Kathy; then I looked around and the cyclo driver had a big smile on his face. Time and again it became evident that she could out bargain all of us.

Gladys experienced the trauma of having to take the shots for rabies.

In November in the middle of the night, Gladys shook me out of my sleep with "I think I've been bitten by a mouse." As I turned on the light, sure enough a mouse jumped out of bed. She said, "Catch it." Fortunately for the mouse, or for me, the mouse escaped.

Gladys went on to teach the next day; but, being concerned about the bite, I went to the 17th Field Hospital and visited with the Colonel in charge. I told him what had happened; he said, "Well, in any other place, I would suggest a tetanus shot, but here I would suggest the series for rabies. Have her come in today to the 'sick call' area; I'll authorize the shots. We will need to make a plot of her stomach; there are fourteen shots in this series and they are painful."

When she arrived at the hospital for her first shot, she went up to report to the Sergeant in charge, who politely said: "What can I do for you?"

"I'm here to take the rabies shots; I was bitten by a mouse."

He responded in a loud voice, "You were bitten by a mouse; get that rabies shot ready!"

By this time, all the soldiers on sick call looked up; and Gladys flushed with humiliation as she could see their amused looks. I felt so sorry for her because as the shots progressed her stomach turned black and blue as if run over by a herd of elephants. She said the most difficult aspect of taking those fourteen painful shots came as she walked into the waiting room to hear the Sergeant's loud response with "Here comes the rat lady; get the rabies shot ready!"

We shared our first Thanksgiving in Vietnam with many.

Gladys invited all the missionaries, the teachers in the Christian school, and several of the military men to share Thanksgiving dinner with us. She baked a large ham and prepared a turkey with all the trimmings. Everyone knew that cakes and pies to be her specialty; her array of deserts tempted everyone.

The servicemen loved to tease Gladys because they knew she would always have a comeback. One said, "Gladys, did you know there are 100 species of snakes in Vietnam!"

She replied, "I'm not surprised with all we see at the pet market."

Then he said, "You need to be on the alert because 98 of them are poisonous and the other two will swallow you whole."

One of the military men looked at Roger and said, "Just think, Roger, in about six years you'll be back here."

Roger really came to and said: "Oh, no, they don't. I'll tell the draft board I've already served my two years in Vietnam!" We all laughed.

The servicemen talked about their families and how they celebrated Thanksgiving. We had a prayer time; often the servicemen's prayers moved me to tears. In all, we had almost 50. In her journal, Gladys simply wrote: "We all had such a good time."

The next day a Vietnamese couple brought us gifts–an alligator skin bag for Gladys and a book for me. They did this because Gladys had visited the man when ill. Since the couple have several children, their generosity overwhelmed us.

A few days later, Captain Jim Hopkins took us to the officers' club for dinner. The steaks tasted so good.

Our children enjoyed being with him because he had been in our home so often he seemed like family. However, we soon noticed the Vietnamese waitresses all lined up some distance from us and pointing to our table and laughing. Soon one came over to our table and quickly ran her finger across Roger's dark and heavy eyebrows. Roger flushed with embarrassment but the waitress went back and reported to the others the eyebrows to be genuine; then all burst forth with giggles.

A major explosion at Tan Son Nhut shattered our feelings of security.

We lived just four blocks from the Tan Son Nhut air base. Our first December started out with a bang! On the night of December 4, the VC attacked the base.

First, the mortar explosions awakened us; then machine gun and small arms fire continued throughout the night. Flares made the night look like day; machine gunfire continued to shatter the stillness of that two o'clock hour in the morning. Several loud booms followed one after the other. Then things really began to happen.

We got up to check on our children. I checked on Roger; Gladys walked into Kathy's bedroom just as an explosion rocked Saigon; we thought the end had come.

Kathy sat up in bed with eyes and mouth wide open and said "Mother! What was that?"

Gladys calmly replied, "Oh! I think the boys decided to play soldier out at Tan Son Nhut."

To which Kathy sighed and said, "Oh," and went back to sleep.

The VC had fired mortars on to the base and hit a transport plane loaded with gasoline. The explosions shook our house and rattled the shutters, as our home did not have glass panes. Also, that night the VC blew up a U. S. Aid building downtown. They killed several VC and an MP. One explosion just missed a military billet where U. S. servicemen live; how thankful none of them were injured.

I marveled at the calm way Gladys handled crisis situations; in each God seemed to be preparing us for more difficult moments. Her faith and trust in God came through loud and clear in many other threatening situations.

About the events of this night, Gladys simply wrote in her journal, "Boy, did we rock and roll last night! In spite of the war and culture shock, we go about the work for Christ with our eye of faith on the Cross and the great mission we have here in Vietnam. We love the people and feel that Vietnam is the greatest mission point on earth at the present time."

Our First Christmas and New Year in Vietnam included our new family.

Several family members and friends in the States, started sending us gifts. This proved so exiting for our children. Because of stories about our work in *The Christian Chronicle,* we received a package from a family in Detroit, Michigan, that we did not know. It contained a large Santa Claus, which our children thoroughly enjoyed and became a family treasure.

One friend sent us $10 to buy a Christmas tree. We went shopping downtown for a tree. Real ones are nonexistent. However, Kathy found an artificial one. Its limbs looked like a fiber bottle-brush dyed green. However, it looked somewhat real. Kathy decided we had to have it; however, the merchant wanted $25 for it; I told her, "The limit is $10 because this is all we can afford."

As we headed for the Volkswagen bus, Kathy said, "Dad, let me bargain."

I said: "We'll drive around the block and then pick you up."

We drove around the block; she waved us on; we repeated this three times. I felt sure she would not get that tree. But on that third trip around, she stood proudly on the curb with the tree. The merchant waved and smiled; I think he had a lot of fun with the intensity of this little girl's bargaining.

That evening Gladys and the kids had fun making our living room look like Christmas. A serviceman brought over two fruitcakes, which his mother had sent him as a present; he asked to put them under our tree.

I never ceased to be amazed how Gladys made the military feel that our home could be theirs while in Vietnam. When we arrived in Vietnam, neither of us drank coffee; but when the GIs came, the first question asked: "Gladys, do you have the coffee pot on?" So we became coffee drinkers!

Not far from where we lived, the 7th Day Adventist owned a compound for their missionaries. I had been to their hospital and one of their doctors invited our children over to meet his. Therefore, I took Kathy over for her to meet other American children. Because of its closeness, Kathy felt she could walk there and back on her own, which she did. She felt a sense of pride and independence by being able to go there and play with an American girl. Later both Roger and Kathy enjoyed playing with these new American friends.

About the middle of December, John Steinbeck, with his wife, came to Vietnam to do research for a book. Mrs. Steinbeck contacted our mission and indicated she would like to worship with us, since she was a member of the Church of Christ. I visited her at the Caravelle Hotel and offered to pick her up for Sunday services and invited her to eat lunch with us following services. We did pick her up and she spent Sunday afternoon with us. She told us several interesting stories about her life with the famous writer. Chidingly "I told her I had a bone to pick with her husband because of making the 'Okie' name famous in his book, *The Grapes of Wrath.*" We had a good laugh.

Gladys had a surprise about a week before Christmas. One of her students, Juliet Tran, and her maid brought a present for our Christmas dinner. It consisted of a live turkey and five-dozen eggs. Our maid volunteered her husband to come, kill, and dress it. Until then, the turkey remained in our small backyard enclosure. Roger decided we should keep it for a pet. But the maid's husband came, with no one home, and did the honors.

Gladys wrote in her journal "My turkey is in the deep freeze–without his feathers!" Also, she started baking pies and cakes and putting them in the refrigerator.

Since Christmas came on Sunday, we decided to have the gang over for dinner on the 24th. Gladys spent the day preparing the dinner. Curt and Eveyln Accord, one of our missionary couples, helped by taking the kids to the zoo; they enjoyed it very much. Curt spent a lot of time keeping church records and he taught in the school.

We enjoyed the dinner, the fellowship, and the exchanging of gifts.

Later that night, the VC activity increased in spite of the truce. They killed six VC just around the corner from our house. We heard the shots in the night but went on sleeping.

Christmas day started with our opening presents. Kathy enjoyed new dolls; Roger received a challenge–a cuckoo clock to put together. After services, since some of the military could not be with us for Christmas dinner, we had four over for lunch and four over for dinner.

Y-Kim, a Montagnard, introduced us to the mountain people.

In December 1966, Y-Kim came to our house for a visit. He spent almost three hours sharing his life's story. He is a Montagnard by birth; honesty became the trademark for his mountain tribesmen. Our military liked to employ them for special roles because of their trustworthiness.

When about 14, Y-Kim started working for Dr. Lanny Hunter, a Christian Military doctor from the States. The good doctor taught Y-Kim English, but more important, he taught him the gospel. Y-Kim spent his off hours watching American films on base. His English expanded rapidly, and he used his expanded vocabulary with the doctor. However, when Y-Kim used certain curse and vulgar words he heard in the movies or among some of the military, Dr. Hunter taught him that such words should not be used.

When it came time for Dr. Hunter to return to the States, he wanted Y-Kim to further his knowledge of the Bible and his education. He made financial arrangements for Y-Kim to move to Saigon and attend the American-Vietnamese International School. In testing him, we found he could probably manage the 7th grade. This is the same grade as Roger and they became bosom friends.

Gladys learned that Y-Kim's 20th birthday came on December 29. She baked a birthday cake and invited Y-Kim over for supper. Y-Kim had never had a birthday cake with candles. Then he became even more excited as the kids told him to make a wish and blow out the candles in one breath.

After blowing out the candles, Gladys served the cake with a dip of ice cream topped with a sugar cube dipped in lemon extract, which she lit.

All of us thrilled to see his astonishment as he exclaimed: "How can ice cream burn?" We all got a good laugh. Roger and Kathy gave him gifts, which really overwhelmed him.

Y-Kim visited us frequently. Gladys learned that he liked fried chicken; therefore, when we knew in advance he planned to be with us, she made his favorite "chicky fri." In time, Y-Kim opened our eyes to the importance of God's Word being available in your mother tongue.

What does God have in store for the New Year?

After church on New Year's Day, several of us went to the floating ship for dinner. Our kids really enjoyed eating there because you walked up a gangplank and you could feel the ship gently rocking on the water; we all liked the peanuts, which had a thin, crispy coat. This joyous occasion had a sad side because the next day Captain Hopkins would be leaving. After dinner, he came home with us to provide some final counsel and encouragement. What a great friend God provided me!

As I reflected on our first few months in Vietnam, a sense of awe came over me because of all the experiences that had been packed into that time. Our family had made good adjustments to a culture so foreign to our own. To overcome the loss of Maurice and Marie Hall to our work, God used this to teach me to depend on Him to a greater extent; gradually, we learned to see how God works in so many traumatic situations. God loved us through our servicemen and our new Vietnamese friends. Servicemen, many with years of experience as church leaders, served as my best advisors and friends.

As people learned about our work through **The Christian Chronicle** and other publications, it became clear that God provided the resources we needed to carry on our work. Daily God opened doors for me to study the Good News of our Savior with an overwhelming number of Vietnamese.

Therefore, Vietnam, once the "Pearl of the Orient," became very special to me and to all who ever entered its borders. Some enter Vietnam and find their faith; some lose their lives; some struggle with the meaning of life; and some just exist from day to day.

As I came to know the servicemen on a personal level, I could sense the inner warfare going on in each heart. All missed family and friends back home; all possessed a patriotism, which often moved me to tears; all came with a desire to give the Vietnamese people an opportunity for freedom without the tyranny of communism.

As my acquaintance with the Vietnamese grew, I came to enjoy some of the most meaningful and memorable relationships of my life. In time, I came to understand the struggles experienced by so many that longed for freedom after having known foreign domination for decades.

The battle for minds is waged on many fronts.

My Vietnam experience convinced me that the greatest battle of all is in the arena of ideas. This great battlefield takes place in the heart of all men and women. Who or what will win the battle for our minds? Life is full of choices. Choices have consequences. The big question becomes: "What choices bring fulfillment and which bring heartache?"

The battle for minds is fought in every century. An ancient writer indicates one solution for seeking knowledge and wisdom: "The fear of the Lord is the beginning of knowledge. (Proverbs 1:7, NIV)" He also wrote: "The fear of the Lord is the beginning of wisdom, and knowledge of the Holy One is understanding. (Proverbs 9:10, NIV)"

Two thousand years ago this same battle brought a challenge to thinking minds. An adversary asked Jesus: "What is the greatest commandment?" He replied, "The greatest commandment is to love

God with all your heart, mind, and soul, and the second is to love your neighbor as yourself. (See Matthew 22:34-40, NIV)"

I became more convinced that the greatest battle of all is a spiritual battle. This spiritual battle is fought every day in the heart and mind of every person–whether Vietnamese, American, or any other nationality. In all of life, there are triumphs and tragedies. From our challenging adventures in Vietnam, it seemed all fell into one of these two categories because rarely did life march on at an even keel. What challenges does God have for us in our mission endeavors as we serve people living in a war-torn nation?

The American-Vietnamese International School

"For attaining wisdom and discipline; for understanding words of insight; for acquiring a disciplined and prudent life, doing what is right and just and fair; for giving prudence to the simple, knowledge and discretion to the young–let the wise listen and add to their learning, and let the discerning get guidance . . . . The fear of the Lord is the beginning of knowledge . . . .

(Proverbs 1:2-5,7, NIV)"

As the war escalated, the U. S. Government evacuated all military dependents. As a result, the American Community School closed; thus, many who had attended this school did not have a place for their children. Many of these patrons encouraged Maurice Hall to open a school, which he did. Hall could see the school had great opportunities for reaching the lost. He recruited Christian teachers from the States, who also came to help mission endeavors. In its first year of operation, Leonard Blake directed the school.

The children in the school came from the international community; their parents included ambassadors, bankers, or prominent businessmen, who wanted their children to be taught in English and who could afford the tuition. The children came from 13 different nations.

The school used the American curriculum plus Bible instruction from kindergarten through grade 10 with plans to add an upper grade each year. In addition, the staff included teachers who taught the Vietnamese curriculum to nationals of that country.

All teachers made a commitment to teach truth with an emphasis on God's truth, which leads to true wisdom and eternal life.

Dedicated teachers made the school.

Maurice Hall recruited all the teachers. Those recruited lived on a subsistence salary. I admired the dedication of all 13 of those young Christians. Each came with a sense of mission far beyond their years. Each had a love for children and a determination to make a difference in the lives of each child who came into their classroom. Each teacher wanted to influence every child and his or her parents with knowledge of Jesus Christ and the hope that He alone can give.

When the school for American dependents closed, USAID warehoused the books, classroom materials, and desks. I went to visit the director of USAID who offered to give us any of these we could use. All the teachers searched the local market for school supplies; many wrote home for materials. Because of limited funds, each teacher demonstrated his or her ingenuity by using these resources wisely.

For the fall term in 1966, my elders gave permission for me to become the director provided I kept the major part of my time on evangelism. Leonard Blake worked diligently to help me get oriented. Later Leonard helped me through a critical situation in which I thought we were going to lose the school.

The Vietnamese government required the Principal to be a national; therefore, we obtained a Vietnamese who served in this capacity.

In order to make contacts, I taught a typing class daily at the Christian school for 30 minutes; each student had to provide their own typewriter. Then I had a 30-minute Bible class. I used a Bible drill format and found the students to be quick learners.

Leecia Bruce served as the secretary and bookkeeper; she had a warm, loving personality. She demonstrated her efficiency by being one of the most organized persons I have known. Susan Chau assisted her and served as interpreter and translator with Vietnamese parents; she also prepared our reports for the Education Department of the Vietnamese Government.

Jim and Betty Casey brought classroom experience to the group and helped each teacher create a warm environment for learning to take place. Everywhere Jim went he used his influence for Christ. He conducted one-on-one Bible studies and preached meaningful sermons. I basked in their love and friendship. Jim had the ability to give love and encouragement and provided great wisdom in helping me deal with the many problems within the team. Later, he helped me in making a survey to determine if a need existed for more orphan care.

Jim had a jovial spirit and had a way of making me laugh when I did not feel like it. But one day, I returned the favor. He grew frustrated in dealing with the Vietnamese Government in an effort to adopt a child. I attempted to make light of the situation and he said, "Oh, Burcham, I know you. Even if I am face down in the gutter, you would say to me 'Roll over and give everyone a good smile.'" We both got a needed laugh.

Because of her training and background, I felt Betty to be especially qualified to teach the beginners. Learning is so critical that first year and a child needs to obtain a good foundation in order to succeed later. At times, she became frustrated because of our lack of resources; but, in spite of this, she made her classroom attractive and an inviting place for her children.

Although Judy Colvin, a graduate of Oklahoma Christian, majored in accounting, she possessed teacher qualities extraordinaire. She came with a tremendous desire to reach out to the Vietnamese people. In a short period of time, she developed a close relationship with five young ladies. They went places and ate together whenever she had a spare moment. After being in Vietnam several months, she came in to share her disappointment that none had become Christians. With an evident note of disappointment, she said, "Maybe I made the mistake of putting all my eggs in one basket."

I assured Judy that her time in preparing the soil for the gospel had been wisely used. I told her, "Our job is to plant the seed by teaching the basics that bring about Christian faith and God will give the increase." In time, all five became Christians. Later, one of these made it to the United States and married a Chinese preacher.

Arlen Ewing became one of my best support persons. He taught social studies in the upper grades. His knowledge of world history and economics challenged me in personal conversations with him. He read from many sources and provided good interpretations on the events taking place in Vietnam and the United States that affected our work. Whenever I faced personal challenges within our mission team, he defended my feeble efforts in keeping our team on track.

Gene Conner taught English and Literature in the upper grades. He had a tremendous desire to see the school succeed. When Gene drove the Volkswagen, I always felt a bit uneasy. In heavy Vietnamese traffic, he had the amazing ability to read; when traffic backed up, he spent his time in a book. With uncanny sensitivity, he seemed to know when the traffic started moving. Of course, cars honking may have caused his alertness to get going.

Gene worked with the military congregation that met on the Tan Son Nhut base. He preached and taught classes. During the Tet offensive, we became extremely concerned for Gene because he lived out from Saigon. After the school closed because of the Tet Offensive, he put forth great effort until it reopened.

Paulette Wright and Diane Powell taught in the elementary grades. Each brought a special warmth to the classroom. Each demonstrated unusual flexibility in teaching wherever needed.

During our second year, Curt Accord taught in the lower grades. He performed a great service for the Saigon congregation by keeping our records. Also, he worked with the Tran Quy Cap congregation and his wife, Evelyn, developed a close friendship with several girls and taught them the gospel. They both tried every way to further our evangelistic efforts. In fact, Charles A. Shelton, the preacher of their home congregation, the Campbell congregation in San Jose, California, came over and helped in a special campaign by passing out tracts, signing up students in our Bible Correspondence Course, and preaching. During their time in Vietnam, Curt and Evelyn had a beautiful baby, Marcia Leigh.

Linda Carpenter taught our Kathy the first year of the school. In addition, she had nursing skills and used them to help in our orphanage program.

Patti Alley taught science in the upper grades. She possessed a beautiful trained voice that helped all of us sound better. She also worked very hard on the Vietnamese language and became good at small talk.

Gladys taught math in the upper grades during our first year of operation.

By the spring of 1967, our enrollment grew to 164.

Dedicated teachers made their impact on missions in Saigon by teaching in the American-Vietnamese International School. They are left to right: Ralph and Gladys Burcham, Arlan Ewing, Paulette Wright, Diane Powell, Gene Conner, Leecia Bruce, Jim and Betty Casey, Patti Alley, Judy Colvin, Phil and Sophie Nhon.

A talented serviceman I converted played an important future role in our mission.

Early on I met Dick DiNucci, a serviceman in Saigon. We studied the Bible together; he enjoyed the fellowship of the entire mission group. When he made the decision to accept Christ, I arranged for a Vietnamese to conduct the baptism. Immediately, he started helping with our mission whenever he had time off. Since he had completed the military language school, he spoke fluent Vietnamese. In fact, his effectiveness with the language could be seen as he shared stories and jokes in Vietnamese.

Dick's tall, lean appearance made him a foot or more taller than the Vietnamese. When we went to the marketplace to teach or hand out materials, Vietnamese who listened and laughed with him would surround him. During his R and R's to Hong Kong, he met and fell in love with Jennifer, a beautiful Chinese young lady.

As the end of Dick's duty in Vietnam approached, he asked me about the school and whether or not he could be used in some way. I told him his math and science degree could be used to fill a needed slot in our junior and high school offerings. To my surprise he replied, "I've completed the required time for my commission. I'm thinking about resigning on my return to the States and I just may join you." When it came his time to leave Vietnam, all of us hated to see him leave.

What a surprise! When I next heard from Dick, he indicated his desire to be with us in the fall if we could use him. Then Dick said, "I plan to marry Jennifer in Hong Kong and we would like to stay in your home while we locate an apartment." I told him, "Come on."

But this required me to move Gladys to a different teaching role. She had her degree in mathematics and had taught in this area her first year. Even though she loved math, she gladly accepted the role of teaching the fourth and fifth grades for our second year.

How I hated to lose two very talented teachers.

Dick's decision answered many prayers because Jim and Betty Casey shared with me their plans to return home upon the completion of their first year. What a devastating blow! But they explained their situation and hopefully desired to complete arrangements for adopting a Vietnamese child.

Jim's perseverance amazed me. He had to move the Vietnamese bureaucracy to get adoption papers approved, get a passport, and an exit visa. When Jim got to the place where everything had to be approved, he sensed their stalling. A Vietnamese secretary told him to return the next day because the one needing to sign the papers had a full schedule.

Jim tried to explain the urgency of getting the papers signed because they planned to leave very soon. Again she stressed her boss to be very busy. Jim said, "I have time to wait until he is free" and sat down. How rare to see an American who can outwait an Asian; but Jim waited patiently for quite some time. Then in an unbeliev-able move the official came out, got the papers, and signed them. So his persistence in adopting a child paid off; he and Betty adopted a precious little girl, Bonnie.

Though I hated to see them go, they went with my blessing.

For the fall term in 1967, Dick and Jennifer arrived in Saigon; they did stay with us for several days. Jennifer and our Kathy struck it off from the beginning. Jennifer played dolls with Kathy and they seemed to enjoy each other's company. They shopped together. Kathy really helped Jennifer in adapting to Vietnam.

Jennifer had a great desire to learn how to prepare American foods for Dick. She followed Gladys around in the kitchen to watch the art of making cinnamon rolls, doughnuts, and cakes.

Jennifer, seeing how busy Gladys to be, offered to make some Chinese food. Gladys asked, "What pork should I get to make sweet and sour pork." Jennifer came back with "From a pig." Gladys simply wrote in her diary, "Oh, me!"

The Christian school faced a new crisis.

But the school ran into unexpected trouble! Just days before the school opened in the fall of 1967, the Vietnamese Principal indi-cated he planned to take over the school and wanted all the funds. We refused because the school had made a commitment to take care of the return fare for each of the teachers. Since most of the funds remained in reserve for the airfare back to the States, we refused to turn over the funds even if it meant closing the school.

I made a visit to one of my closest friends, Tran Van Can. After explaining the situation to him, I said, "I'm so discouraged; I believe our only alternative is to close the school."

Tran understood my discouragement but he offered his help: "Don't give up. I know the Minister of Education personally. I believe I can get a new American school authorized." We prayed about it.

But it seemed impossible. I felt the only alternative to be to turn that school building over to the Principal. Yet, with Tran's encouragement, I determined to seek to start a new school in another location. Yet, this seemed impossible to me because of the time factor; also, I had experienced over and over how long it takes to move the Vietnamese government.

Questions kept cropping up: Where can we find another Vietnamese Principal? Will the parents send their children to our new school? Can we get Government approval? Where can we get a new building? How can we move all the furniture and supplies in a timely manner to begin on time? How can we notify the parents and get their endorsement of our plan?

With Tran's encouragement, I called a meeting of the teachers and explained the situation to them with the questions and problems facing us in starting a new school. They gave their endorsement to apply for a new school and promised to help in every way possible. We prayed about it. Then we did some strategic planning.

First, they assigned me the job to make the application with the Government, find another Vietnamese Principal, and get approval for a new school. I went back to Tran, who had helped me on many occasions in meeting with government officials. He knew the protocol and he knew many of the officials on an acquaintance level.

Tran Van Can went with me to the Minister of Education and we explained our problem. The Minister listened with sympathy. We requested all the credentials of the teachers and withdrew all documentation for the old school. We inquired about the possibility of finding a Vietnamese Principal. He put us in contact with Mrs. Ngo

Tuan Ha. He gave us the application for a new school and promised to cooperate in every way possible.

I visited with Mrs. Ha; she showed an interest and promised to help us in our application for a new school.

Second, you can't operate a school without students. Since all the students had already pre-enrolled, the teachers divided the list and personally visited each parent of each student; they invited them to a public forum to discuss our situation. When we met for the forum, we explained the necessity of closing the old school and the difficulties we faced in beginning a new one. The parents promised to give solid backing.

How gratifying to get such a strong endorsement from the parents! They expressed appreciation for the quality of education their children received the prior year; they expressly commended the teachers for the moral and spiritual values taught.

Third, Leonard Blake took on the monumental task of finding a building.

His experience proved to be invaluable because he had helped locate our present school building; also, he had helped the church locate a meeting place when it became necessary to move.

He and Tran located a small hotel on a good street not far from USAID headquarters. I along with Tran, Gene Conner, Arlen Ewing, and Dick DiNucci–all teachers in the school—began negotiating with the owner to get the price within the range of something we could afford. Dick served as our interpreter. I took Kathy along, as a representative of the students, and that did it; we got the building. It seemed as though Kathy in dealing with the Vietnamese could perform "magic!"

Fourth, all the teachers and parents promised to pack and help in the move.

Everything seemed to be going smoothly. We submitted our new application with the teachers' credentials. The application included the location and layout of the school building. The Education Minister indicated tentative approval of our application.

"Excitement" barely describes the feelings of myself, the teachers, and the parents. With the negotiations of the building completed, we started the monumental task of moving.

I felt helpless when caught in the cross fire of
bullets coming my way.

At this time, the tension in South Vietnam could be felt among the populace because of the coming election for a new President. Throughout South Vietnam, the communists waged a campaign of terror. They killed or wounded over a thousand civilians throughout the country.

During this time, the military observed strict curfews. Most Americans tried to stay off the streets as much as possible. Our warnings included not going downtown; these warnings we observed.

On the Thursday before the election, I helped in the move to the new location. I parked in front of the new building and started carrying a box of books. For the first time, since arriving in Saigon, the bullets whizzed by me as I approached the school. Half way between the parked bus and the school, the bullets started coming my direction.

On down the street a policeman had whistled a man on a motorcycle to come to a halt. Instead the young man sped up the street; the motorcycle passed on my side of the street; consequently, I found myself in the line of fire. The first bullet hit a street sign behind me; the second bullet whizzed by my head and broke the plate glass in front of me. Besides the glass, nothing shattered but a few nerves!

With the election over, all of our mission team felt a sense of relief. Again, we knew the providence of God had provided protection for our mission team.

Would the school be able to reopen?

But even more nerve racking, the former Principal strongly opposed our move; and this raised our level of concern because he possessed many influential friends in the upper circles of Vietnamese politics. The former Principal had designs to get more involved in Vietnamese politics. Then we got word from the Minister of Education that we could not open the school.

Many of the parents had helped us in the move to the new location. When told the school could not open, the parents drafted a letter to the Minister of Education indicating their full support of our program. They indicated their children planned to attend the new school. Many indicated they would not send their children to the old school even if we did not get permission to start a new one.

This favorable letter had been signed by many which read like a "who's who" list for Vietnam. Many of the children in the school had parents in the diplomatic corps. Some of the positions of these parents included the Consul General of India, the Ambassador of Korea, and the Military Attaché of the Philippines, doctors, professors, and several bank presidents. I really believed it would be difficult for the Minister of Education to deny our application.

Morale among the teachers began to slip, because the "on again, off again" approval for the school went on for almost a month. Because of the uncertain situation, many of the teachers felt it necessary to make alternate plans.

During this time, Gladys and I worked diligently to let the teachers know we were putting forth our best efforts to get the school reopened. Many frequented our home for counsel and Gladys did an unusual amount of baking and had many over for lunch or dinner. But I kept encouraging all to pray. And pray they did!

Finally, the signed school papers came and we opened the school again even though about a month late. With all of the struggles of the past several weeks, the school opened with a record enrollment of 184. What a commendation for the Christian school!

The unseen player in all of this had to be God. Over and over again I brought this whole business before the One "Who is able!" Again this reminded me of Maurice Hall's closing advice: "God will provide." As I looked forward to a new year, I wondered what challenges God had been preparing us to meet!

The Vietnamese People[1]

"...Go and make disciples of all nations, baptizing them in the name of the Father and of the Son and of the Holy Spirit, and teaching them to obey everything I have commanded you. And surely I will be with you always, to the very end of the age."

Matthew 28:19,20

My most memorable times came as I shared with the Vietnamese the "love of Jesus Christ." I am thoroughly convinced the Bible to be inerrant and the very Word of God. Because the Bible teaches that Jesus is the only way to eternal life, I wanted every person I meet to be saved and possess the hope that is only in Christ. My mission to the Vietnamese people provided an exciting challenge each day as I constantly sought guidance from God in ways of reaching out with God's love and truth.

From the beginning of our ministry, I taught the Bible in English to both individuals and groups.

Like everyone going to the mission field, I asked: "What is the central issue of my teaching?" Thus, before leaving for Vietnam, I spent

---

[1]Note. In order to give a better flow to our mission endeavors, the events in this chapter occurred over a seven-year period.

months in answering the question "What must be the focus of my teaching?" From that study, I developed a series of Scriptures I entitled "Framework of Christianity," which involved basic teachings to bring one into faith in Jesus Christ. These basic concepts I included in some way with every person or group I taught. Also, I used this material in a personal work class for our missionaries on Wednesday evenings.

Before teaching doctrinal concepts, I knew people must first come to fall in love with God as seen in the life of Jesus. Therefore, the life of Christ, as presented in the gospels, had to be central in all I taught. Consequently, I looked afresh at the gospels on how each presented the humanity and the divinity of Jesus Christ. I felt that John's writings in the gospel of John and his writings in I, II, and III John helped in seeing the significance of how Christ demonstrated love in His life and teachings.

In my earlier studies, I knew the impact the book of Romans had on my own life. I wanted the Vietnamese to know this book. In Romans, I discovered salvation to be a gift from God; this gift of grace is not something I deserve or earn but is based on my acceptance of Christ's sacrifice for my sins. When our missionary group asked me to teach Romans, I encouraged all of us to focus on the righteousness from God that leads to faith in Jesus Christ.

Jesus' words in Matthew's Gospel are my challenge. Jesus said, "go and make disciples of all nations. (Matthew 28:19, NIV)" *My question: "What does it take to make disciples?"*

It is my firm conviction that "making disciples" requires me to teach the Bible as God's inspired word because His Word tells us who He is and answers the great questions of life. "All Scripture is God-breathed and is useful for teaching, rebuking, correcting and training in righteousness, so that the man of God may be thoroughly equipped for every good work. (2 Timothy 3:16,17, NIV)"

I wanted the Vietnamese to know the evidences for God.

How does one get to know God? Upon arriving in Vietnam, I could see God's beauty all around. As I look up at the heavens, I am thankful for such a wonderful Creator. It amazed me that the same sun, moon, and stars in Vietnam are the same ones I enjoyed in Oklahoma. "The heavens declare the glory of God; the skies proclaim the work of his hands. (Psalm 19:1, NIV)"

When I saw all the different kinds of flowers, fruits, and vegetables in Vietnam, I wanted the Vietnamese to know that God created these for all to enjoy. I love plants and gardening. The overwhelming beauty of tropical plants possessed a fascination for me. Seeing my first "flame tree"–with its bright orange-red blossoms–reminded me how God created special beauty for each part of our world. At times, when "the flame tree" caught the sun's rays, I had the feeling of witnessing a ball of fire.

The majestic coconut palms fascinated me as I saw young boys shimmy up the trunk with their bare feet and cut off a large fruit and toss it to the ground. The coconut's thick outer layer served as a cushion to keep the fruit from bursting. One of my Vietnamese friends took me to a restaurant where they served a drink made from the milk of a green coconut; after a few sips, I knew that it takes time to develop a taste for this drink.

Being surrounded with beauty and an abundance of fruit, I wanted the Vietnamese to recognize these as evidences for God. Design is evident in every one of these plants and trees and in every aspect of our world. The order of our universe allows us to count time by days, months, and years because the earth's rotation around the sun on a schedule allows us to predict seasons. The Vietnamese ancient calendar is based on the lunar orbit.

I wanted to remind the Vietnamese that one of the great marvels of God's creation is the human body with its built-in senses–sight, hearing, smell, taste, and feelings. The body's computer-like brain, its digestive system, and its heart with its blood system–all sustain the functioning of every aspect of the body. Order and design–not only in the human body but throughout our world–all point to an intelligent being who is the architect of our world.

As I looked into the eyes of Vietnamese children, it seemed God carved their beauty with a slightly olive skin with dark eyes and hair. Their slight build allowed them to stay in a squatting position for long periods of time. How agile! But more important, I marveled at their intellectual capacity.

There is something about nature that speaks to every person about God. "For since the creation of the world God's invisible qualities–his eternal power and divine nature–have been clearly seen, being understood from what has been made, so that men are without excuse. (Romans 1:20, NIV)" I constantly thanked God for creating our world and giving me the ability to see and enjoy it; I wanted the Vietnamese to know the God of creation.

God is not silent because He speaks to us through His Word and His creation–a loving Creator who made the world and everything in it. God created us in such a way that we can see and enjoy His world. "In the beginning God created the heavens and the earth. (Genesis 1:1, NIV)"

Knowing God involves seeing how He loves us and wants a personal relationship with each one of us. Though God wants a personal relationship, He does not force Himself on anyone. He has built within each of us the ability to make choices. He has given us the power to love Him or hate Him.

But knowing God requires us to appreciate His greatest characteristic, which is love. God's desire for His creation is that we love Him and our neighbor as ourselves. John says, "let us love one another, for love comes from God. Everyone who loves has been born of God and knows God. Whoever does not love does not know God, because God is love. (1 John 4:7-8, NIV)"

When one does not love his or her fellow human beings, that person "cannot love God, whom he has not seen. (1 John 4:20)"

I wanted the Vietnamese to know that sin separates one from God.

God is holy; therefore, sin and evil cannot be a part of His nature. When God created man, He gave him the awesome freedom to make choices; but early on, God's first man and woman–Adam and Eve–violated a direct command of God. Their choices brought sin and death into the world. "Therefore, just as sin entered the world through one man, and death through sin, and in this way death came to all men, because all sinned . . . (Romans 5:12, NIV)"

But what is "sin?" Sin is defined in the context of the nature and personality of God. Sin is ungodliness. To be like God is godly. To be unlike God is to be ungodly. This may be illustrated simply: God is love; therefore God loves us. If we love each other, we are like God. If we hate each other, we are unlike God. Our hate is sin.

Sin is declared wrong because it is to be different from God. It brings the consequence of death because God and sin cannot co-exist and the sinner is thus separated from God, as darkness must flee when light comes. We are created to live with and be sustained by God. When we are separated from God, who is the source of life, we will die.

Throughout the Scriptures, God has defined behaviors that are sinful, such as, unwholesome talk, anger, falsehood, greed, gossip, sexual immorality, hatred, jealousy, and idol worship. Sin is any behavior that comes between God and us and is destructive in developing effective human relationships. Anyone who commits such sinful behaviors cannot inherit the kingdom of God. (I wanted the Vietnamese to know these passages: Galatians 5:19-21; Ephesians 4:19-31; 1 Corinthians 6:9-11; Romans 1:18-32.)

But where does sin originate? Sin entered the world by human choice; consequently, when any person sins, we separate ourselves from our Creator. (Romans 5:12) When we turn our back on God, God has no choice but to give us up. When we leave God out of our lives, sin becomes the ruling force and leads us into all kinds of evil and immorality. (Romans 1:24-32) Sin is the great chasm erected by us that separates us from our God. When we sin, we do not possess the power within ourselves to return to God. We find ourselves in a helpless, hopeless state crying for a deliverer. Paul expressed this hopelessness with a declaration of despair: "What a wretched man I am! Who will rescue me from this body of death? (Romans 7:24, NIV)"

Therefore, destructive behaviors originate in the heart and mind of each person. (James 1:13-15) Therefore, our wrong choices bring a separation from God, which is spiritual death. Every person is accountable to God and will face Him in judgment. (See Romans 14:12) "Just as man is destined to die once, and after that to face judgment . . . (Hebrews 9:27, NIV)"

Thus "making disciples" means that I will explain how sin separates us from God. "But your iniquities [sins] have separated you from your God; your sins have hidden his face from you, so that he will not hear. (Isaiah 59:2, NIV)" Though sin separates us from God, from the beginning God started working out a way to show mercy and to restore that lost relationship with every person.

I wanted the Vietnamese to appreciate why Christ had to die!

The problem of every human being then is to find a way back to God. We are unable to provide the way because we are impotent by sin. We are unworthy, helpless, lost. Since sin is the inevitable captor of the soul, every person is under the penalty of death. Justice demands death for the sinner, but God's love for us expresses itself in His mercy and grace which provide the Savior as a substitute for our death. Jesus Christ becomes the Savior.

Thus, "making disciples" involves developing a clear explanation of why God sent Jesus Christ to be the Savior of the world. "In him we have redemption through his blood, the forgiveness of sins, in accordance with the riches of God's grace that he lavished on us with all wisdom and understanding. (Ephesians 1:7, NIV)" "So Christ was sacrificed once to take away the sins of many people; and he will appear a second time, not to bear sin, but to bring salvation to those who are waiting for him. (Hebrews 9:29, NIV)" How wonderful to know that Christ, by His death on the cross, can bring us back into fellowship with God. It is essential for all to understand that the Sacrifice of Christ on the cross allows God to show mercy because the penalty for sin has been paid.

Truly Christ came to earth in human flesh and conquered the devil, sin, and death in the atonement made for our sins. (Hebrews 2:9,14-18) Because Jesus suffered the temptations common to all, He is able to plead our case before God. (Hebrews 4:15) "Salvation is to be found through him alone; for there is no one else in all the world, whose name God has given to men, by whom we can be saved. (Acts 4:12, TEV)" (Also, see John 1:12,13; 12:32; 14:6)

Jesus saves then is Gospel–Good News or Glad Tidings. The total fact of Christ–His life, death, burial, resurrection, ascension, and mediation–is God's only saving resource.

The fact, the reality of the crucified, resurrected Savior is the drawing power to bring us to God. I will encourage the Vietnamese to kneel at the cross and prayerfully declare, "Behold the Lamb of God, that takes away the sin of the world. (John 1:29, KJV)"

I wanted the Vietnamese to understand
one's response to the Cross–the significance of "faith."

What is the proper response of the sinner to the cross? Our response is logically based on the nature of grace and the atonement. What response does the Savior call forth? He calls for faith or trust. This faith is the principle of depending on Jesus Christ to do what we cannot do for ourselves. By God's grace we are made righteous. "This righteousness from God comes through faith in Jesus Christ to all who believe. There is no difference, for all have sinned and fall short of the glory of God, and are justified freely by his grace through the redemption that came by Christ Jesus. God presented him as a sacrifice of atonement, through faith in his blood. He did this to demonstrate his justice, . . . at the present time, so as to be just and the one who justifies those who have faith in Jesus. (Romans 3:22-26, NIV)"

"Making disciples" requires me to teach so that those who hear will come to possess faith in the saving power of Christ. " . . . Faith comes from hearing the message, and the message is heard through the word of Christ. (Romans 10:17, NIV)" God is able to extend His loving grace because Christ has paid the price in full on the cross for the wages of our sins. (Romans 6:23) Since salvation is depicted in the gospel as the gift of God's loving grace through the merits of Christ, we cannot earn or deserve it, but only accept or receive it through faith. (Romans 4:25; 5:1,2)

Faith includes complete reliance and dependence–belief and trust–in Christ's power to save. May God help me to teach so that "faith" will be produced in Jesus Christ as Savior; that "faith" involves repenting, confessing, believing, trusting, and obeying

Christ's teachings. All of these faith responses are made in accepting the gift of salvation and relate to Christ and Him crucified.

I wanted the Vietnamese to understand why "repentance" is required.

Further, God's Word teaches that before anyone can become a follower we must repent of sin. May God help me to develop a clear explanation of "repentance"; His Word instructs us that "repentance" is a turning away from sin to God and is an expression of "faith." Since all sin is committed against God, the Scriptures teach that one "must turn to God in repentance and have faith in our Lord Jesus Christ. (Acts 20:21, NIV)"

Since "sin separates," it seems a natural requirement that to be a follower we must turn away from that which separates us from God. "The Lord is not slow in keeping his promise, as some understand slowness. He is patient with you, not wanting anyone to perish, but everyone to come to repentance. (2 Peter 3:9, NIV)"

I wanted the Vietnamese to understand why "confession" is an expression of "faith."

Confession must also reflect our faith in Jesus Christ as a sin offering. The Christian confession is faith spoken–a verbal expression from the heart of our belief and trust in Jesus' power to save. (Romans 10:8-10)

When we have heard the Good News that "Christ bore our sins on the cross," a faith is produced in the Savior that demands public acknowledgment. When Christ is confessed before others, He has promised to confess us before the Father. (Matthew 10:32)

I wanted the Vietnamese to understand why "baptism" is an essential expression of "faith."

Faith is naturally expressed in turning from sin and becoming one with the Savior in a new birth that is spiritual in nature. Therefore, "making disciples" involves "baptizing them in the name of the

Father and of the Son and of the Holy Spirit. (Matthew 28:19, NIV)" May God's Word help me in explaining the purpose of "baptism." God's Word teaches that "baptism" is an expression of faith. "You are all sons of God through faith in Christ Jesus, for all of you who were united with Christ in baptism have been clothed with Christ. (Galatians 3:26,27, NIV)"

Baptism is a spiritual expression of faith–an outward act that shows trust and reliance upon Jesus Christ for salvation. Therefore, since baptism acts out the death, burial, and resurrection of Christ, it pictures our faith. When we go down into the grave of baptism, we are acting out our repentance. Baptism demonstrates our death to sin by being buried in a watery grave. This allows a spiritual birth because we are united with Christ; for here the Christian is conceived. The believer is raised from the watery grave to live a different kind of life. Thus, the believer is showing to the world one's death to sin. This marker event of faith brings us into a saved relationship with Jesus Christ and a new life. "Or don't you know that all of us who were baptized into Christ Jesus were baptized into his death? We were therefore buried with him through baptism into death in order that, just as Christ was raised from the dead through the glory of the Father, we too may have a new life. (Romans 6:2-4, NIV)"

Mark's gospel puts the missionary charge as "Go into all the world and preach the good news to all creation. Whoever believes and is baptized will be saved, but whoever does not believe will be condemned. (Mark 16:15,16, NIV)"

From the moment one has been brought into union with Christ, the believer has been reconciled to God and belongs to Jesus Christ. The world no longer has control over the Christian because we have been crucified to the world, have become free from the power of sin, and now belong to the Savior. The baptized believer is a new creation; this is the new birth. The old person is dead and all is become new. (See II Corinthians 5:17)

To the believer who has accepted Christ by repentance and baptism, sin has no further claim on the individual for the penalty for sin has been paid; its account completely settled through the merits of Christ. Now the redeemed person has the Spirit of Christ living in one's soul, giving strength to live for the redeemer.

God has promised two great spiritual gifts in Christ when we repent and are baptized: the forgiveness of sins and the gift of the Holy Spirit. "Repent and be baptized, every one of you, in the name of Jesus Christ so that your sins may be forgiven. And you will receive the gift of the Holy Spirit. (Acts 2:38, NIV)"

I wanted the Vietnamese to recognize how the "Holy Spirit" helps one in living the Christian life.

"Making disciples" requires that I stress the help God gives the Christian through His Holy Spirit: " . . . the spirit helps us in our weakness. We do not know what we ought to pray for, but the Spirit intercedes for us with groans that words cannot express. And he who searches our hearts knows the mind of the Spirit, because the Spirit intercedes for the saints in accordance with God's will. (Romans 8:26,27, NIV)"

Not only does the Holy Spirit intercede on our behalf, He is constantly working in our hearts for a clearer understanding of God's Word and motivating us to help others. The Holy Spirit works in our hearts to see our lost world and leads us to share God's Good News.

I wanted the Vietnamese to understand the significance of "the church."

"Making disciples" means that I must teach about Christ's church. When Peter confessed, "You are the Christ, the Son of the living God," Jesus said "on this rock I will build my church. (Matthew 16:16,18, NIV)" At the conclusion of Peter's first sermon, the Scriptures indicate "Those who accepted his message were baptized, and about three thousand were added to their number that day. (Acts 2:41, NIV)" The purpose of this Christian community is to encourage each other in the faith. "Let us not give up meeting together, . . . but let us encourage one another–and all the more as you see the Day approaching. (Hebrews 10:25, NIV)" This fellowship provides weekly worship.

Truly, God provides for our support needs in keeping us saved in Christ's church. Christ shed His blood for the church (Acts 20:28) and is the head of the church (Colossians 1:18). The church is essential in keeping us saved, in growing in service, and in reaching out to the lost.

I wanted the Vietnamese to appreciate
what is involved in "worship."

"Worship" has always been a part of God's plan. God has built into every being the desire to worship. If one does not worship God, that person will find something to worship–material things, idols, selfish fulfillment, or our universe. (See Romans 1:21-23) What is taught in Scripture about the kind of worship God desires from those who want to follow Him? Christian worship involves participating in the Lord's Supper in memory of Christ's death for our sins, the teaching of God's Word, singing, praying, and giving.

The Lord's Supper. "Making disciples" must include something about "the Lord's Supper." In the beginning of the church, this community of believers met on each first day of each week to partake of the Lord's Supper. "On the first day of the week we came together to break bread. (Acts 20:7, NIV)." "For I received from the Lord what I also passed on to you: The Lord Jesus, on the night he was betrayed, took bread, and when he had given thanks, he broke it and said, 'This is my body, which is for you, do this in remembrance of me.' In the same way, after supper he took the cup, saying, 'This cup is the new covenant in my blood; do this, whenever you drink it, in remembrance of me.' For whenever you eat this bread and drink this cup, you proclaim the Lord's death until he comes. (1 Corinthians 11:23-26, NIV)"

Teaching God's Word and Singing. In "worship," the Christian community dwells on the word of Christ and engages in singing. "Let the word of Christ dwell in you richly as you teach and counsel one another with all wisdom, and as you sing psalms, hymns and spiritual songs with gratitude in your hearts to God. And whatever you do, whether in word or deed, do it all in the name of the Lord

Jesus, giving thanks to God the Father through him. (Colossians 3:16-17, NIV)"

Praying. The Christian community engages in prayer. Christ's "intent was that now, through the church, the manifold wisdom of God should be made known . . . according to his eternal purpose which he accomplished in Christ Jesus our Lord. In him and through faith in him we may approach God with freedom and confidence. (Ephesians 3:10-12, NIV)"

We can take all of our concerns to God. "Do not be anxious about anything, but in everything, by prayer and petition, with thanksgiving, present your requests to God. And the peace of God, which transcends all understanding, will guard your hearts and your minds in Christ Jesus. (Philippians 4:6,7, NIV)"

Giving. The Christian community is instructed to give. Paul provided instruction for the Corinthian church with "On the first day of every week, each one of you should set aside a sum of money in keeping with one's income . . . (I Corinthians 16:2, NIV)" God desires that we not only give our money but ourselves. (See Romans 12:1)

Within the various avenues of worship, God really wants our hearts and our minds. Worship provides us the opportunity to express to God our love; our praise; our adoration; our devotion; our appreciation for His Word; our awesome recognition of His power; our thanksgiving for His generous gifts–including the greatest gift of salvation in His Son, Jesus Christ; our gratitude for His Holy Spirit that helps us live the Christian life; our hope of eternal life in His Son; and our recognition of God's sovereignty and will that will ultimately be fulfilled in all things.

I wanted the Vietnamese to recognize
the kind of life the Christian is to live.

"Making disciples" involves "teaching them to obey everything I have commanded you." May God help me in teaching and living those attitudes and characteristics of the kind of life Jesus expects of His followers! May God help me to be faithful to His Word, as He has given in it a clear explanation of the new life in Christ!

In Romans 12, we are to offer ourselves "as living sacrifices, holy and pleasing to God–which is your spiritual worship"; we are not to "conform to the pattern of this world, but be transformed by the renewing of your mind"; our "love must be sincere"; we are to "hate what is evil"; we are to "be joyful in hope; patient in affliction, faithful in prayer"; we are to "share with God's people who are in need"; we are to "practice hospitality"; we are to "bless those who persecute you; bless and do not curse"; we are to "live in harmony with one another"; we are not to "be conceited"; we "do not repay anyone evil for evil"; we are to "be careful to do what is right in the sight of everybody."

In 1 Corinthians 13, Christ's disciples are challenged further to show a kind of love that is rare in this world. "Love is patient, love is kind. It does not envy, it does not boast, it is not proud. It is not rude, it is not self-seeking, it is not easily angered, it keeps no record of wrongs. Love does not delight in evil but rejoices in the truth. It always protects, always trusts, always hopes, always perseveres. (1 Corinthians 13:4-7, NIV)"

Christ holds His disciples to a high standard. That standard in Ephesians challenges: "But among you there must not be even a hint of sexual immorality, or of any kind of impurity, or of greed because these are improper for God's holy people. Nor should there be obscenity, foolish talk or coarse joking, which are out of place, but rather thanksgiving. (Ephesians 5:3-4, NIV)"

Christians are to put off the acts of the sinful nature, such as "sexual immorality, . . . hatred, discord, jealousy, fits of rage, selfish ambition, . . . envy; drunkenness, orgies, and the like. I warn you . . . that those who live like this will not inherit the kingdom of God. (Galatians 5:19-21, NIV)"

However, the Christian is to put on the fruit of the Spirit, which includes "love, joy, peace, patience, kindness, goodness, faithfulness, gentleness and self- control. (Galatians 5:22,23, NIV)"

I wanted the Vietnamese to know that God provides help in living the Christian life. Prayer is a great avenue in which God gives us strength. I wanted to share the Gospel in such a way that people would come to love God and His Son and would bring them to faith in Jesus Christ. My teaching must convict them of sin that separates from God and would cause them to repent. Following Jesus' instructions for making disciples, I wanted to baptize them "in the name of the Father and of the Son and of the Holy Spirit." I wanted them to experience the forgiveness that comes when one is baptized and I wanted them to know the empowerment of the Holy Spirit. This acceptance of Christ by faith, which is expressed in repentance and baptism, would allow God to add one to the Christian community, His church.

How do you answer the question about God's love from a young man who knew tragedy after tragedy?

One day when teaching a group about how God loves us, we looked at Scriptures showing God's love and concern for every person. A young Vietnamese man challenged me to show evidence of God's love in his life.

He stood up and said, "Sir, please show me how God loves me! The Viet Cong killed my father when I was three. Relatives helped my mother after his death. Then my mother was killed when I was seven. From that time on, I have lived with various relatives and often left to my own devices for livelihood. How can you say that God loves me?"

My reply: "I am truly sorry for the tragedies you have experienced in your early life. Let me ask you a question: Who would you say caused the loss of your father and your mother; was it God or man?"

After a moment of deep reflection, the young man replied: "Well, I would have to say it was man?"

Then I emphasized that God does not tempt His creation with evil. The sequence of sin is seen clearly in the book of James. "When tempted, no one should say, 'God is tempting me.' For God cannot be tempted by evil, nor does he tempt anyone; but each one is tempted when, by his own evil desire, he is dragged away and enticed. Then, after desire has conceived, it gives birth to sin; and sin, when it is full-grown, gives birth to death. (James 1:13-15, NIV)" According to Scripture, evil cannot be a part of God's nature but evil originates in the heart of man, who is influenced by Satan and the sinful influence of others.

I sensed the deep agony this young man had faced all his life. Then I said: "All of us ask about how life came to be." We ask,"Did life just evolve or were we created?" I believe that life is the creation of a loving God who desires a relationship with us. This God provides the air we breathe; He created the food we eat and the water we drink. There is design and order in our universe. But the Bible reveals that evil came into the world. Therefore, as many of your writers indicate, there is an on-going struggle between good and evil. Do you think it is possible for a loving God to see your need and provide relatives to care for you?"

He replied: "I suppose that is possible. But why did a loving God allow all these bad things to happen to my family?" Then I tried to explain that we live in a sin-cursed world and God does not promise that we will be free from trials or problems; for example, look at the sufferings of Jesus Christ! But God does promise that He will be with His followers during those trials and sufferings and will not allow us to be overcome by them.

In the class, we continued to discuss the problem of good and evil. But I could see that the young man had many unanswered questions. I felt somewhat inadequate to give him really satisfying answers. I could remember Paul's struggle; even with his superior education and background in the Scriptures, he still asked the Ephesians to pray for him. "Pray for me, that whenever I open my mouth, words may be given me so that I will fearlessly make known the mystery of the gospel. (Ephesians 6:19, NIV)" If Paul needed help, I had a greater need. I asked a silent prayer for God's wisdom and the words to answer this young man's search for answers.

Since I did not have a Bible study following this class, I asked the young man if he would stay after class so that we could continue our discussions. He stayed; we walked to a nearby park and I listened sympathetically to his frustrations and tragedies. For several weeks, we made this a regular routine to walk through the park discussing some of the great questions of life. I came to love this young man and prayed for our discussions to lead him to the Savior. We maintained our friendship and Bible studies until the Vietnamese military called him up to serve. I had given him a Bible and he promised to continue his search for meaning to life.

***Ralph Burcham is teaching a Bible class
to a group of Vietnamese men.***

*American servicemen desired
to start a congregation at Bien Hoa.*

After we arrived in Vietnam, the servicemen at Bien Hoa indicated a desire to start a Vietnamese congregation in their area. Therefore, the servicemen invited us to worship with them at Bien Hoa. In the meantime, I had talked with Nguyen Dan Bao and his wife about the possibility of them starting a congregation. So after worshiping in Saigon, the Baos and our family drove out about 20 miles to Bien Hoa for the afternoon service. We enjoyed being out of the city for a while. The beautiful drive to Bien Hoa refreshed us all. This highway is considered to be unsafe at night but not too risky during the day.

The Baos had been converted and faithfully served Christ before we arrived in Vietnam. They loved teaching children's classes and taught most effectively.

After the service, the servicemen asked us to stay and discuss the possibilities of starting a congregation. The servicemen offered financial support for their move. The Baos promised to give this prayerful consideration. In time, the Baos did start a congregation.

I felt a real sense of pride because the Baos accepted this challenge to begin a new congregation. Their worked proved to be very successful.

Almost immediately, Bao started studying with a Buddhist priest. Bao made an appointment for me to go with him to visit the priest. The priest graciously received us and provided tea and some candied ginger. I took a small bite of the ginger and felt I had bitten into liquid fire. It burned all the way to my stomach. Watching me intently, the priest gave a big smile.

As we talked, the priest looked at me and asked "What are your views on creation?"

I replied, "I believe that God created the world as is explained in the Christian Bible." Then I gave further details from Genesis.

The priest listened intently and then confessed he had written a book on creation but he had very different views from mine. We talked further; then he said, "I believe I need to make some revisions in my book!" Later, Bao baptized this priest and another one into Jesus Christ.

Some time later the Baos asked me to perform the wedding of their daughter. As we discussed their plans, the couple told me they wanted a typical American wedding. Then I discussed with the bride and the groom what such a wedding entails. We had a rehearsal and everything seemed to go very smoothly.

The Baos planned the wedding to be at Bien Hoa so American servicemen could be present. They asked Tran Van Can to translate. We rehearsed.

On the appointed day for the wedding, everything went exactly as planned. At the conclusion of the ceremony, I told the groom "You may kiss the bride." Nothing happened; the translator remained silent. I repeated, "You may kiss the bride." Then the translator whispered to me, "We don't do this in Vietnam." To which I concluded the ceremony by saying, "I would like to introduce Mr. and Mrs. . . ." The servicemen all had a big smile. They then congratulated the couple.

It really takes time to become familiar with the subtleties of a culture. It is through several of our Vietnamese co-workers—who loved us, who tactfully taught us, and who guided us—that we came to appreciate Vietnamese history and culture.

Radio and TV seemed to be the best way to reach the Vietnamese population.

Maurice Hall worked diligently in getting permission to present Gospel messages on Vietnamese radio stations. In July 1965, the Vietnamese government granted permission for a 30-minute weekly Sunday morning broadcast on Saigon Network Channel C. When Maurice left Vietnam, he asked me to coordinate this program. Talented Vietnamese prepared the program each week.

During 1966 and 1967, radio turned out to be an excellent medium in Vietnam for reaching the people as the masses did not own nor could they afford a TV. Maurice Hall made the original arrangements for the radio program, sponsored by the White's Ferry Road Church of Christ. Each week radio messages went throughout the southern part of South Vietnam over three radio stations.

The thirty-minute radio programs included singing, Bible reading, and a sermon. We negotiated for time on the radio station in DaNang. This unfulfilled dream would have allowed the Good News to be broadcast into the very heart of communist territory in North Vietnam. Also, eleven other radio stations offered to give us free time but we lacked the funds to supply the tapes.

Tran Van Can helped with our radio program.

Then the Viet Cong blew up the radio station, which put us off the air for a time but Tran Van Can helped me in keeping in touch with the Administrator of the radio station who offered to help us get a new program.

The number of people requesting our Bible Correspondence Course could gauge the success of this program. Eventually we had several hundred enrolled.

Then in the fall of 1967, the VC blew up the radio station again, and the program went off the air for a time. When the new station re-opened, after some difficulty, we gained permission for a new program. However, with the destruction of the radio station during the Tet Offensive of 1968 our program went off air again. Not to be discouraged, Tran put forth his best efforts and obtained a new program entitled *"The Voice of Christianity."*

Tran worked for the U. S. Government in dubbing in Vietnamese on military training films. I told him about the Herald of Truth television programs. I asked: "Can you dub in Vietnamese on these films?"

He replied: "Of course, I can." I thought "How wonderful God has trained a man with the technical know-how to prepare gospel films for Vietnamese television audiences."

Tran excitedly responded: "Since television is in its infancy in Vietnam, the local television station is looking for good programs." I felt these new opportunities to be tremendous for taking Christ throughout this war-torn country. But I wondered: "Will we be able to take advantage of this media?" I prayed to God for direction.

As I reflected on these opportunities, I felt our Lord actually gave me the answer in the story of the Good Samaritan (Luke 10:30-37). The priest failed his fellow man because he had become calloused as a slave to daily routine in the temple. The Levite's responsibilities kept him busy in caring for the temple and the worship services. When the priest and the Levite became so temple centered, they lost their sensitivity to the needs of others. But the Samaritan, being person centered, possessed a love for his fellow man; the needs of the man touched his heart.

Somehow I wanted to reach out with the loving heart of the Samaritan to the spiritual needs of the Vietnamese people and to the children that have been robbed of family and possessions by the Viet Cong. I prayed that I might be an instrument of God to demonstrate that God cares. I knew they could not know God's love unless I loved them and unless they heard and understood the good news of a Savior. I felt the physical and spiritual wounds of these people— who had suffered the hardships of war for decades–had waited too long to be bound up and healed. I couldn't be like the priest and Levite and pass them by!

We did not have the resources to produce our own films. Therefore, I wrote to the producers of the Herald of Truth in the States and told them of the unique opportunity we might have. By return mail, they sent five reels of some of their most popular programs and gave me permission to have Vietnamese dubbed on the film.

Immediately, Tran started dubbing in Vietnamese on the film. Then he told me, "These programs are of a better quality than anything being shown on our TV stations."

Being thoroughly convinced that God had led us to Vietnam, I felt a tremendous obligation to use my energies in bringing the true peace of Jesus Christ to hearts that knew well a lifetime of conflict and war. How I prayed for God's wisdom to use me in giving life and hope. My vision for Vietnam included getting the Good News of Christ out to the nation in every way possible. This included the media–radio, newspapers, correspondence courses, TV, and tracts; teaching both one-on-one and in groups; and benevolence.

I thanked God for opening up these new avenues for taking the Gospel to people who had known nothing but war throughout their lives.

Speakers for the Gospel Meeting standing in front of the Thong Nhut Theater are Ralph Burcham and a Vietnamese minister.

*The challenge of gospel lectures in the
Thong Nhut Theater seemed a possibility.*

One of the largest auditoriums in Saigon is the Thong Nhut Theater. It is next door to the British Embassy and on the street that leads up to the Presidential Palace. Some of the Vietnamese Christians learned that we could rent this facility for two nights–Saturday and Sunday–at a very reasonable rate.

In planning sessions with several of the Vietnamese Christian leaders, they decided to have two lectures; I would speak on the first night and one of the Vietnamese preachers on the second. My topic–"The Greatest Questions of Life." The speaker for the Vietnamese radio program prepared to speak on "Humanity in Christianity."

As we discussed advertising, someone made the suggestion that we invite members to hand out invitations at bus stops, particularly at transfer points with a tremendous amount of traffic. In discussions on what kind of invitations to prepare, someone suggested using a theater type ticket to be stamped with the word "complimentary" across it and with a clear explanation of the purpose of the lectures.

Those receiving a special invitation in the Saigon area included: each local listener writing in to our radio program, to the names and addresses received in hospital visits, to those enrolled in our Bible Correspondence Course. Also, we sent invitations to the parents of the children attending the American-Vietnamese International School. In local newspapers, we placed ads. We placed cloth banners in front of the theater and above the stage.

My concern: "Will anybody come?"

To my surprise over 450 attended the first evening. Each person attending received a response and registration card. The card could be used to enroll in the Bible Correspondence Course, to request a private Bible study, or to order literature. We printed the songs used for congregational singing on cards that advertised the three radio programs carried on different stations in South Vietnam. Even though many of the Vietnamese were unfamiliar with the songs and congregational singing, I wondered how this would turn out.

During the lectures, a group of Vietnamese Christians prayed off stage "for souls to be touched by the message of Christ." The song leader explained the songs and, to my surprise, the people responded enthusiastically to congregational singing. At the close of that first meeting, 18 indicated a desire to be baptized into Christ.

In the audience an American, Bill Moffitt, who lived in Columbus, Indiana, came forward and said he would like to study the Bible. Captain Gordon Stalcup studied and baptized him.

Another 150 attended the second lecture with five responding to the invitation. At the close of each lecture, the audience submitted questions. This proved to be a forum that the audience enjoyed.

The success of these lectures excited all of us because we felt God's Good News to be going out and changing lives.

Locating a baptistry is a challenge.

I had studied with a young man for several weeks, so when he indicated his desire to become a Christian, I then started making arrangements for his baptism. Since we were in the process of relocating our congregation, our large portable baptistry had been moved to the orphanage. When we arrived at the orphanage, the cover had not been properly placed on the baptistry and a thick green slime covered the water. I asked Yen, the local preacher and orphanage director, where we might go for the baptism. He suggested a place he knew nearby where the ocean tide flowed in and out.

Yen accompanied us and we drove as far as we could. Then we took a trail through the jungle. As we went along, people living near the trail started asking questions and following us. I thought to myself: "I wander are these friends or enemies?"

When we came to the clearing, the scene reminded me of Bible times. Because of the fast moving tide, we looked and found a good place on the beach. Fishermen were cleaning their nets–repairing and stretching them on large bamboo frames.

Since we had quite an audience by this time, Yen thought it would be good to give an explanation of the purpose of baptism. So he preached a mini sermon on Jesus Christ and how one becomes a Christian. After his brief lesson, I took the young man's confession.

As we both prepared to go into the water, I took off my shoes and the audience started whispering and pointing at my toes. They found amusing my white feet and my hairy toes; the body hair on a Vietnamese is almost transparent. After I stepped into the water, the audience changed their focus to the young man's baptism.

I baptized the young man into the name of the Father, the Son, and the Holy Spirit. I explained the significance of his confession and baptism because two things happen: his sins will be forgiven because of Christ's sacrifice and he will receive the gift of the Holy Spirit, who will help him live the Christian life. Being in Christ, he has the hope of eternal life.

As we started out of the water, the tide was rushing out and I couldn't help but recall what Roger said about how God flushed everything.

We started an outreach in the Vietnamese Military Hospitals.

Some of the members of the Saigon church served as soldiers in the Vietnamese military. Their faithfulness encouraged us. As a result of these friendships and the injury of one of our members, we started visiting the Vietnamese military hospital. As we saw the wounded, it reminded us of "man's inhumanity to man." Someone told us that the turnover in the largest military hospital to be about 2,000 patients each month.

A steady stream of casualties poured into the military hospitals. But for each killed, many more were wounded. At the Cong Hoa Military Hospital, we learned it had over 2,500 patients and more come in daily. This was only one of several other such hospitals in the Saigon area.

I visited with the Administrator of the Cong Hoa hospital. I told him about our mission. He gave permission for us to visit any of the wards at any time we chose.

From these experiences, I determined to try to do something in some small way for these men. I made an appeal for funds to buy Bibles and small gifts; as a result, we received funds, servicemen provided boxes of soap and other items to give. The members of the Saigon congregation sacked these special gifts. Also, we offered a free Bible with an insert, *"Introduction to the Bible."*

Realizing most who received the Bible lacked an understanding of it, I prepared an introduction to the Bible entitled *"You are invited to walk the path that leads to eternal life."* In the opening paragraph I opened with questions to tease their spiritual intellect. "Man is constantly searching for meaning to life. In this search, he often turns to religion. He desires to know more about the supernatural. Is there a God? Can man know God? How does God reveal Himself to man? Where did man come from? What is the purpose of man's existence? What will happen to man after death? Is it possible for man to have eternal life?" (See "Appendix C" for a complete copy of the insert.)

This insert included an outline of key passages that gave the reader a framework for understanding Christianity. I concluded with "May God bless your efforts as you begin your search for eternal life, which is available only to those who accept the Son of God and who follow in the path given in the Bible. 'A crown of life' is promised to those who are faithful to Him until death." (See Revelation 2:10)

In addition to the Bible with the insert, we gave each the first lesson of a Bible correspondence course. To some patients, we gave a tract.

A sea of suffering humanity overwhelmed us.

The great tragedy of war has to be those injured or maimed in some way. The Lord gave us an opportunity to work with the wounded of the Special Forces of Vietnam. When visiting the Cong Hoa Military Hospital, I met Captain Vu Vinh Thung, who worked with the Special Forces in Psychological Warfare. He offered to show us through the hospital. We asked Tran Van Can and Thuong Van Nguyen to accompany Gladys and me.

On the appointed day, Captain Vu greeted us in the administrative section of the hospital. As we walked down the dirty corridors, the open wards had no partitions and you could look in on scores of wounded with no privacy. We saw human suffering that cannot be equaled on the face of this earth. Some of the patients had a leg or an arm in suspension; the unfortunate ones had no limbs to be placed in suspension. Somehow the scores of amputees touched me deeply. Particularly moving are the young men who would have to live out their lives without an arm or leg or neither. Captain Vu indicated that because of the scarcity of medicine they often do not have enough anesthesias to sustain an amputee for the entire operation.

As Captain Vu walked with us down the aisle of the first ward, we could see rows of hospital beds with a patient in each. Then screams and cries of a man having a cast put on from the waist down startled and disturbed us. On either side of that aisle we saw scores of suffering young men.

The Captain stopped by the bedside of the first man selected for us to visit. After the introduction, a hush fell on all of us as we looked into the eyes of a man who had no eyes. The eye wounds had not healed. I immediately thought of a poem I once read: "Oh, God, forgive me when I whine, I have two eyes, the world is mine!" As we looked down to his arms, we saw that they ended just where the hands should begin.

By this time, I felt ill; the tears began to slide down my cheek as I realized this man had no eyes and no hands. Then my eyes cleared enough to look again and I see that only stubs ended where the feet should be.

A silent prayer came across my quivering lips. "Oh, Lord, give me wisdom to say some words of encouragement to this man. What could I say to this victim of a booby trap?"

As I groped for words, I heard myself saying: "I appreciate the great sacrifice you have made for your country so that your people might enjoy freedom. There is a God in heaven that loves you and is concerned about you. He, too, made a sacrifice by giving up His Son so that you could enjoy eternal life." Then it seemed no other words would come.

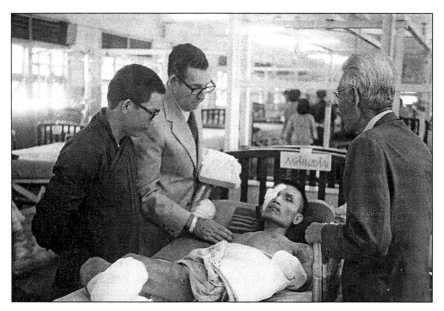

***Ralph Burcham looks with compassion on a Vietnamese
soldier who lost both eyes, both hands, and both feet.***

Impulsively I wanted to take him into my arms; I found myself
putting my arm across his shoulder as he raised himself partially in
the bed. If this man does not come to know Jesus, what a hopeless
future! Death would seem to be a sweet release. Yet, without Christ
what does eternity hold for this man?

I asked: "Do you have relatives who live nearby?" He said, "My
mother has come to stay and take care of me." Then I presented him
with cookies, small gifts, and a Bible. He expressed appreciation.

After encouraging him to have his mother read to him from the
Bible, we moved on to our next patient. Fortunately, this man had
eyes and one whole arm; however, the other limbs ended in stubs. He
thanked us for the Bible, gifts, and cookies. I told him how the love
of Jesus Christ had impacted my life, and how this book points to a
God who loves him and wants an eternal relationship with him.

I thought to myself, "What kind of future do these amputees have
before them? Vietnam is an underdeveloped country; there are limited
opportunities for the handicapped as well as for the poor living in the

countryside. What kind of life? At best, a difficult one! Many will become beggars in a city with beggars on every street corner."

Nearly every patient had a family member who served as a practical nurse because of the overtaxed regular staff. We saw young wives with their small children visiting their husbands and fathers– all had given so much that they might have the right to live as free people.

While making the hospital rounds, a helicopter landed with new patients from the war area. Helicopters constantly streamed in bringing the war's latest victims.

We walked through several wards before we came to the ward for paraplegics. The degree of paralysis differed for each man we visited. Each patient had a family member or volunteer, who exercised and turned the patient, read to him, and just talked. The first man visited suffered paralysis from the waist down. I told him: "This book contains a great story of how God loves you and wants to provide for your greatest needs. God can bring hope to your life!" He thankfully accepted a copy of the Bible. A seven-year old brother cared for him and we gave him some gifts.

The next patient suffered paralysis from the neck down. His spinal column had been injured and he could only move his head. His wife told us they had four small children; then she sorrowfully explained that she had no hope for his recovery. As I looked at this patient, I felt that as long as he had love, he would exist; but what a bleak existence!

We moved on from patient to patient. Each had to be rotated to keep bedsores from forming. Yet, we saw bedsores so repulsive to human senses. Someone must exercise their limbs to keep the muscles from deteriorating. Some would be lying face down. It became more and more difficult to give true words of encouragement. To each, I tried to express appreciation for their sacrifice and point them to a God of sacrifice who provides eternal life.

How moving to see this young wife turning her husband face down. The construction of the bed had a cut-away, which allowed the patient to read or look at items placed on a small shelf below. Gladys gave this young woman a Bible. How touching to see the wife place the Bible on the shelf below the husband's face. Gladys looked back to see this little wife in a kneeling position as she held up the Bible for her husband to see and as they read the Bible together. I prayed that both would be blessed.

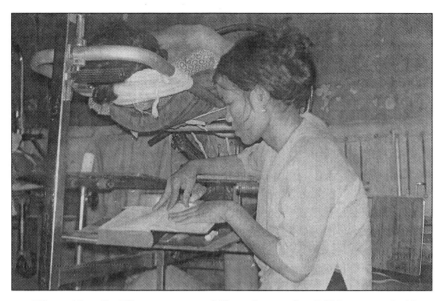

The wife of a Vietnamese soldier places the Bible on a shelf below the cut-away as she reads to her paralyzed husband.

As we walked through the wards of the war wounded, I prayed that somehow these men might come to know Jesus Christ, the great healer of men's souls.

I received new insights into hurting Vietnamese prisoners–outcasts of society.

Maurice Hall started a prison ministry. After he left, one of our missionaries, Phil Carpenter, continued the prison work in Saigon for several months. When Phil moved to Nha Trang, I started working in the prison as a temporary replacement. These prisoners made up the outcasts of Vietnamese society–prostitutes, drug dealers, thieves, murderers, the aged, homeless children, and the crippled.

Each Friday from 150 to 400 prisoners assembled to hear sermons and lessons.

On my first visit, one of the officials of the prison escorted me around the prison. I saw prisoners preparing the next meal. They prepared the food in a squatting position. The food's unpleasant aromas seemed to permeate the air. I found the odor to be stifling.

I went into the wing of the prison for those with leprosy. Here tucked away from society were the true untouchables. Some had missing fingers or toes, or a partial ear or nose. Being my first time to see a leper, I felt ill in what I saw. Therefore, I prayed fervently for a cure for their physical disabilities; but, more important, healing for their leprous souls.

The large room where I held the class consisted of large concrete slabs about 18 inches thick with a walkway around each block. The guards brought the prisoners in before they allowed me to go in. The prisoners squatted on the slabs crowded next to each other: a smelly place with some smoking while some looked at me with great disdain and arrogance.

As I looked into their eyes, I saw hurting individuals who needed forgiveness and the love of God. As I surveyed their situation, I prayed for wisdom. I told them about a God of compassion who created our world and loved them so much that He sent His Son to die for them in order that each might have eternal life.

I wanted them to know the God who sent His Son to the earth to become their Savior. He had a natural birth like all of us. He grew up in a poor area of the world. He never possessed much of this world's goods. He lived a sinless life. Wicked men killed him. But after three days, He came out of the grave alive. For the first time, a hush came over my captive audience.

Then I said, "He lives today and wants to do something for each of you."

For like Paul, I "resolved to know nothing while I was with you except Jesus Christ and him crucified. (2 Corinthians 2:2, NIV)" Over and over again, I tried to help them get the message of the cross.

When my schedule became overloaded, I asked Ron Matthews if he would take over. Matthews, one of our single missionaries, worked hard in winning the hearts of the Vietnamese. Faithfully each week, he would go to the prison and preach to the very outcasts of Vietnamese society. Many Vietnamese and missionaries helped with the prison ministry.

Then Nguyen Van Minh, my translator and interpreter, filled in for Ron on occasions. Minh, whom I taught and baptized, immersed 13 of these prisoners into Christ. I knew all of these would have a real struggle in remaining faithful to Christ. But I am thankful for the Good News being presented and prayed for those who continue to teach the outcasts of society.

Ron Matthews wrote a poem and dedicated it to the Vietnamese.

After spending some time in Vietnam, Matthews gave me his poem:

Vietnam! Vietnam!
  How many tears have you cried?
  How much blood have you shed?
  How many bombs have torn your land?
Vietnam! Vietnam!
  How many young boys have you lost?
  How many geniuses have you buried?
  How many musicians have you sent to war
  To play the horrible tune of war?
  How many children have you pushed out of the cradle
  To tend rice fields?
Vietnam! Vietnam!
  You know war.
  What does peace mean to you?
  A dream? a happy day? a love returned? no war?
  Must you pay a price so dear?
  Must you give all?
  Must you always live with fear?
Vietnam! Vietnam!
  Your geniuses, your young men, your musicians
  Will play their parts well.
  One day, one day they'll bring peace home to you.

They'll wave a tall and mighty banner.
Your mothers will know rest.
Your daughters will know love.
Your men will know peace.
So worry not
Vietnam! Vietnam!
Worry not
Your day is yet to come.

When Matthews gave me the poem, I kept it a few days before taking the time to read it. Then I realized what a talent this young missionary possessed. How I prayed that his dream of peace might be fulfilled.

Failing to get our servicemen's advice before traveling put us in harms way.

Matthews spent some time helping a Vietnamese family with seven children. The thirteen- year old daughter could not move and had to be waited on hand and foot. She could not talk and showed no response when others did things for her. Because of the poor health of the mother, the family had decided to put the child in a Catholic institution outside of Saigon.

Matthews asked if I would take the family out to this special home. I asked about security and he assured me the area was safe. I did not check with any of our military.

We drove out to the institution, which was off the main highway that leads to Vung Tau. When we arrived, a Priest met us; he arranged for one of the helpers to take the family with the handicapped child. However, the Priest wanted to show us around.

He took us into the different wards. In one, the patients had paralysis that did not allow them to walk. Busy making brooms, all seemed to be content. In another ward, the blind patients kept busy weaving mats used for beds.

The Priest showed us the ward where the handicapped child would be placed; in it, several other children lay helpless in their cribs. The helpers showed tender loving care for each child. The sparkling cleanliness of the ward made such a favorable impression on me. I have never witnessed greater compassion. Next the Priest took us into their storage room filled with sacks of rice marked—"U. S. Aid."

Then some distance away, I could hear shelling. I asked the Priest, "Do you ever have trouble from the Viet Cong?" He said, "No."

I told Matthews that I thought we should try to wind things up as quickly as possible. On our way back, I could see smoke between us and the main highway.

As we got closer, I could see fire and the smoke about a half-mile from the highway. Then a military truck could be seen with dust flying from a dirt road that led up to our highway. We pulled over and stopped.

As the military truck pulled onto the highway, Matthews yelled to the driver, "What's going on down there?" In the most caustic tones, the serviceman replied, "You know, there's a war going on! Buddy, why don't you go down and see?"

Matthews said to me, "Let's go."

I replied, "Ron, you could tell by the tone of his answer that he was telling us we have no business being out here. We're heading back to Saigon."

When I got back to Saigon, I saw Jim Reynolds, a Christian serviceman, at the school and told him what had happened. Reynolds' response, "I can't believe you went out there. That really is Viet Cong territory. As you know, when our planes come back with bombs not used, I instruct the pilots to drop them in that area."

I thanked the Lord for being with us and apologized to Reynolds for not seeking his advice before this trip.

The Vietnamese churches needed training in leadership.

After teaching and preaching to the Vietnamese for several months, I started asking the question: "What can I do to further the leadership abilities of all the new converts in case all Americans have to leave?" After prayer and consulting with others, I decided to offer a leadership-training program.

I sent a letter to all of the Vietnamese congregations sharing with them the content of a leadership program and requesting their help in sending young men with the potential for being preachers or leaders. For preachers living locally, I invited them to attend whenever possible.

Their initial response excited me because they sent me names of 17. Immediately, I started planning the curriculum and selecting materials for translation. I wanted all the materials to strengthen, to inspire, to give in-depth knowledge of the Scriptures, and to teach Christ-like ways and attitudes.

Because of the in-depth nature of the studies, the classes would meet five days a week from 8 to 12:30. In the afternoons, students would spend their time in study, sermon preparation, and visitation.

The curriculum covered a survey of Old and New Testaments, textual studies, basic Christian doctrine, sermon and lesson preparation, organization of the Church, personal work, and ways of reaching the people with the Gospel. I indicated the summer session would last for two months. Then we would evaluate the program and make a decision about a fall term.

We had a filmstrip projector. Jule Miller gave permission to translate his filmstrips: *The Life of Christ, Acts, The Parables,* and his cottage meeting series on the Old Testament. We obtained the filmstrip manuals and translated the dialogue. We made a flyleaf in Vietnamese to match each frame to place over the English; this allowed them to raise the flyleaf and see the English for each frame.

I wrote to Dr. Stafford North, Bible professor and Dean of Oklahoma Christian, about the class and he sent me excellent materials on lesson and sermon preparation. Also, I had many Bible lessons in my file which I started the process of translating. Almost from the beginning, I had been putting together materials that covered doctrinal issues that every Christian needs to know. A friend sent funds for having it published; we printed it in both English and Vietnamese on facing pages and entitled it *"Framework of Christianity."*

On the first day of classes, instead of 17 students, we had 23. How good to see in the class two of my converts, both family men and both had been public school teachers. I believed they would be able to handle a mission congregation after completing the summer program. Many of the older Vietnamese attended the classes regularly. All of them received copies of everything translated into their language. They reacted favorably to the excellent quality of the materials.

After initial instruction, I asked each student to prepare a short sermon, which they delivered in class. However, I felt they needed more preaching experience with exposure to an audience. I proposed to the class that we go to the marketplaces on Saturdays; each could present a sermon; and the rest of the class could hand out tracts or enroll students in our Bible Correspondence Course (BCC). They responded favorably.

I asked the older preachers to critique the sermons. It became evident early on that we had an outstanding future preacher in Le Nho. He possessed charisma and delivery that kept the class in awe for each of his lessons.

On our best Saturday, they enrolled 543 in the BCC. All enrolled large numbers; but Nguyen Van Minh, my translator, enrolled 127 in one day. Another member of the class, Danh, made out the permanent records on those enrolling; and the entire class helped in addressing, stuffing, and stamping the envelopes with the lessons. They also had the responsibility of grading returned lessons.

The BCC had a particular appeal for high school and college students because of its being printed in both English and Vietnamese. One of Vietnam's leading architects enrolled in the BCC by mail; he had received one of the tracts on the street that had an ad for the course in the back.

In this class of young men training to be ministers or church leaders, I presented the challenge of visiting the military hospitals; they decided to try to visit the veterans' hospital once a month; visit with the patients; give small gifts of personal items, such as soap, toothpaste and brush, and a washcloth; they planned to talk with them about the greatest gift of all–Jesus Christ.

***Some of the men in the Leadership Training Class
as they prepared to preach in various markets in Saigon.***

At the end of the summer session, I invited all to our home for dinner. Gladys described it this way: "Twenty-two men came and they ate what I fixed. We bought rice bowls and chopsticks enough to serve everyone. I decided that fried chicken must be a universal food so I fried eight chickens and all disappeared. Of course, I had steamed rice. I even made some fried rice; I mixed the rice with scrambled eggs, chopped ham, and crabmeat. Even, if I say so myself, it was tasty. Then we topped off the meal with fresh pineapple hunks, bananas, and homemade cinnamon rolls. Sometime ago, I learned they have a weak spot for cinnamon rolls. I've been trying to figure out a way to get a pan full up to Ho Chi Minh!"

As I taught the Vietnamese the Word of God, I felt satisfaction in knowing this to be the calling for which I came to this war-torn country. I found the classes challenging. The students' love and interest provided me with the motivation to spend every spare moment in preparation. As the young men in the leadership training class preached at the market places or visited in the military hospitals, I thanked God for moving me to this great mission field. My prayer to God: "Please help me to faithfully plant seeds in hearts that will love God with their entire being, that will love Jesus Christ with a passion to proclaim His message, and that will love others with the love of God's only Son." Who knows what the future holds but I felt thanksgiving to be working for a powerful God who knows!

New Challenges to Life in Saigon In 1967

"Therefore, as we have opportunity, let us do good to all people, especially to those who belong to the family of believers."

(Galatians 6:10, NIV)

In early January, Roger and Kathy started teaching English using Bible stories with some Vietnamese children. Kathy surprised my interpreter, Nguyen Van Minh, who offered to help her start her classes. He became so fascinated that he stayed for her entire first class because her abilities as a teacher intrigued him. He visited her classes frequently.

As a result of their studies, **The Daily Oklahoman,** in its March 12, 1967, magazine section of **Orbit,** ran an article about their classes. The article is entitled "Booms Don't Bother Young Sooners." In part it reads:

"Terror is a stranger to Roger and Kathy Burcham. They never knew it in Oklahoma City. However, bursting mortars in Saigon are easier for the children to bear because they grew up with Oklahoma City's sonic booms . . .

"Back in 1964, during the time the Federal Aviation Agency tested effects of sonic booms on the Oklahoma City populace,

Roger and Kathy had no idea they were preparing themselves for the sounds of war . . .

"As the children of missionaries, Roger and Kathy are expected to do their part in helping teach the Vietnamese children about Christianity and the Bible . . . The children started Bible classes in English for eight Vietnamese children . . .

"'Our children,' Burcham said, 'have found their mission in Vietnam. In the hearts of some of the youngsters they hope to plant the good news of Jesus Christ.'"

As the number of students grew they eventually divided the students–Roger took the five older boys and girls and Kathy's class grew to eleven. One of the parents of a child in Roger's class started studying with me. They studied twice a week for two hours each time.

Often all four of us found ourselves swamped with opportunities to teach the Bible. Concerning this Gladys wrote,

"Ralph stays busy all the time
 The days run into night.
These people want the Bible taught,
 They'd like to know what's right.
"The war is all about us,
 The Viet Cong are near.
We hear the guns; we hear the bombs,
 But we do not live in fear.
"We came to teach about a God
 These people know not of.
It makes you feel your time worthwhile
 To see them seek His love."

Nguyen Van Ming served as a faithful translator.

Shortly after we arrived, I started working with a translator, Nguyen Van Minh, on a Bible correspondence course. I found him to be very intelligent and capable of communicating fluently in three languages–English, Vietnamese, and French. He made his living by teaching school. Ming and his wife had three lovely children.

Though not a Christian, he wanted to translate everything accurately. Therefore, we had rich discussions about the meaning of Bible passages. Through these discussions, we became very close personal friends. We confided in each other and he kept me abreast of happenings in Vietnam, particularly in Saigon.

Ming also served as my interpreter and translator for many of my class sessions.

How I wanted to win Ming for Christ! A few months after arriving in Vietnam, I preached at the English-Vietnamese service and Ming interpreted. But just before I started the sermon, he whispered "May I accept Christ as my personal Savior today?" He seemed so moved by his conviction of sin and his need for Jesus Christ. The joy welled up within me to the point I found it difficult to preach. At the conclusion of the service, I baptized Ming into Christ.

Nguyen Van Ming puts Christ on in baptism.

Ming possessed an unusual sensitivity for those with unusual needs. A Vietnamese preacher came up to Saigon from the Delta seeking help for rebuilding his church damaged by a typhoon. At the time, I indicated my work funds to be depleted but I indicated I would try to find him some help. But Ming gave him the needed funds from his own pocket. Knowing Ming's financial situation, I felt this to be one of the most generous contributions ever given in Vietnam.

We open an orphanage.

The New Year saw us involved in the opening of an orphanage at Binh Trung village. The Village Church of Christ in Oklahoma City authorized us to find a place for children living on the street or separated from their parents by the war. The events surrounding this work are in a separate chapter.

The Vietnamese Tet is a most unusual holiday.

All the Vietnamese holidays had a special flavor of their own and very different from any we had ever experienced. Even though we found each to be fascinating, nothing compared to Tet.

We could easily understand why the Vietnamese refer to Tet, as the holiday of holidays. It possessed a level of excitement like holidays around the world! The hustle and bustle of preparations for these events heightens the level of anticipation. The Vietnamese Lunar New Year celebration–called "Tet"–contains such excitement. Each "Tet" is named after an of animal. We arrived in Vietnam during the "Year of the Horse."

Tet contains characteristics of all of our holidays rolled into one. It corresponds to America's Christmas, New Year, Easter, Memorial Day, Fourth of July, and Thanksgiving combined. Family reunions take on special significance. Since it ushers in spring, it is a spring festival. Being a national holiday, many employers give an extra month's wage with time off. In fact, some businesses close for several days. It is everybody's birthday because everyone is considered to be a year older! Regardless of the time of year one is born, that individual is considered to be a year old when experiencing his or her first Tet. Like our Thanksgiving, there are special oriental foods.

Like our Christmas, the Vietnamese exchange gifts. As Roger noted, "Everyone gets new clothes on Tet; and if they don't, they are considered very poor. (Guess who didn't get new clothes?) They also give the children money in red envelopes, and I sure like to celebrate Tet."

Preparations for Tet start weeks in advance. Nguyen Way, the palm-tree- lined boulevard in front of a government building, becomes a sea of flowers–highlighted by yellow mums and pomegranates. Special foods are prepared and stored away for the big event. There are all kinds of candied fruit. A special treat is the plump and juicy watermelon; these are about the size of a soccer ball.

As Gladys wrote, "The flowers at this time of year are simply beautiful. One evening we went downtown to see the Street of Flowers. They block off several streets and flowers are brought in from everywhere for Tet. Never have I seen anything to compare with it. Every color of the rainbow could be seen as well as several varieties of exotic tropical plants. Kathy purchased a fuchsia bougainvillea covered with a mass of flowers. Roger purchased a miniature orange tree; the fruit is more tart than a lemon; his tree is loaded with fruit–all the way from the blossom stage to ripe oranges. Ralph purchased three large dahlias."

Our first Tet celebration ushered in the Year of the Goat. As one writer put it: "For the Vietnamese, it is a time of solemnity, gaiety, and hope. It is a time to pay homage to ancestors, visit family and friends, observe traditional taboos, and, of course, to celebrate. They look back on the past, enjoy the present, and look forward to the future. All Vietnamese give it full observance for it has centuries of traditions behind it; some say the first observance may have been 200 years before Christ."

During this holiday, the military call a truce and Gladys expressed her concerns: "Both the VC and the Vietnamese nationals lay down their arms to celebrate. Believe me, they celebrate. It is too bad that the arms will be taken up again after the truce. The rumors are that the VC are taking advantage of the truce by moving tons of war goods down to the South."

Roger wrote his friends about the coming Tet: "Tet is coming next week and we get a whole week off. Wheeeeee! That means that we will be half way through this school year, and I believe that I am going to be pretty happy.

"Flovine, our dog, jumps up on my bed or runs right between my legs every time she hears a firecracker go off. I can't imagine what she'll be like on Tet night when the firecrackers really start popping by the millions! Now I guess I'll tell you something about Tet. Tet is the big holiday for the Chinese and Vietnamese. Tet is made up of all our holidays rolled into one big bang.

"For Tet they prepare large amounts of food, exchange gifts, get new clothes, shoot lots of fireworks, and wear masks in dragon dances. I really enjoy the dragon dances.

"For Tet they have a bush with yellow flowers on it, and if it isn't in bloom on Tet day, they will have a very bad year. They do everything to get these bushes to bloom. The bush means happiness, good luck, and a year of plenty."

Families invite visitors to their home for the Tet feast. One of our Vietnamese friends talked with us about proper protocol. The honored guest arrives early. Then he gives flowers to the hostess. This advice helped us in preparation for our first Tet feast.

The celebration for our first Tet started early with a bang! The cost of firecrackers and fireworks run into thousands of dollars. Just before midnight the fireworks started in earnest and we have never heard louder booms! One of our neighbors across the street had a double row of firecrackers from his second floor down to the ground with an extra large firecracker every five or six inches. They seemed to be quite honored when Gladys asked to take a picture. Believe me, when they lit the first firecracker, a deafening roar followed for several minutes. So many red firecracker wrappers covered the yard you had to wade through them like snow.

Our family enjoyed the New Year feast as honored guests in the home of one of the Vietnamese ministers, who supervised the new orphanage just off the Bien Hoa highway. Before taking the family, the minister assured us that his village to be safe and the road to it secure. Some five months before, the VC blew up the main bridge into this village; but it has been repaired and more American and Vietnamese troops guard it. While there, we saw several American patrols.

The meal started with rice noodles and vegetables in a meat broth. Then, carrots, radishes, and green onions–all cut in fancy shapes and served in a delicious sauce. Kathy's favorite soup turned out to be the one with duck cut in bite size pieces. Of course, they served plenty of rice with every course. One of our favorites had to be a roll with chopped chicken, cream, vegetables, and spices rolled in a very thin rice sheet and fried in deep fat. The dessert consisted of fresh fruit and Tet candies. The peanut brittle tasted good. But from my previous experience with the candied ginger slices, I avoided this liquid fire! The hot tea had lotus blossoms in it; as Kathy told us privately, "It tastes like perfumed face powder."

Gladys wrote, "Kathy and Roger are doing a fine job in winning the love of the Vietnamese; both enjoy food–too much–and it makes the Vietnamese extremely happy to see Americans eat their food with such pleasure.

"Food takes on a special importance during Tet. Among the most popular dishes is 'Banh Tet.' It is to a Tet feast what turkey is to our Thanksgiving. It is a cake made of sticky rice, green beans, and meat with fat. It is usually seven inches square and about two inches thick. Banh Tet is wrapped in banana leaves until it is served. A Vietnamese friend told us it represents 'the good earth in the time of spring.' It originated by one of the Ancient Kings, who made it square because at that time they believed the earth to be square."

The Vietnamese excitement surrounding Tet made us excited. We assured our hosts that this had to be our most enjoyable day since arriving in Vietnam.

Being overly protective of our children,
Gladys gave me sage advice.

Roger joined a Boy Scout troop that met on base at Tan Son Nhut. The Scout leader, who served in the military, made each meeting exciting. Each Monday evening I would take him to his meeting. For his first meeting, I went to pick him up. Several Vietnamese boys watched me while I waited. Since I have a double chin, one of the little boys pushed the skin up on his chin giving it a double look.

All the little boys laughed. Then I pushed my nose flat and pointed at their noses and we all got a good laugh.

But after this, Roger decided he would catch a pedicab home. Gladys wrote in her journal, "Roger's real proud of himself cause he can do it all by himself. And it's an accomplishment when you consider that none of the drivers speak English."

Roger thoroughly enjoyed his scouting. One day he came home with a military pack for use in a cookout and hike. I asked: "How did you manage to get that?"

Roger replied: "The Lieutenant told me that it had belonged to a Major who was shot down in the field." This made Roger very proud of his pack.

The next time he went out on base; he wore the military cap given him; and a Vietnamese soldier saluted him. This made him especially proud. Gladys said: "You'd think the man really mistook him for the major."

Then Roger reported: "We're going on a hike out in the woods by the Bien Hoa highway."

Gladys felt some relief when he assured us with "the Lieutenant says it's safe!"

She expressed her feelings with "I believe Roger would go see Ho Chi with that Lieutenant."

Y-Kim, a Montagnard, gave us insights into the process of putting the Scriptures into his mother tongue!

When we had been in Saigon a few months, Y-Kim came to live with us. Dr. Lanny Hunter had taught Y-Kim the gospel. When it came time for Dr. Hunter to leave Vietnam, he made arrangements and provided financial support for Y-Kim to move to Saigon to further his education.

Y-Kim started working with the Wycliff Bible translators, who were putting his native language, Rahde, into written form. Y-Kim opened our eyes to the great work of the Wycliff Bible translators. He gave us an appreciation of how these translators put his language into written form and then use that in recording the Scriptures. Y-Kim became so excited to see and learn to read and write his mother tongue; this helped us realize how much we take for granted the blessings of being able to read the Scriptures in our own language.

After learning to read and write his own language, he helped Wycliff translate the Gospel of Mark. As the Scriptures unfolded in his language, the story of the life of Jesus Christ moved him more deeply.

Y-Kim's experience made me feel a sense of shame for not fully appreciating the centuries of struggle to get the Word of God into my own language. What a challenge for translators to take the original languages and put them in other languages. In the beginning, the Scriptures had to be reproduced by tedious hand copying with only a few people being able to read them because of the lack of education by the masses.

With the invention of the printing press, with faithful translators, and with broader educational opportunities, it became possible for most of the world to read the Scriptures in one's native language. What a blessing!

Y-Kim taught Roger to ride his bike in traffic.

Y-Kim attended our Christian school; he enjoyed being in Roger's class; at home they shared a room together. In time, he taught Roger how to ride his bicycle in traffic. It is impossible to describe the traffic.

One day I came home and asked Gladys, "Where's Roger?" She replied, "I let him take his solo trip in traffic."

I responded, "Don't you think it is too dangerous?"

She said, "Think! I know it is dangerous, but a 12-year old has to do something. He can't live in a glass cage."

In about two hours Roger came home, but you should have seen him. He rang the bell at the gate and called out, "Mom, let me in; I'm still alive!"

What a relief I felt. Gladys wrote in her journal, "He really was 'shook,' but he's been out since; and it gets easier. We just hope he doesn't get too brave."

Seeming tragedy in my Volkswagen accident.

One Wednesday evening on our way to church, the bumper-to-bumper traffic seemed to engulf us. As we traveled down one of the main thoroughfares, we approached a river bridge with a high center. As we got to the crown of the bridge, I happened to be in the lane next to the oncoming traffic. Vehicles filled every lane.

A motorcycle with a passenger faced us in our lane head-on. Because of full lanes, I could see the impossibility of the motorcycle getting back in its lane. So I stopped the bus. The driver tried to get back in her lane but the front wheel of her motorcycle struck the wheel of a taxi and this threw them into the front of our bus. The male passenger fell into this stream of traffic.

A policeman on the bridge blew his whistle to stop traffic. I jumped out and picked up the man. When I did, one of his legs dangled in one direction and the other simply flopped. Also, the cuts on his forehead started to bleed. I felt nauseated because of the condition of this little man.

The policeman came over and helped me get the man into a cyclo; the policeman instructed that he be taken to the nearest hospital. The uninjured woman driver started yelling and attracted a crowd of people. She pointed to her wrecked motorcycle and yelled at me for being responsible. The crowd seemed to be growing angry with me as they heard her version of the accident.

The policeman helped me get the bus across to a place where traffic could proceed; he made an effort to calm the woman. Since I am an American, he told me that I would have to wait for the joint patrol that would write a traffic report. The joint patrol consisted of an American, an Australian, a Korean, and a Vietnamese. He telephoned for the joint patrol. He assured me that I had nothing to worry about because he had seen what happened.

I asked, "Is it necessary for the whole family to stay?" He said, "They could go." I hailed a taxi and sent the family to church to let everyone know I would be delayed.

I felt such compassion for the injured man that I thought to myself: "I'm going to help him if he needs medical attention. When

I get back with the family, we will make a trip to the hospital to find out about his condition."

The joint patrol arrived, took our statements and that of the policeman, and indicated that I would need to be in traffic court the next day. Then they told me I could go. About to leave, I saw the injured man on a cyclo. His bandaged head covered the cut I knew he sustained. I asked the policeman to find out for me the extent of his injuries. He whistled the man over.

When the policeman asked about the injuries, the man pointed to his head and the cut; he indicated this to be his main injury. Then I asked: "What about his legs?"

The man replied, "I'm an amputee and my wooden leg came unhooked." Oh, what a relief!

The next day I went to traffic court; they dismissed the case.

Our house is robbed.

In late spring, someone broke into our house during the night. From the looks of our place, the robber went into every room. How sobering because the robber did not awaken any of us. The robber had dumped Gladys' purse on the den floor; however, he must have been disappointed because he did not find much money in it. He got Roger's billfold off his nightstand.

Evidently, the robber wanted money as he had pulled books off the shelves and had moved things around where money might be hidden. How amazing he missed the money I had just cashed even though it lay with some of my Bible notes on the corner of the dining table.

This made us all a bit jumpy. A few days later, we came home to find the back door open and the screen unlatched. Immediately, we all felt that someone might be in the house.

I started a "hunt and destroy" mission with a broom by going through every room in the house. When I got to Kathy's upstairs room, I got down on my knees to look under her bed. Then I sensed someone standing behind me.

Just ready to swing the broom, I heard "Daddy, what are you doing?"

I said, "You spoke up just in time." We both had a good laugh. In thinking back, we decided we had left the back door unlocked. Oh my!

Tran Van Can became more and more valuable to our mission.

I first met Tran Van Can in 1966, shortly after our arrival in Vietnam. At the time, he worked for the U. S. Government in translating American military training films and dubbing Vietnamese on them. Because of his linguistic ability and his familiarity with Vietnamese officials, I found him to be invaluable as an interpreter and translator. His background as a former Buddhist helped me in my teaching. In addition to Vietnamese and English, he spoke French, Mandarin and Cantonese Chinese, and Japanese. The more I worked with Tran the more I came to appreciate his background and intellectual gifts.

From his birth on August 19, 1914, Tran grew up in North Vietnam. He never knew his father because he died three months before his birth. In time, I came to know his wife and six children on a very personal basis. God blessed him with talented children–three boys and three girls.

His mother considered herself to be a spiritualist and necromancer (one who conjures up spirits of the dead in order to predict the future). While a boy, he followed his mother to the pagoda or a temple to worship idols and ate foods offered to statues of Buddha. When visiting the temple of female gods, he watched his mother and her friends practice witchcraft and sorcery; as Tran put it, he watched these women "pretending communications with the dead and spirits."

Tran once said, "Almost all Vietnamese people believe horoscopes and divinations; by natural instinct they believe that there is a god they call Highest King or Mr. Heaven. The Vietnamese pray to God and Buddha for peace, good health, and prosperity."

At the age of 22, he left his home for Hanoi for advanced study and work. In Hanoi, he got acquainted with an English missionary lady, Homera Dixon, who claimed to be a relative of the British Royal Family. Ms. Dixon belonged to the Christian and Missionary

Alliance. She talked to him about Jesus as the Savior of sinful mankind; she taught him about the God of the Bible.

Tran gave me good insights on what Vietnamese believe: "Like my fellow countrymen, I believed in a God in Heaven, who knows everything and is everywhere and has power to give life and cause death, but I flatly rejected Jesus because the name Jesus was condemned everywhere by the Buddhists. Buddhists invented many bad stories to defame the name of Jesus, and instilled great prejudice against Christianity in general and Catholicism in particular.

"A friend of mine had the same prejudice against Jesus Christ as I did. My friend became a believer in Jesus and was converted by the Evangelical church. He told me the Biblical stories of Jesus and advised me to read the New Testament. I did read the New Testament and became enlightened with Christianity, and this banished all my prejudices against the name of Jesus.

"Finally, the Word of God convinced me of my sins against God and men to the point that I could not help being repentant for my sinful condition. I then accepted Jesus as my Savior and confessed my sins to Him and prayed to God for forgiveness. I also accepted the creed of the Evangelical church and was baptized by its pastor to join his congregation. In 1938, I was elected a deacon of the Hanoi Evangelical church, and also assisted the lady missionary in her work.

"I came back home and told my mother about the true God who revealed Himself to man in Jesus Christ as the Savior of Mankind. At first, she rebuked me and refused to hear me talk about Jesus. But she loved me as her only son. Taking advantage of the moments, when she agreed, I read the Bible to her and explained about the Biblical God and the Savior Jesus Christ.

"One day, my Mother said to me, 'I know that Buddhism cannot save me from sins against God, and that spiritualism and sorcery are trickery. What I did in the pagoda is false and deceptive; therefore, I do not see the way to Heaven. Now I want to be saved from Hell.'

"In 1940, I took her to the Evangelical church. She expressed her faith in God and Jesus Christ as her Savior, and was baptized.

The Gospel of Jesus so strongly touched her that after conversion, she no longer went to the pagoda, and gave up her spiritualist and witchcraft practices and idol worship. Her friends mocked her and said that Buddha and Mr. Heaven would punish her even unto death because she had turned away from their idols. But nothing happened to my mother, which surprised her friends greatly. My wife was converted through my mother to the Evangelical church, two years before we were married in 1944."

Tran leaves North Vietnam as a refugee. Later he is introduced to the Church of Christ.

After the Vietnamese defeated the French in 1954, the Geneva Agreements partitioned the country–the Communists would control North Vietnam and the South would be independent. At this time, Tran and his family fled Hanoi for Saigon, the capital of the new South Vietnam where he worked for the U. S. Embassy as a translator.

Captain Joe Hale conducted worship services in his home. He and Sergeant Wilson invited their Vietnamese friends and other servicemen to these services. Captain Hale asked Tran to translate the sermons for the Vietnamese present. When Captain Hale completed his assignment in Vietnam, Sergeant Wilson moved the services to his home and Tran continued as the translator. The Vietnamese asked the servicemen to help get a missionary family. A plea went out and in 1964 Maurice and Marie Hall arrived to accept the challenge. Tran continued to serve as translator.

When the Halls left in mid-1966, we continued to use Tran as our translator. Tran continued his study of the Bible and he tells of his further conversion: "In late 1967, I was baptized by a missionary into the body of Christ and became a member of the Saigon Church of Christ. Through my study of the Scriptures, I became fully aware of the baptism by the Evangelical Church was unscriptural and decided to be re-baptized scripturally for the sake of my conscience."

I asked Tran to share his experiences with our mission; he wrote: "The Halls and the Burchams built several congregations in Saigon and Cholon, and in other provinces such as Bien Hoa, Long Xuyan, Rach Gia, and DaNang with a total of over 500 members.

"They also operated the American-Vietnamese International School in Saigon, which was approved by the Minister of Education. This was the first school in South Vietnam that applied the American-Vietnamese curricula with a Bible teaching program. The students at the school were children of the personnel of the diplomatic corps, foreign residents, and well-off Vietnamese.

"Also, the mission conducted a radio-broadcasting program titled *'The Voice of Christianity'* for Vietnamese radio listeners. This excited the religious men in South Vietnam to discussions and questions on the air over Christian Protestantism and Catholicism. This program also effectively promoted the mission's Bible Correspondence Course. The most striking result of these broadcasts resulted in a return to New Testament truth and the Church of Christ by two Catholic priests and many attendees from Catholic seminaries and members of other denominations."

I performed the wedding
for an American with a Vietnamese bride.

Bob Fairless asked me to perform the ceremony for his approaching wedding. Bob originally came to work in the missionary team. Because of a lack of finances, he started working for the U. S. Government. During our counseling sessions, I got better acquainted with Chau. She possessed that special Vietnamese charm and grace.

The engagement party in Chau's home possessed the best of Vietnamese customs. With great ceremony, a friend presented Bob to the family; in turn, Bob gave all the family gifts. Next, Chau's mother introduced her family to him; then Bob introduced his friends. The engagement dinner followed at the Dong Kong Hotel; it started with the most delicious appetizers. Waiters served the many courses with a sophisticated flair.

Gladys summed it up with "Would you believe we ate for two hours? My figure is really suffering over here. But, boy, do I enjoy it. I told Ralph I felt cheated and we should probably get married all over again." She especially liked the fact that the groom had the financial responsibility for everything. We wished that our friends back home could experience a Vietnamese engagement party.

Bob and Chau chose traditional American vows. Gladys planned the wedding reception. At its conclusion, Gladys expressed her true feelings with "I felt just like a mother when it was over–tired!" The wedding reception also had a special charm about it.

This wonderful couple played a special role in our lives when the war came into Saigon.

We are amazed at the many new foods and a new fruit.

Discovery of the many new varieties of fruits and vegetables amazed us. After having been in Vietnam for almost a year, we still found new fruits and vegetables. Each seems to have its season even though things can grow the year around. As Gladys wrote to some of her friends: "Recently, we have eaten three new fruits we've never seen the likes of before. Two were delicious, but the third—well, I wouldn't go 17,000 miles for it. In fact, I'd walk across the street if I thought I could avoid the smell.

"Ralph brought this fruit home one evening and put it in the kitchen. About 30 minutes later someone said, 'What's that terrible smell?' Now you must understand, for someone to use the expressions, 'terrible smell,' in Saigon, it's gotta be awful. Ralph said, 'It's the fruit; ever since I heard about this fruit, it has teased my curiosity.' Then he moved it out to the garage.

"The next noon we got Chi Hai to kill (I mean cut) it (it already smelled dead). But we were determined to see if it could be eaten. Need I say more—one small nibble convinced Roger and me, but Ralph had to start with a big bite. He lives dangerously! The taste and smell stayed with him all day and all night. Kathy was too smart to even try it. Chi Hai normally served us and went back to the kitchen, but this time she stayed in the doorway and watched. We gave it to her and she ate it with gusto. I know the Vietnamese 'smeller and taster' must be dead for some of the things they eat."

We learned this fruit to be a special treat; some call it "bread fruit." It is the national fruit of Singapore; it is called "durian." It is a large citrus type fruit, about the size of a small watermelon, and is divided into sections. The texture is very different and the dictionary says it has "a prickly rind and a nasty-smelly odor." It is an expensive fruit; it is quite an honor to be given one as a gift.

When "lichee" arrived at the markets during the rainy season, I had to try some. It has a bright red hair-like covering and is about the size of a large plum. When peeled, "lichee" has the texture of a grape and is very sweet.

All of us enjoyed "mangosteen." This fruit has a thick, purple skin. It takes a sharp knife to cut and peel through the outer layer. Inside, the transparent white pulp is divided into sections; it has a sweet-sour taste.

The "custard apple" became another of our favorite fruits. When ripe, it is easy to peel the thick, green scaly covering; the meat is white or light yellow with a sweet-sour taste and contains many black seeds.

Papaya, mangoes, pineapple, and several varieties of bananas–all add to the great variety of fruits found at different seasons.

In time, we learned to eat "nouc mam," which is a Vietnamese fish sauce. When served, it is diluted and sprinkled with dried red hot peppers and placed in a small dish by each service. You dip your spring roll or other food into the nouc mam with your chopsticks.

We discovered we really liked sharks' fins soup.

We never had the courage to try two of their delicacies: a half hatched egg and a hundred-day old egg. As Gladys said privately, "The half hatched egg is hard boiled; I guess they have their meat right with the egg. I've never been offered one, but I'd have to get out of that some way."

Roger and Kathy loved the pet market.

Roger seemed to be getting braver all the time. He decided that he and Kathy could go to the pet market all by themselves just to prove they could. As Gladys tells it, "I came home from school and Roger and Kathy both met me at the gate with those 'you-won't-believe-it' expressions. Sure enough they each had a baby guinea pig.

"Kathy went into great detail how the man at the pet market fed a guinea pig to one of the big snakes while they watched. All the while, she had that real sad look so Roger helped her out with, 'Look at it this way, Mom, we saved two lives.' Guess we'll make the pet market 'off limits.' I'm just thankful that pets aren't so cheap at home."

We enjoyed a family outing at the Saigon zoo.

Our children had a day off on May 1 for the International Labor Day. We decided to get away and went to the zoo. We enjoyed the beautiful flowers and the cleanliness of the park is a tribute to Saigon. The colorful tropical gardens had such a soothing effect. The stately palms and other trees provided shade and a place to rest. Visitors seemed to be enjoying the paddleboats in the water gardens. The grounds, the flowerbeds, and the grass–all had a manicured look.

The healthy looking animals and the tropical birds attracted quite a crowd. But our children also seemed to attract attention everywhere we went. I said to Gladys, "I don't believe all eyes are on the birds." She replied, "Mine are."

We attend a Buddhist wedding.

Chi Hai, our maid, invited us to her daughter's wedding. She wanted to be sure that we came so she brought her son, who speaks English, to give us a special invitation. Since we had not been to a Buddhist wedding, we didn't know what to expect, but we felt honored to be invited.

They lived in a little house over the river. The guests consisted of close friends and relatives. Chi Hai made us feel very special and ushered us to a table. They served a big meal.

We kept waiting for the ceremony but none occurred. With the introduction of the couple, we decided this represented the culmination of all the paper work with the Vietnamese government.

Each table had liquor on it, but Chi Hai came over and took the bottle away from our table. When we got home, I said, "I wondered how we would get out of that!" Roger came back with "Oh, I just thought ummmmm!"

We felt the tension surrounding the election for the Vietnamese Presidency.

The campaign for President in Vietnam had to be more amusing than in the States. The eleven candidates all traveled together to campaign. They gave each candidate 15-minutes to present his platform. Gladys said: "I'm afraid I'd get tired of listening to all those speeches if I were in the crowd."

A nearby neighbor ran for the Vietnamese Senate. Gladys told his wife "Sorry, we can't vote in your election." We hoped he behaved, as we'd have hated for our street to be blown up. But a U. S. Senator felt the election in Vietnam should be put off a month. Gladys said, "Forget it! Things get pretty tense around here before an election and we are ready to get it over. Just another one of the things you can't understand when you are half a world away."

But the tension seemed to be on the increase as the war came closer in on Saigon. The bombings and exploding shells could be heard most evenings. Nighttime became almost like day with the bright, eerie glare of many, many flares. Saigon seemed to be expecting most anything until the conclusion of the elections.

After one of our Sunday evening church services, I took one of our visitors home in the Cholon district; we passed by the Capitol Hotel that served as a military billet. We came back about 5 minutes later and everyone seemed to be out with ambulances tearing up the street. We just missed a bombing of the Capitol Hotel. Ten American soldiers inside suffered injuries; many Vietnamese casualties lay on the street or sidewalk. Gladys wrote about this by saying "I don't even discuss anymore whether or not we have a guardian angel."

Our servicemen at Tan Son Nhut started using a new type of rocket. As Gladys put it, "It really shakes things around here. They fire from Tan Son Nhut at a target 25 to 30 miles away. Sometimes this goes on day and night. The first few nights, we found it hard to sleep; but I guess we are used to it now. Just another war noise to keep the enemy at bay."

The Viet Cong terrorists did all in their power to undermine the election. The dead or wounded count came to more than one thousand civilians after a weeklong wave of communist pre-election terror throughout South Vietnam.

The Vietnamese won my admiration for their bravery in going to the polls in spite of the terrorists' threats and violence. I felt it a real tribute to their courage and determination to have a democratic form of government.

All Americans were restricted to their quarters over the weekend. Since the schedule called for me to preach, I felt I had an obligation to go to the morning service.

One of our servicemen called Gladys to find out our plans for Sunday. When she told him we planned to go to church, he asked if he might ride along. He came over in his civilian clothes and accompanied us. He had his overnight bag. Of course, I gave little thought to what he had in his bag. Later, our family had a discussion about the contents of the bag. Finally, Roger confessed that he had asked. In the serviceman's bag, he had a pistol and plenty of ammunition.

Over and over I felt God protecting us through our military. I prayed constantly for their well being; but we knew many others kept their prayers going up to the Father on our behalf.

I received an invitation to the National Day Parade.

Because of the tensions associated with the Presidential election, we were glad to get it behind us. But because I served as a member of the Press, I received an invitation to the National Day Parade; this followed the inauguration ceremony the day before. The new President was scheduled to speak. Of course, rumors indicated that the VC might take advantage of this situation and disrupt the program.

I debated about whether or not I should attend. However, some of my servicemen friends indicated that every effort would be made to provide good security. So I decided to go.

The decorated speaker's platform was on the street leading down to the Presidential Palace. Bleachers had been set up for guests to watch the parade. What a festive occasion with flags everywhere!

Security remained tight. Surprisingly, however, with my invitation in hand and my press card, security agents ushered me to a seat with the Press, located next to the platform where the special events were to take place. I had a good view of the area reserved for world leaders and special guests; the speaker's stand seemed so close.

The parade and the whole ceremony impressed me very much.

Eating out became a part of our family routine.

On most days, we had guests for lunch or dinner or both. I didn't realize how little time we had together as a family until one evening at the dinner table Kathy said, "Can you believe it. Just our family for supper!" Then it struck me that I couldn't remember when we had last had a meal alone. Almost every day we had someone in our home for lunch or dinner or both. Even though we had a maid, Gladys found herself baking and cooking most every day.

Therefore, I put forth extra effort to give our family a chance each week to be alone and away from the pressures at home.

The floating ship in the Saigon River became one of our favorite places to eat out. Howard and Mildred Horton, our co-workers, invited us to meet them at the floating ship for dinner. Just as we crossed the street in front of the ship's dock, we heard shots on the water close by. We could see the bullets hit the water. We ducked behind some cars. We decided it might be a good evening to go on a diet, but the shooting stopped so we walked the board gang plank up to the ship.

Howard greeted us smiling. He said, " Mildred got down under the table pretty fast and had to look up to see the floor." As it turned out, a small Vietnamese boat got too close to a big military ship and fired these warning shots.

Another time I told Roger he could choose the place where we would eat out. After much serious thought, he said, "How about Adairs in Oklahoma City!" And Gladys said, "You can't win even when you try to be nice." We settled for the Vietnamese Officer's Club on Base. It is a nice place; but halfway though eating, Gladys saw a mouse running around under the tables. She excitedly responded with "Thinking of fourteen rabies shots, I put my feet in my lap."

About that time, some guy across the way decided to light a string of firecrackers inside the restaurant (early Tet celebration);

such a noise, Roger almost swallowed his chopsticks. It really startled all of us.

One evening Vietnamese friends invited Gladys and me out to eat. We went to a Vietnamese restaurant called "Sing-Sing." Our first natural association linked with a prison in San Francisco, so Gladys came back with "We may not get out without a black and white striped suit with a number on the back." The tasty food included "nuoc mam" with everything; surprisingly our taste buds were beginning to enjoy it.

The Vietnamese holidays and our family outings colored our weeks and gave relief from the stresses we faced on a daily basis.

Adjustments seemed to be easier after being in Saigon for several months.

Many indicators pointed out that we enjoyed a new comfort level in Vietnam. When Kathy celebrated her birthday for the second time in Saigon, she invited some friends over after school. The party included Vietnamese, Filipino, and Korean guests. As Gladys put it, "Kids aren't smart enough to know they shouldn't be able to get along so they had a good day. Oh, what lessons we need to learn!"

Several evidences pointed out that Kathy's Vietnamese to be improving. It really shocked the cab drivers when she told them to "turn left" in Vietnamese. In fact, they became so pleased that they forgot to fuss about what I paid. She did a good job when we went shopping, bargaining in Vietnamese, too. I tried to learn some, then usually said the wrong thing when I tried to think of it in a hurry; however, I worked hard on their religious vocabulary.

Because we had been without electricity so much, Gladys had gotten in the habit of saying, "Kids, blow out your lights!"

As time passed, we noticed that Roger and Kathy just ignored their novelty to the people. Age wise, our children are much larger than Vietnamese children of the same age. Also, Roger is catching on that he is much heavier than the average Vietnamese child. One of his friends, who is a fan of "batman," kids Roger with "I'll bet the fat man goes home in his fat mobile." Several times on the street, they looked at him and said "Boo Coo (too much) Kilo" (their weight measure instead of pounds). As Gladys says, "When they say that to me, I just pretend it's a compliment and go on."

God helped us to learn to depend on Him.

Being in a war situation required many emotional adjustments because the events of the first several months in Vietnam became somewhat overwhelming. Even though we could hear shelling outside the city and an occasional burst of bullets or an explosion in the city, we did not live in fear because of God's day-to-day protection.

We came to be more and more convinced that God could do more than we could think or ask; He had demonstrated His power through our weaknesses. Our trials and problems served as stepping-stones in teaching us patience. God had constantly overruled to make blessings out of our trials.

It seemed God used those early adjustments and struggles as preparation for more difficult times. However, we had experienced that God does provide and would help us in our times of need.

Somehow I could relate to Christ's final hours on earth. He had spent three years preparing His disciples for His own crucifixion and the struggles His followers would face. He promised to send His Holy Spirit to strengthen them and lead them in their work. My greatest struggle seemed to be allowing God and His Spirit to do their work! However, I felt God had led us to experience the challenges of reaching the lost of Vietnam. Many lost souls had been baptized into Christ and were enjoying their new Spirit-filled life.

The Vietnamese Orphans

"Religion that God our Father accepts as pure and faultless is this: to look after orphans and widows in their distress and to keep oneself from being polluted by the world."
(James 1:27-28, NIV)

Shortly after arriving in Vietnam, Dennis Rush, a civilian worker, described the condition of many young boys who lived on the streets. He invited me to go with him about 5 a.m. to see where the boys slept.

As we walked, my bewilderment increased at what we saw in many of the shops' entrances with the doors set back from the front of the building with glass show cases on either side. In these small alcoves, groups of little boys from four to nine years of age huddled together sleeping on cardboard. As I looked on these little fellas from storefront to storefront, compassion for these little guys welled up within me.

During the day, these little fellas could be seen rummaging through garbage cans, begging for food, selling pornographic pictures, or picking pockets. When picking pockets, they worked in groups of at least three. While the target was unsuspecting, one child grabbed the victim's right hand while one grabbed the left and the third child grabbed for the billfold or passport. "Lightening quick" best describes their actions!

When the war escalated in an area, the people scattered by being torn from their homes as the Viet Cong moved into their villages and confiscated property. Then the men, women, and children left all they had and drifted to refugee centers. The most appalling needs belonged to the boys and girls whose parents had been killed in the war or who got separated from their parents or relatives. Truly, one of the greatest tragedies of war has to be the hardship placed on innocent children.

If these boys and girls do not find a relative or friend to take them in, they will be left to their own devices to sustain life. It never ceased to amaze us to watch the little boys gambling. They played cards on the streets and maybe had one cigarette they passed around; the winner getting to smoke until he lost. These boys, as little as 7 or 8, could play cards like professionals.

As I returned home, I shared my concerns with Gladys. For the next three days, the sight of these little guys weighed heavily on my mind. This, not only dominated my conversation, I became weary just wondering if I could do something. Finally, Gladys came at me with, "Why don't you stop stewing and do something?"

Unusual circumstances surround the beginning of the Binh Trung Orphanage.

Immediately, I started writing letters with a plan of action for my sponsoring church and to Kenneth Hobson, an elder in the Village Church of Christ in Oklahoma City. Before I left for Vietnam, the Village Church asked me to survey the situation; and if a need still existed for additional orphan care, they would sponsor such a program.

My sponsoring church gave approval with permission to raise funds provided the work would be under the oversight of the Village church since they had indicated a desire to develop a long-range plan for orphan care.

In visiting with some of my Christian friends, I asked about the requirements of the Vietnamese Government for establishing an orphanage. I discussed this with Jim Casey, one of our missionaries and teacher with the Christian school, who had an interest in orphan care. He indicated the landlord of his apartment worked for the Social Welfare Department. Jim made an appointment for us to meet with Mr. Trieu Phong, the Associate Minister of Social Welfare. At the appointed time, Jim went with me to see Mr. Phong. I asked him "Is there a need for orphan care?"

Mr. Phong replied: "Because the war continues, our department has 77 orphanages caring for up to 10,205 orphans; it must be increased and is always needing moral and material support from all social organizations throughout the country and abroad."

I explained to Mr. Phong about the desire of the Village Church of Christ to sponsor an orphanage program. I said, "Please tell me what is required for this church to be able to operate an orphanage."

He replied in a most formal way: "For an orphanage to operate with the approval of the Vietnamese Government, a formal agreement will need to be drawn up with your organization. Therefore, we look forward to more relief from your society. With a sound belief in your compassion, we request your acceptation of our sincere thanks in advance."

Mr. Phong went on to say, "For over ten years, the living conditions of the population, especially the laborers in the cities and the farmers in the countryside, are most distressing and unpleasant: not enough food to eat or clothing to wear, housing facilities have been extremely scarce, medicines, transportation facilities, farming and industrial tools have been short. In a word, the basic needs of the population have not been properly met.

"What is the reason for this unhappy situation? It is because ours is an underdeveloped country, but we also have had to endure many terrible natural calamities: floods, storms, fire, etc. More than that, the Communists, with their un-humanitarian, savage and wanton acts, have incessantly brought us many sufferings, sorrows and distress.

"The social picture which was not too bright has been more darkened because hundreds of thousands of people, victims of this war, have had to leave behind their homes, their ancestor's tombs, their possessions, to seek freedom."

Then Mr. Phong pointed out the urgent need for additional orphan care because his Government was stretched in its resources in providing assistance to almost a million persons. These refugees had been relocated to 267 temporary camps and resettlement centers as a result of the war. He provided an application and information needed to receive governmental approval.

In speaking of the many things the orphan program could do for Vietnam, Mr. Phong said, "We would like to emphasize the strong unity this precious friendship creates between free people. This friendship becomes deeper and closer day by day and will be a remarkable strength in conquering poverty, hunger, and most of all, communism." Because of the urgent need, Mr. Phong gave me permission to proceed without a formal agreement and indicated his office would cooperate in every way possible.

However, Mr. Phong stressed the need for a formal agreement between the Government of Vietnam and the Village Church. He indicated an agreement would allow us to import items for the orphanage "duty free." He provided me with a sample of an agreement from another social agency.

After visiting with Mr. Phong, I went to see Tran Van Yen who lived across the river from Saigon in a small village. He preached for a small congregation and had indicated an interest in childcare. I presented this plan to Yen and his wife; they had indicated an interest in providing shelter for some. I asked, "How much will it cost to feed and clothe an orphan for a month?"

After giving it some thought, he said, "Approximately $15." Yen went on to say that his congregation paid for his rent and for the church which occupied half the building; in addition, the other half of the building remained vacant and could be rented for the orphanage for $30 a month.

Behind the Yen's home, the grounds included a large garden– buoi trees (something like a grapefruit) and orange trees. It contained between two and three acres and would make an ideal place for children to play; also, the garden would give them something to do. They could raise their vegetables, fruit, and possibly, chickens.

Then Jim Casey and I started working out a formal agreement, which took several weeks to complete with the Vietnamese government. When the details had been worked out and Ken Hobson had given approval, Jim informed me that there would be an official signing in the Minister's office. Jim indicated that his friend had arranged for the press to be present.

An historic moment as we obtained
legal recognition to operate an orphanage!

April 27, 1967, became an historic moment as the Vietnamese Government granted a legal agreement to operate an orphanage with the Village Church of Christ. On this day, Jim and I arrived at the Minister's office slightly before the appointed time. We had a briefing by the Minister's aide, and I answered questions about the future development of the program. Since there was another orphan program operated by other Churches of Christ, he asked about the relationship of the two. I indicated that eventually the two programs would be merged into one; and when policies were completed in the States, Howard Horton would be coming to work out the merger.

We were ushered into the office of Mr. Nguyen Xuan Phong, the Minister of Social Welfare, for the official signing of the agreement. With cameras rolling, the Minister asked me: "What is the purpose of your program?"

I replied, "We are interested in providing quality child care for orphaned children. This will include physical care–food, clothing, shelter, and medicine. It will include educational development–basic courses of reading, writing, arithmetic and social skills to help the children in becoming useful citizens in society. Also it will include moral and spiritual development including instruction from the Bible."

He responded, "These are worthy goals. You can be sure that our office is here to assist you in any way possible."

The Minister of Social Welfare and Ralph Burcham sign the agreement to allow the operation of an orphanage.

After the official signing, Jim Casey and I walked out feeling good about the completion of an agreement that would help many, many children in the future to have a chance for a better life, hopefully as Christians. I will always be indebted to Jim for his great work in getting governmental approval for our child-care program.

Then I started making appeals for funds. To my surprise the Lord opened the hearts of a former missionary couple who now worked for USAID, Dennis and Toni Ruch; they gave $500 for the temporary care of these children; what a generous gift! Dennis is the one who went with me on that early morning tour to see how these homeless children live on the street.

Dennis and Toni continued to take an interest in the work even when transferred to NhaTrang. When Dennis had business in Saigon, he stayed in our home.

Many servicemen became the first to give. Soon we had enough funds for a year's rent on the other half of Yen's place and for funds to care for twelve. I asked Yen, "Why don't you pick out 12 of these children and tell them we will provide food and care for them."

Picking up those first children will be etched forever in my memory. On the appointed day, Yen and I picked up nine children from a refugee camp near the Saigon River.

These children–all so filthy–looked as though they had been dipped in grime all their lives. Nearly every child had sores and heat rash. One of the little boys had a potbelly caused from worms; all children suffered from malnutrition and needed much care. They ranged in age from 3 years to 12.

You could see the apprehension on each little face. They loaded into the Volkswagen and we headed for the Yen's home. All remained quiet most of the way even though Yen tried to tell them about the possibility of school and where they would be living.

Four of the first nine children
to receive care in the orphanage.

As we arrived at the future home of these children, I felt great emotion as Mrs. Yen welcomed them and gave each child a new handkerchief. She asked if they had ever owned one before–none had. Then she explained its purpose and gave a demonstration— being so cute I had to chuckle inside.

After the children had been in our care for a week, I notified the Yens that some of us planned on coming out to see the children, including a nurse, Linda Carpenter, who would examine each child. When we arrived for our visit, you could see such a remarkable change in each child because the boys looked clean and had on fresh clothes. However, it takes time for sores to heal and deficiencies to be corrected.

Also, a large number of people crowded around the Yens' place. I asked, "Are these members of your congregation?"

To which he replied, "No, these are people from the village who want to see the nurse!" From the time the Yens received my note, the news had spread throughout the village that a nurse would be coming to visit the children.

After taking care of the orphans, Linda examined many from the village and made notes of various ailments so that proper medicines could be obtained. It is difficult to imagine the urgent need of these people for medical care. One lady had a scaly substance over her feet and ankles.

Y-Kim, the Montagnard boy, who lived with us and had been trained to be a medic, gave assistance and translated for Linda. The people expressed their gratitude and appreciation for Linda's help and concern. Some started attending the services of this village church.

Since these children had not been in school, we started developing plans for teaching them the basics and moral training in the Christian Scriptures.

The child with worms, parasites, sores, and malnutrition touched me deeply. How grateful I felt that the Lord had led us to this child for no one would have the heart to turn down this lad whose eyes showed the anguish and pain of extreme hardship, neglect, and starvation. Yet, I felt this same child to be impoverished spiritually. But first, we had to take care of his physical needs.

Soon all children participated in classes to learn the basics of reading, writing, and arithmetic. But just as important, daily Bible classes taught these children about God, His love, His Son, God's word, His world, and how to live peacefully with others. It turned out most of the children had the capacity to learn. Actually, some were very bright. Eventually, some of the men from my leadership training class taught their classes. Le Nho, one of these students, conducted daily Bible classes.

Background of some of the orphans moved me deeply.

When I looked at each child, I knew each had a story to tell. Some of these moved me to tears. Nguyen Dan Bao, a Vietnamese minister at Bien Hoa, found Thanh and placed him in the orphanage at Binh Trung. This is what Thanh related about his life:

"My day started like most days in Vietnam. Before it ended my world turned upside down."

On this never-to-be forgotten day, the VC terrorized his village. When the VC came into his home, Thanh hid in a water storage jar. Eventually, they destroyed his home and killed his parents. With no family to turn to, no place to go, Thanh slipped out of the village, went down to the river, caught a boat, and landed at Bien Hoa.

When you have known nothing but war all your life, the war becomes an every day topic, like the weather, until its menacing arm strikes your home. When tragedy knocked on Thanh's home, everyone knew. One look at Thanh's face and you could see the tears and the fears that made him look much older than eleven.

Thanh described how he survived: "For a time, I slept wherever I found a sheltered place–the steps of a building, an alley, a cardboard box. I got food by stealing; sometimes I begged for it." A gang of "cowboys," a term used in Vietnam for young hoodlums, found him, and he joined them to steal and plunder. Being smaller than most of the gang, they began to use him as their "stooley" with the police. Again and again young Thanh found himself in trouble.

After going without food for some time, Thanh, half starved, went up to a Vietnamese home to beg some rice. The mother of five children answered the door and invited him into her home. No one had shown him any real kindness for some days. He showed the neglect of living on the street because of his being so very dirty, grimy, and hungry.

The woman placed rice before him, and with a few animal-like gulps, he emptied the bowl. As the kind woman gave him more rice, the tears welled up. Thanh said, "I thought how nice it would be to have a mother." As he told his story to the woman, her heart melted when Thanh said, "then the VC killed my parents!" A mother's love and compassion surged forth and Thanh had a new home.

The new home lasted but three days. The "cowboys" found him and wanted to take Thanh with them; he refused and his "new" mother defended him. The gang made threats. In fear the "new" mother took Thanh to Nguyen Dan Bao.

In turn, Bao placed Thanh in the orphanage at Binh Trung. As I saw Thanh, his successful adjustments to the orphanage could be seen in his appearance; he liked his more ordered world. Also, his laughter had returned.

Thanh craved love and affection from anyone. When shown a kindness, he "clung like cloth." He tried hard to please and made real efforts in adjusting toward his new life. Even though eleven, he had to start in the first grade because all schools had been closed in the area where he grew up because of VC activity.

Thanh enjoyed his Bible classes and he sung hymns with gusto.

A TV station in Oklahoma City and Tulsa filmed a report on our work; they selected Thanh to represent one of the orphans in our program.

The Christian Chronicle, a church related newspaper that I served as a reporter, ran several articles on our work. As a result, the Lord moved people to open their hearts and their pocketbooks. In addition, the Village church put out a flyer indicating the dire need of these children.

Churches and Bible school classes started sending us clothing and gifts. When several packages arrived, we made visits out to the orphanage. One Bible school class sent us balloons. Roger and Kathy thought it would be fun to blow them up before going for our visit. On our way the heat in the Volkswagen caused some of the balloons to burst. I became fearful that someone might get the wrong idea about these popping noises. But we made it to the orphanage without incident.

While at the orphanage, a Vietnamese military patrol came by. Their curiosity with the excitement of all the children caused them to start lining up along the fence. Soon we had 30 to 40 soldiers peering over the fence with rifles in hand. Gladys took their picture; they all smiled. For a moment, it looked like the war stopped for lack of soldiers to fight!

Many American servicemen became more and more involved with the orphanage. The Yens did not have electricity. Their water came from a well. One serviceman came up with the idea of getting a gasoline pump and building a shower house with a storage tank on top. When the shower house was finished and the pump installed, all of us stood back to watch what would happen.

How exciting to see that first water gush forth! But then our faces drooped after little squirts, then no water. The shallow well needed to be enlarged as it did not have enough space for recovery for a large pump; eventually the servicemen enlarged the well to accommodate the pump. The excitement of the children made all of the effort worthwhile.

Servicemen at Cat Lai Camp offer assistance.

Yen, the orphanage director, suggested we put a sign on the busily traveled main highway to Bien Hoa. The lettering in both Vietnamese and English included the location of the orphanage at the Binh-Trung Village and indicated it to be sponsored by the Village Church of Christ in Oklahoma City, U. S. A. The sign included the Bible School and Worship times with special children's activities in the afternoon.

Located on the main highway between Saigon and Bien Hoa, this sign attracted many servicemen who freely offered assistance.

Since servicemen stationed at Cat Lai passed the orphanage regularly, the Company Commander of this base contacted me and requested I visit him.

On my arrival at the Cat Lai camp, Captain Andrean received me cordially and indicated his men had seen the sign and noticed the children playing near the road. He said, "I have over 300 men serving in my unit; they work seven days a week from 12 to 14 hours on duty each day. Morale is quite low because the nearby towns are off limits and there is not a USO facility in our camp. We saw the orphanage sign on the highway; since my men pass by it regularly, they want to help the children. Please allow us to take these children on as a project." We discussed ways in which they might help.

And help they did! They gave gifts of candy and gum to the children, played with them, and provided food and clothing items.

In time, Captain Andrean requested I visit him again because he had a proposal for a major project for the orphanage. When I visited him, he said, "My men took on a new attitude almost overnight after deciding to take the orphanage on as a project. Their morale has shown marked improvement ever since they started playing with the children. But my men are concerned for the cramped quarters where the children are living.

"We want to make a proposal. If you will obtain land, we will build an orphanage for you. Here are the plans my men drew up for the building." To my amazement, he spread out the plans that consisted of separate areas for girls and boys' sleeping quarters, bathroom and shower facilities, an indoor play area, and a dining hall.

Then the Captain said: "The men will scrounge some of the building materials; they are collecting money to buy things they can't scrounge. We are holding a reserve of funds to outfit the orphanage upon its completion."

I asked, "What do you mean by 'scrounge?'" He recognized my concern and said, "This is just a military term; my men will be using surplus materials or we will get permission for using questionable materials. They will not be stealing." I felt somewhat embarrassed by my concern.

This overwhelming response from these servicemen, who sacrificed so much, almost left me speechless. I expressed appreciation for their plan and indicated I needed approval from the elders of the sponsoring congregation. I could sense his disappointment because his men hoped for an immediate response.

Therefore, I felt compelled to give them an expanding role in helping the children. I gave permission for its medical unit to examine each child. This they did; they provided free medicines and shots. These children received some of the best medical and dental care possible, as each day their medical unit checked for any potential health needs; they provided the orphanage with pure drinking water. In addition, they obtained the clothing size and shoe size for each child, which the servicemen sent back to family and friends asking for these items.

Captain Andrean then said: "Just as soon as you obtain property, please let me know and we will start the orphanage." I thanked him for his generous offer.

After leaving the camp, I went immediately to share the good news with Yen and to ask his help in obtaining property. In turn, he made an appointment for us to meet the Chief of the Province at

Thu Duc. Yen said, "I know it is important to have the approval of this official because he has the power to give us land or can help us obtain a piece of land."

On the day of our appointment, I took a small gift to the Province Chief. We laid out our plans for an orphanage. He told us he would assist us in every way possible to build; however, he suggested we meet with the Chief of the Hamlet in the district where the orphanage was to be located.

When we met with the Hamlet Chief, we laid out our plans for the orphanage and told him we needed his assistance in locating a piece of property. He endorsed our plan and offered to help. He indicated there were 33 homeless children living in his village that he would place with us if we could provide for them.

I agreed to take these children after completion of the orphanage. My heart said "yes," but my mind raised the question, "Where are you going to get the funds for the care of these children?" With the promise of help from the servicemen, I felt these children would be better off than living on the street.

Sometime later, Yen invited me out to see a piece of property that he had located. Rarely did I travel alone. However, on this occasion, there seemed to be no one available and Gladys and the children were in school. After looking at the property, I started back to Saigon. In the ditch on my way back, I saw a dead man in black pajamas. I wanted to stop but the servicemen had warned me not to touch a dead body because these are often rigged with explosive devices. I resisted the temptation and, with a heavy heart for this unknown man, I headed on back to Saigon.

The owner of a piece of land at Binh Trung indicated his willingness to sell. It seemed to be an ideal location. However, it came with an asking price that far exceeded what I felt we could raise. Where could I get this?

I wrote to the Village church and to several Christian friends with "Somehow we must reach out with the loving heart of the Samaritan to these children who have been robbed of family and possessions by the Viet Cong. Somehow we must be instruments of God to demonstrate today that God cares. These children cannot know God's love unless we love. Physical and spiritual wounds of these suffering boys and girls waited to be bound and healed. Do we dare pass them by?

"Florence Nightingale once spent a whole night caring for a wounded soldier during the Crimean War. When the dawn arrived, the soldier gave her the highest compliment ever paid to a human being: 'Miss Nightingale, last night you were Jesus Christ to me.' Let us determine to make Christ and Christianity relevant in the lives of the boys and girls who are victims of this cruel war."

Immediately the Village put out another flyer with pictures of some of the children in the orphanage. In response to these efforts, funds began to pour in. With these funds, we soon cared for over fifty children and purchased the land for the orphanage.

The great sacrifice of our servicemen weighed heavily on my heart. I prayed daily for their safety and well being. Then I received a letter from an associate minister of a church in Houston, Texas. He wrote: "Enclosed we are sending you a check to be used in your program of work with the Vietnam Orphanage. This money is from our Vietnam Orphan Fund—which is a memorial arranged by Mr. and Mrs. D. P. Dennis in memory of their son, Dan, a casualty in Vietnam . . . We shall be remembering the church and Ralph Burcham in our prayers . . . thanking our Father for those who dare to reach out to help the unfortunate to know Christ." (Several years later, I visited the Vietnam Wall memorial in Washington, D.C. and made a tracing of Dan M. Dennis.)

The death of young Dan, whom I had never met, moved me deeply. I found myself going to the Scriptures to gain insights on death. As I read there is victory in death for the believer in Jesus Christ, I felt encouraged. In I Corinthians 15, Paul discusses the meaning of life and death from a Christian point of view. After pointing out the significance of Christ's death and resurrection, these words are reassuring: "For this perishable nature must put on the imperishable, and this mortal nature must put on immortality, then shall come to pass the saying that is written:

'Death is swallowed up in victory.'
'O death, where is thy victory.
O death where is thy sting?'

145

The sting of death is sin,
and the power of sin is the law.
But thanks be to God, who gives the victory
through our Lord Jesus Christ. (I Corinthians 15:53-57, RSV)"

As I reflected on the gifts given to the orphanage in memory of loved ones, I received new insights on the significance of these gifts in the words of Sir Walter Scott, who wrote: "When death comes . . . then it is not what we have done for ourselves, but what we have done for others that we think on most pleasantly." Somehow I wanted to help these families to feel some comfort in knowing the memory of their loved one lived on to make a better way of life for boys and girls, who also lost their loved ones in this great struggle for freedom. An unknown writer put it this way:

"God often sends me joy thro' pain;
Thro' bitter loss, divinest gain.
Yet thro' it all, dark days or bright,
I know my Father leads aright."

I received permission from the Village elders to proceed on the construction of the orphanage. The servicemen at Cat Lai gladly received this welcome news. Only God knows what all these men did to give a better quality of life to so many homeless children.

Upon the purchase of the land, the servicemen at Cat Lai began working. Within a few days, Captain Andrean invited us out to see the progress on the building. To our amazement, the foundation had been laid; how good to see the framing going up. He indicated his men were making swing sets and slipper slides; he said "This will be one of the few orphanages in Vietnam with a well equipped play area."

Servicemen from Cat Lai hire some Vietnamese laborers to help them in the construction of the building to house the orphans.

The orphanage sat back off the road a short distance with a water puddle– from recent rains—between the building and the road. After inspecting the building, my wife and I started back to the road where we had parked. But between the van and us, a herd of water buffalo had moved in and blocked our path. They looked rather vicious. About that time a small boy saw our predicament, came out with a little switch, and moved the buffalo out of our path. I felt like the big brave adult!

Servicemen started requesting their home congregations to send items for the orphanage. Roger wrote his friends about receiving some of these packages; he said, "I met a V. C. (Vietnamese Communist)! One Sunday morning Sergeant Major Billy W. Williams, a soldier, said he had about a hundred packages for us at his office for the orphans. Kathy had gone with a friend so she was not with us. Billy had gone on to his compound, where his office was, and was waiting for us. The guards let us in and we took the bus around to the front of his office. There we met this nice translator who was Vietnamese and he seemed like a very nice man. He even helped us carry the packages to the bus.

"Billy told us that his friend knew all the good places to eat in town and that he had lunch with him every day. Billy really liked this man and he was so nice and he could speak perfect English, which surprised me.

"One day some Vietnamese policemen came and arrested Billy's translator. Billy asked them why they were doing this and they said that they had proof this man was a V. C. Later Billy found out that he was one of the top V. C.s in Cholon. (Cholon is another town that is hooked on to Saigon and I can't tell when I am in Cholon or Saigon.) Billy also found out that his translator had many maps of terrorist activity that the V. C. planned for Saigon. They found a map and plans for striking the Bob Hope show—where the show would be, where the audience would be seated, and where Bob Hope and the other performers would be. Now this was the same man I talked to!

"Dad had given this V. C. the address of the church and even our *home*. Dad had also invited him to come out and see us. He could have blown us to smithereens if he had wanted to. But now he is caught and they are probably sending him to your City Jail–so you better lock your doors because he might get loose!"

Of course, Roger had a way of putting things in a lighter vein. But both Roger and Kathy enjoyed the support and encouragement given to us by our servicemen.

Servicemen from Cat Lai attended a feast with the Vietnamese orphans.

Howard and Mildred Horton arrived to help.

As plans moved forward for the orphanage, the Village church sent Howard and Mildred Horton to Vietnam to survey the situation. I met the Horton's plane on July 28, 1967. They stayed with us for a few days as they looked at the various orphan programs; other congregations of the Churches of Christ sponsored some of these. All Churches of Christ involved in orphan care desired a unified care program overseen by a professional staff.

The Hortons brought a breath of fresh air to our mission team. They had a rich background in mission work, having served as missionaries in Nigeria in the 1950s. I had also worked with Howard during the time he worked at Oklahoma Christian as an administrator. He provided counsel, encouragement, and loving friendship. Most of all, he became a Christian mentor. His in-depth studies of the Bible over the years, his preaching experience, his love for people, and his rich faith in Jesus Christ provided the support I needed at the time.

The Hortons came at a time when I found myself mentally, emotionally, and physically exhausted from dealing with the many problems within our missionary group. Also, unknown to me, I had a health problem sapping my physical strength that would soon require medical attention.

When the Hortons finished their survey, they returned to the States with plans to bring to Vietnam some experts in child care to study the situation and provide advice and recommendations.

We learned of a plane crash in Hong Kong.

After working out the details with several churches for merging the orphan care programs, the Hortons wrote indicating their arrival time to be on November 5, 1967. Also, they were bringing with them Gayle and Mary Oler; he had served as the Superintendent for Boles Home in Quinlan, Texas, for a number of years and had a rich background in child care. I had their flight number and the projected arrival time. I went out early to the airport and waited and waited past the time for them to arrive.

While waiting, a Christian serviceman, that I knew, saw me and asked: "Whom are you waiting for?" I told him about the Hortons and Olers scheduled to arrive earlier in the day. He said, "Let me see if I can find out something for you."

He came back shortly with "I didn't find out anything about their flight. But a plane did crash in Hong Kong scheduled for Vietnam."

My heart sank as I thought they could be on that plane. I asked: "Is it possible to find out who was on that flight?" He left to see if he could get any information. He came back with "I can't get any information about the flight number or the names of passengers on board the crashed plane." I felt this would be the case but I had hoped.

I continued to wait. In time I saw a plane land. I recognized the Olers as they came into the terminal. My heart skipped a beat as the Hortons were not with them.

After hugs, the Olers quickly explained that the Hortons' plane had crashed. Because of the heavy air traffic with servicemen going on R. and R. to Hong Kong, the two families could not get passage on the same plane. Questions and answers tumbled out at a rapid pace.

"What happened?"

The Olers explained about their being unable to get on the same flight with the Hortons. With both planes loaded and ready for take off, the Hortons' plane was scheduled to leave first.

Then the pilot of the Olers' plane said: "There has been a plane crash. We are asking all passengers to disembark and go into the terminal. As soon as we are able to reschedule your flight, we will announce it over the speaker system."

Gayle said: "We knew the Hortons had to be on that plane. I tumbled over everyone to get off as quickly as possible to find out what happened. As soon as we got off, we saw the Hortons walking across the tarmac."

After an emotional reunion, Howard explained, "Our plane was headed down the runway when the pilot discovered a problem. He tried to reverse the engines but the plane was too far down the runway and crashed into the bay of Hong Kong harbor; the plane hit the water at about a hundred miles an hour. On impact the nose of the plane broke off and sank.

"We stepped out onto the wing. Almost immediately, a small boat pulled up and we stepped into it without even getting our shoes wet.

The Hortons had to stay in Hong Kong for the investigation of the crash and to file claims for lost luggage. The airline promised to take care of all hotel and other expenses.

The Hortons arrived in Saigon at noon on November 10. They came out to our place for dinner and spent the night. This gave me an opportunity to ask Howard about their experience. I said, "Did you know you were going to crash?"

He replied, "We did."

"What did you do?"

"When a plane is traveling that fast, you don't have much time to do anything; I simply took Mildred's hand and said 'He's able.' Then we crashed.

"It is unbelievable but only one Vietnamese woman died of a heart attack; 20 others were injured; but everyone else survived." Howard credited the pilot with calming the passengers in the face of disaster: "If it were not for our pilot, we would have been in real trouble."

Howard explained more about their situation. " The runway in Hong Kong juts out into the harbor. Planes can either take off over the ocean or towards the mountains. Because of the wind currents, our plane was the only one that day to take off over the water."

Then with emotion, he said, "The Lord looked after us. Just think where we'd be if we had flown into the mountain! My biggest loss–luggage full of about 150 sermons."

Howard could not have arrived at a better time when I needed help. Several days before their arrival, I had no energy and had to make myself work. Gladys insisted I go to the doctor. When I did, they ran several tests and discovered I had amoeba dysentery. Then I started a series of daily shots. After each shot, I felt disoriented and deathly ill.

The missionary team took my classes. Since I always prepared several days in advance, they continued to follow my outlines. How grateful I felt that the classes continued.

Then Dick DiNucci offered to take the preacher-training boys on Saturdays for visits to the military hospitals or to share the gospel at the markets.

Ready to leave Vietnam, a serviceman and an American worker wanted to visit the orphanage. Our children had some gifts to take out so they went along. On our way out, we had to go around some hand grenades on the Bien Hoa highway. Since visiting the orphanage often, we felt it safe during daylight hours.

When we got to the orphanage, Yen had received a new orphan with blond hair. Evidently he had an American father because the child stood out from the sea of black heads all around. He really looked out of place. Because of his difference, the other children seemed to be picking on him. Kathy wanted to bring him home with us. I explained: "I'm sorry but we can't!"

But on the way back to Saigon, Roger and Kathy tried to put me on a guilt trip with "Dad, you are not going to leave that little boy out there, are you?" I tried to explain that our world was already overloaded.

When we got back to Saigon, Roger and Kathy wanted to visit with Florence Vinyard, who originally worked with the mission team but had gotten a job as a civilian worker. Florence had developed a close relationship with our children; frequently she would invite Kathy over to spend the night. Since Florence had adopted a child earlier, Kathy enjoyed babysitting for her.

Florence had a dog that had puppies. She gave one to the kids but told them not to name it "Florence." Of course, this gave them an idea; so they combined her first and last names into "Flovine."

When they saw Florence, they immediately started telling her about this blond boy at the orphanage. They told it so well that Florence decided she had to go out and see the child. Before long, she went through the adoption process and gained another child.

As Gladys wrote in her journal, "Oh, there's many things to learn here. Even down to giving the baby a bath. Since Florence is keeping two orphan babies in her apartment, she has a maid to care for them during the day. One day upon arriving home after work, she heard one of the babies screaming as loud as he could. She hurried in to find the maid giving him a bath. She was holding him in the stool, washing and flushing. Maybe that's why it's hard to house-break these babies. I'd be afraid of the bathroom, too!"

I took the time to learn the background of each orphan.

As mentioned, each of the orphans had his or her story to tell. These stories touched me deeply and made me feel even a greater compassion for their circumstances.

After Howard Horton started working full time to merge the orphan programs, he went out to Binh Trung to see about the children and to encourage the work on the new building. He wrote: "As soon as I reached the orphanage my schedule of activities went out the window.

"An American serviceman was sitting on the porch of the orphanage with children literally all over and around him. He had seen our sign and had come to see if we could take another little boy. Immediately I went with him out to a Special Forces (Green Berets) Camp to see if we could help. Here is the story:

"'Little Captain' is twelve years old, but his size is about right for eight. His mother died when he was an infant and has been reared by his father. When the father went into the Vietnamese army, his son went with him to the dependent's camp. The father was selected for training as a Vietnamese Ranger by American Special Forces (Green Berets), again 'Little Captain' went with him. The bright-eyed youngster became a kind of mascot, adopted by Vietnamese Rangers and the American Green Berets.

"During the Tet attacks, the father disappeared. No one knows whether he was killed, kidnapped, fled AWOL or was a Viet Cong sympathizer. He has not been seen nor heard from since.

"For a while, the men of the Special Forces Camp tried to care for 'Little Captain.' He got some attention from everybody, but no adequate care and training from anybody. At this point, the MACV adviser came to us.

"I first saw 'Captain' when he was brought into the headquarters building and introduced to me by a Vietnamese Major. The little fellow stood erect, saluted stiffly with eyes upon the floor, outwardly almost concealing the inward fears that caused his little shirt to throb with every pounding heartbeat. I'm no good in this kind of situation. I'm afraid my heart melted all over him. Rough and tough, superb soldiers arranged to assign him to us and sent him on his way with the tenderness that has become the recognizable badge of American servicemen here.

"One week later when I was again at the orphanage 'Little Captain' was already learning to read and to copy writing, although he had not been to school. On my last visit the car had hardly stopped before he bounded to the gate–no stiff salute, no downcast eyes nor pounding heart, just a happy, intelligent, bright-eyed boy of twelve, still in a skin made for an eight-year old."

Every time I looked into the eyes of one of those children, my gratitude to God increased for Dennis Ruch who moved me to make that early morning visit to see the street children huddled in store fronts. Words could not express my thankfulness for the wonderful direction given by the Brookfield and North Park Churches of Christ and to the Village Church of Christ, especially to Kenneth Hobson, who possessed a heart of gold and compassion.

May God continue to richly bless all the workers and servicemen who provided loving care for so many children! But I am extremely thankful to all contributors and memorials that made it possible to care for these homeless boys and girls. A special feeling of gratitude welled up in my heart for all the servicemen from Cat Lai and from other units who used their spare time to make a difference in the future for the boys and girls of Binh Trung. But I especially held in high esteem the servicemen of Cat Lai Camp who built and equipped this excellent facility. All over Vietnam servicemen spent many off-duty hours in helping to build a better life for the Vietnamese.

Some of our orphans pictured with Bao Nguyen,
staff of the orphanage, and our children.

The American Servicemen

"But thanks be to God, who always leads us in triumphal procession in Christ and through us spreads everywhere the fragrance of the knowledge of him. For we are to God the aroma of Christ among those who are being saved and those who are perishing. . . . in Christ, we speak before God with sincerity, like men sent from God."
(2 Corinthians 2:14-15,17b, NIV)

Though the churches that sent us to Vietnam wanted our work to be primarily among the Vietnamese, the American servicemen came for counsel, helped with the work, provided encouragement and support, and demonstrated a love for Jesus Christ and for our country that we found to be very inspiring. Most every evening we had one or more for the evening meal.

J. C. Ward became one of the first servicemen to look us up. Some of his children had been campers with us when I directed a summer camp. J. C. came to church; after the morning services, we had a short visit before he had to return to duty. Not long after this, he had a severe heart attack. I visited him in the hospital and wrote his wife giving her assurance of our prayers and visits.

Servicemen started congregations throughout Vietnam.

Truly, our servicemen are the "aroma of Christ" spreading God's good news everywhere. Not only did the servicemen meet on their various bases, several of our mission team gave encouragement to them to start Vietnamese congregations at nearby villages or cities. I found the servicemen eager to share their faith with the Vietnamese "like men sent from God." We offered them any materials we had translated in Saigon.

As a result, congregations began to spring up in various parts of Vietnam near military bases. I felt tremendous gratitude for these men spreading the gospel. I became convinced that being witnesses for Him helped the servicemen remain faithful. Don Yelton and Lieutenant Frank Ship started a servicemen's group at Can Tho. Eventually, they hoped to reach out to the local Vietnamese population.

Lieutenant Louis Armstrong started a servicemen's group at Pleiku. He requested that Gladys make communion bread and send to him; Gladys happily complied. The servicemen at Pleiku, too, had hopes of starting a Vietnamese congregation in their area.

J. C. Watkins wrote that the servicemen at DaNang had their own service and supported their own orphanage. Nguyen Van Cau, a Vietnamese minister, worked with them.

At Bien Hoa, the servicemen met in the base theater and supported Nguyen Dan Bao in the Vietnamese effort. Bao baptized 15 into Christ within the first five months of his work. Major Harber started one in Vung Tau; congregations started up in Phu Tho Hoa and several other places.

Servicemen began the Vietnamese work in Saigon. In addition, the servicemen met on Sunday afternoons at the Base Chapel at Tan Son Nhut; Gene Conner worked with them; they provided some support for the Saigon congregation.

Phil Carpenter worked with servicemen at Nha Trang and had plans for beginning a work among the Vietnamese.

A serviceman came to me for help.

Early in our mission, one of our servicemen stole some things from the military. His conscience got the best of him, and he came to me for help. I advised him to turn himself in, which he did.

He seemed so remorseful; I assured him God would forgive him provided he truly tried to make things right. We prayed.

I wrote a letter on his behalf to the military court pleading for mercy; the penalty could have been hard labor for a period of time and a dishonorable discharge. At the Court Martial, my letter was read. He received a light sentence of forfeiture of pay for three months. He did not lose his rank. He called me on the phone to share the good news of his second chance.

He came out for a visit. He felt this to be an awakening experience that gave him a clearer vision for the future. We thanked God. I felt this young man possessed the potential for becoming an outstanding soul winner.

The patriotism of our military often moved me to tears.

After we had been in Vietnam about four months, one of the servicemen took us out to the base for dinner and a movie. Before the movie started, the American flag came on the screen and all servicemen rose and stood at rapt attention. As "God Bless America" played, the screen projected the waving stars and stripes with images of life in our great nation–fields of golden grain, majestic mountains, crystal clear streams of water, forests of trees, children at play, and people going to church.

Homesickness overcame me as I could feel chill bumps up and down my spine and the tears started sliding down my face at their patriotism. I knew each felt strong commitments to serve our country; each faced death regularly; and all wanted to return home alive.

One morning, while passing by the Military hospital, I noticed soldiers being unloaded from the battlefield. I thought "War is one of the great blights of every age; how I wish that men everywhere could live in peace."

A serviceman and Christian teachers came to my aid.

On another occasion, Jim Reynolds, a Christian serviceman with much wisdom, provided the emotional support I needed for a crisis

I faced. Our mission had a regular program on several Vietnamese radio stations. Since most Vietnamese did not trust checks, I had to pay in cash.

On one occasion, I had exchanged a large amount at the bank to make our quarterly payment. I took a taxi to the school to pick up the family; as I stepped out of the taxi, the driver started off as I reached for my briefcase with the money in it.

A patron of the school saw this and shouted for me to get in his car; we gave the taxi a chase. But the little taxi wove in and out of traffic and we soon lost sight of him. We could not see a visible license plate or number to give us any clue. We went to the police station; they could not help without more information. I felt completely dejected with the loss and knew I could not personally make up the loss since we lived from month to month on our salary.

I relived the situation over and over. " Why didn't I take my briefcase out first? How could I be so careless with the Lord's money?"

When I returned to the school, I shared my experience with Reynolds, who served me as a counselor, fill-in preacher, and personal friend. He encouraged me and tried to help me overcome my guilty feelings.

A day or two later Reynolds slipped a little poem into my hand, which turned the tide in my depression. Rudyard Kipling, who had spent so many years in Asia, wrote:

"It is not good for the Christian health
To hustle the Asian brown.
For the Christian riles and the Asian smiles
And he weareth the Christian down.
At the end of the fight lies a tombstone white
With the name of the late deceased.
And the epitaph drear, 'A fool lies here,'
Who tried to hustle the East."

Truly, Kipling caught the essence of a Westerner trying to move things faster than the Easterner has been taught to live life. Over and over again, I learned great lessons of living in a totally different culture.

About three days later, the teachers invited me to the roof of the school building for a devotional. At the conclusion of the devotion, they presented me with an envelope. In the envelope, ten teachers had given me a large part of their month's salary to make up the loss. Since all of the teachers at the school live on a subsistence salary, I felt overwhelmed at their love and generosity.

How generous! How grateful! How thankful! God does move in mysterious ways. God constantly works behind the scenes in our lives. Jesus and the Holy Spirit constantly intercede for us.

I needed some spiritual strength and went to Romans, Chapter 8–one of the great chapters in the Bible. "In the same way, the Spirit helps us in our weakness. We do not know how we ought to pray, but the Spirit himself intercedes for us with groans that words cannot express. And he who searches our hearts knows the mind of the Spirit, because the Spirit intercedes for the saints in accordance with God's will. And we know that in all things God works for the good of those who love him, who have been called according to his purpose. (Romans 8:26-28,NIV)"

Reynolds provided counsel and became a very close personal friend. I found out he liked to preach. His Bible-centered lessons usually contained three easy to remember points. I commented on his excellent lessons, which seemed unusually short. He said, "A good lesson need not be eternal. If a preacher can't condense it to 15 minutes, he hasn't spent enough time in preparation."

When Reynolds had completed his time in Vietnam, he asked Gladys if he could invite some over after church for supper. Of course, Gladys agreed; he said: "There will be about 15 and I'll provide the steaks." Gladys prepared the food including a freezer of ice cream and pecan pies. However, instead of 15, we had 30; probably some heard about it and felt Reynolds meant to include them. But, believe it or not, we had plenty of food.

Oh, how I hated to see Reynolds leave. He had encouraged and provided wise counsel from the moment we first met.

Servicemen often came to us looking for encouragement.

John Bacon, a former Oklahoma Christian student we knew, came in to see us. He had been in Vietnam for several months and had been on the front lines from the beginning. He said, "It has been a living hell." According to him, more had been killed in his unit from accidents than from the enemy.

Someone had sent John an article about our orphanage. He brought a case of Dial soap. He came to Saigon for materials for his unit. He asked if he might spend the night. Of course, we agreed. Being so dirty, I offered him a shower and a bed. He refused saying "My buddies would know and give me a hard time." He slept on our porch in a sleeping bag.

We found it so amusing by the names of some places in Saigon. They used American names on many buildings. One day a G. I. walked up to Gladys and asked: "Lady, can you tell me where the San Francisco Hotel is?" Gladys looked at him and said: "Friend, you are not only in the wrong city, I think you are in the wrong country." They both laughed and he walked away looking for his hotel.

I found myself doing almost as much counseling as I did as a professor at Oklahoma Christian–husbands unfaithful to their wives, wives unfaithful to their husbands. One serviceman told me that of the 36 men that came in his unit, 15 have VD, some twice, and over 90 percent had made a visit to Tu Do Street, which is filled with bars and prostitutes.

On the other hand, I found most Christian servicemen exercised great self discipline by remaining faithful to their spouses and families. They used their time off by serving others. Several examples are described in the chapter on "The Vietnamese Orphans."

Servicemen constantly faced life and death.

Some of the servicemen I came to love and appreciate were not so fortunate.

Before Maurice Hall left Vietnam, he visited James, his son, who was stationed in the military at Monkey Mountain. Later, when

Maurice and Marie prepared to leave Vietnam, James offered to pack and ship their goods as soon as he could arrange a visit to Saigon.

How happy we felt to meet James when he came to get his parents' things, which we had packed and placed in our garage. James had such a love for his parents and a real servant attitude.

Truly, the Halls had given of themselves in making it possible for the Vietnamese to hear the Good News. How sad when another of the Hall's sons, Bill, gave his life for the Vietnamese people in order that they might have freedom. No one will ever be able to thank the Halls enough for all the sacrifices they made for the Vietnamese people.

***At the Vietnam War Memorial in Washington, D.C.,
Ralph Burcham made tracings of names of servicemen
he knew who made the ultimate sacrifice.***

Counseling servicemen provided great challenges!

William (Bill) Jerkins came to me for spiritual counseling. His family lived in Florida and his wife had read about our mission work and encouraged Bill to visit with us. Over a period of time, we developed a close relationship. He shared information about his wife and two children. Bill wanted to know more about becoming a Christian; therefore, we had studies together. As we studied, I would write down the Scriptures, which he would take back to review at his quarters.

Some time later, Bill came by for another visit; I noticed immediately his uneasiness, which marked his face and his movements. I asked, "What's the matter?"

His voice had a tremor to it as he replied, "Yesterday, I told my commander, 'I'm not feeling well. Could I go into Saigon and visit with a friend?'" His commander gave permission.

Bill poured out the concerns of his heart: "You know I am to go home in about a month. I am so anxious to see my wife and children."

Often servicemen got "the eleventh month jitters" just before their scheduled departure for home. As we talked, I tried to reassure him. "Perhaps part of your fear is that you do not feel you are in a right relationship with God."

With a reflective tone in his voice, he said: "Maybe you are right. I have decided to accept Christ as my Savior. I want to be baptized in the presence of my wife and children." I urged him to put Christ on immediately. "We can go down to the church and you can be baptized right now."

After a lengthy discussion and prayer, he indicated he must return to the base. I can remember so clearly how he walked slowly to our gate; as I let him out, he walked hesitatingly down the street, and I watched until he turned the corner.

A few days later, I received a letter from his wife indicating Bill had been killed in action. In his things, his wife found the Scriptures and notes Bill wrote during our visits together. Some thirty years later, I met Bill's wife and son along with their daughter-in-law and their three lovely little granddaughters.

What a sacrifice Bill gave for his country; what a sacrifice for his wife and children; and what a sacrifice the grandchildren are making in never knowing a loving grandfather, who served his country by making the ultimate sacrifice!

Servicemen often asked: "What would God have me do?"

Captain Robert Bradley came for advice and counsel. He served as a helicopter pilot. He shared his love for his family and looked forward to the time when he could return to the States.

But the weight of the killings had burdened his heart. He said, "I've come to feel that I need to make a change. I've considered joining the medical evacuation corps. I know there is more risk involved because you fly into enemy territory to pick up wounded soldiers. This makes you vulnerable to small arms fire. What do you think?"

I quickly responded, "I cannot recommend or suggest the direction you should take. This is between you, your family, and God. Do spend some time in prayer before you make your decision." We spent some time in prayer asking for God's direction and wisdom. When he left, I felt he had made his decision.

A few weeks later, I received a letter from his wife, Virginia. She wrote, "At a later date, I will send you the letter Bob wrote me about visiting you in Saigon. When I received his letter about his decision, I went crazy. The next letter about three days later granted his request to fly for the medics. He knew it would be more dangerous. He was sent to Pleiku and then from there flew to many other cities or hot spots . . .

"Then Bob flew from Pleiku on the morning of March 21, 1967, on a mission and crashed while hovering in enemy territory to get a wounded soldier . . . I want to thank you both for the pleasant day you gave to my husband, Captain Robert Bradley. You were the only civilian Christians he was to meet during the four and a half months he was there. He sent us two pictures of you and your home.

"He was transferred to the Medics as he requested. He knew it was more dangerous as it proved to be. Thank you for being Jesus' messengers in a foreign land . . . Continue Praying–that's the power,

Love, Virginia." She set up a memorial fund in his name and sent funds and clothing to help the Vietnamese orphanage.

Captain Bradley motivated Gladys to write an article, *"As A Living Sacrifice."*

"A sacrifice is defined as an offering of the life of a person or an animal to a god or deity. In the 12th Chapter of Romans, Paul pleads for Christians to give their bodies as a 'living sacrifice.'

"In seeking His followers, Christ never asked for people who would give Him one day a week and their spare evenings. Neither did He ask for individuals who would give Him only one-tenth of their money. Christ asks us to give all. When we truly give our hearts to the Master, we will give everything. John defines Christians as those that 'let Christ be a home to them and they are the home of Christ . . . (I John 3:23-24, Amplified Bible)'

"How many of us have known a wonderful Christian mother who began very early in her child's life to teach that child to love Jesus! As the years passed, she convinced the child that his or her life must be consecrated to Christ's service if the child is to please God. Then, one day, that son or daughter came home and announced a desire to give all–a life dedicated to Christian service in a foreign, backward, uneducated, disease-infected country. Yes, that mother taught her lesson well; but can you hear the reaction to an announcement like that. Too many mothers back down and offer all kinds of reasons for not doing it just yet.

"How many wives are guilty of holding back when a dedicated Christian husband is ready to give all? 'The children are too small,' 'What will we do with the house and car?' 'Can we afford it now?' 'Is it wise to leave a high-salaried job?–and security?'–on and on it goes.

"Have you ever known anyone who gave his entire being to his job? He used his time, talent, and energy in order that his business might succeed. His life is dedicated to some cause. Since I am in Vietnam, I would naturally think of the soldier. And Christ used the soldier to teach some of His greatest lessons! Not many weeks ago, one of our Christian servicemen visited our home. He related his desire to transfer to a medical evacuation team even though it involved greater risk. He felt he could be of greater service to his country and to his fellow man. With his request granted, the new assignment required his life in his efforts to save others. He gave his life in the great struggle for freedom. Can we give any less in the service of our Master?

"'I beg of you, my brothers, as an act of intelligent worship, to give him your bodies, as a living sacrifice, consecrated to him and acceptable to him. (Romans 12:1-2, Phillips)'"

Then Gladys concluded with this from an unknown author:

"Lord help me live from day to day
In such a self-forgetful way;
That even when I kneel to pray
My prayer will be for others."

Events like these helped me realize how those who paid the ultimate price live on to help other boys and girls have a better way of life through freedoms won or for memorials set up by family and friends.

Several years after being in Vietnam, we visited the Vietnam Memorial in Washington, D. C. This turned out to be a very moving, emotional experience as I looked up the names of servicemen, who had touched our lives in some way. As I made tracings of these, I felt deeply for the loss experienced by their families.

Over and over again, I thanked God for our Christian servicemen. My heart filled with admiration and appreciation as I remembered those men who were willing to make the ultimate sacrifice for their country and for a people desiring freedom. Truly, they are the "aroma of Christ" sent by God to strengthen the saved and to reach out to the lost with a message of salvation.

More and more I came to realize how rare it is for anyone to be willing to give up his or her life for someone else. This scripture came to mind: "Very rarely will anyone die for a righteous man, though for a good man someone might possibly dare to die. But God demonstrates his own love for us in this: While we were still sinners, Christ died for us. (Romans 5:7-8, NIV)" Christian servicemen that I came to know and the ones I baptized served as my example of true dedication to the cause of Christ.

Vietnam — "I Shall Not Die"

"I will not die but live, and will proclaim what the Lord has done."

Psalms 118:17, NIV

During December 1967, the military was on alert quite often. One serviceman, Gary Simpson, a Military MP, expressed concern for our well being when he learned that I did not possess a gun of any kind. To cover his concern, he said: "My company is having an IG inspection and I have a machine gun that is not on our property books. May I leave it with you for a few days until the inspection is over?"

I gave permission and in a few days Gary left a machine gun with a large belt of ammo. It had been over 12 years since I completed basic training in an armored-infantry division and fired machine guns and other weapons. Later, he brought over a machete that he had chromed.

After several days had passed, Gary visited us and I asked: "Have you had your IG inspection?" When he indicated the inspections to be over, I requested, "Please take the machine gun and the machete." As events unfolded, that may have been a serious mistake on my part.

Gary also provided regular comic relief in helping me overcome the serious side of my nature. One day, while on duty at the Port, he saw a Vietnamese worker leaving who appeared to have things stuffed in his clothing.

He went up to the worker and gave him a hard pat on the back and said: "Papa San, I hope you are having a good day." The eggs stuffed in the worker's clothing smashed and started running everywhere. As Gary related this experience, I thought how good to have a friend who helps me see the lighter side of life!

Also, Gary showed his concern for our safety just prior to the time when the war came into Saigon. More will be discussed about this later.

The war has touched every Vietnamese home. One of my Bible students told me he had lost two brothers and an uncle; another when two months old, lost his father; and later, when seven years old, the VC killed his mother. All felt great pessimism about an early end to the war. Most felt that, even though the war would probably escalate to major proportions very soon, a "cease fire" would not bring peace to this land. Most believed it would go back to guerilla warfare.

The VC had terrific losses in the weeks before Christmas, 1967; when this happened, they usually resorted to terrorism in the cities. In many ways, we could feel the growing tension over the military situation in Saigon as the Vietnamese expected something to "blow" at any time. Also, most here–who were familiar with the history of Ho Chi Minh–did not feel he would come to the peace table. As one told me, "Ho Chi Minh waited out 33 years in exile believing he would some day come into power in North Vietnam."

Another serviceman, Sergeant Fred Hall, spent most every evening with our children watching TV. He lived in a billet about two blocks from our place. He worked in the mortuary at Tan Son Nhut. He reported that business had been "disgustingly good." On average, they processed about 30 bodies each day; but during the battle of Dak To, they processed over 400 in three days.

One day Sergeant Hall reported that something big must be in the making because the mortuary had received the biggest shipment ever of embalming fluid from the States. He felt this to be an indication of plans to intensify the war in the near future. Since we knew so many servicemen on a very personal level, we felt a deep sense of concern for those out in the field.

Increased terrorist activities in Saigon kept us on the alert, but no major war within the city. We kept hearing rumors that something would blow at Tan Son Nhut on Christmas Eve, but the Security Guard must have been Number One as nothing happened.

We looked forward to our second Vietnamese Tet.

After Christmas, 1967, we began thinking about our second Tet. From our previous Tet, we knew this to be an exciting, enjoyable time.

All the Vietnamese make all the money possible for this celebration. We found it is not the time to go shopping, as the Vietnamese merchants did not bargain.

During the Tet season, as Gladys learned from experience, "Even the Police fine taxi and cyclo drivers for anything especially if they have an American passenger. I feel sorry for the taxi drivers when it happens to them. It's happened to three I've been riding with recently. When the third one whistled us down, I got out with the driver and walked over to the policeman and wrote down his badge number. Of course, I couldn't have done a thing, but he let the little fellow go without having to pay."

As Tet approached, the fireworks and firecrackers seemed to be going off in every part of the city; the explosions seemed to be bigger and made more noise than any we had ever heard. Roger put it this way: "These fireworks are like fifty American New Years and Fourth of Julys combined."

At first we jumped every time we heard a firecracker as it reminded us of explosions heard nightly outside the city. After a while, we just ignored the noise.

Our children wanted firecrackers, and they felt somewhat cheated by the small ones I purchased. Our watch dog, Cindy, slept on our front porch; when she heard gun fire or firecrackers, she started scratching and rattling our front doors. At such times, we had to bring her in to calm her down.

For the Vietnamese, it is a time for celebration; they hoped the new year would bring peace and an end to the war. An ancient custom involves paying homage to ancestors. Family and friends are invited to dinner. Protocol demands that the honored guests arrive early. At dinner, honored guests would be seated first. All day during Tet, they put on their best clothes and make unannounced calls on family and friends with yellow "mums" or miniature orange trees. Buddhists visit pagodas for ceremonial rituals in honor of ancestors.

This holiday demands that one spend time in reflection. It is a time for making amends with one's friends and family. Forgiveness is sought and given. An attempt is made to pay off debts.

One Vietnamese writer put it this way: "This is the time when the Vietnamese look back on the past, enjoy the present, and look forward to the future. It is truly a comprehensive holiday, and all Vietnamese give it full observance. Tet simply means a renewal of the body and spirit, a brand-new disposition to greet the New Year. It is a communion of the living and the dead, past and present merging in the broad current of today, looking back and gazing forward, sorrow for things done and hope for tomorrow, nostalgia and prayerful contemplation of the new."

Bang! Bang! Boom! They aren't bombs tonight. This is the eve of the Chinese New Year, January 29, and I had forgotten how noisy it got last year.

We are just ending the "Year of the Goat" and tomorrow begins the "Year of the Monkey." Roger summarized it this way: "Well, a lot of butting went on last year and we can probably expect the same old monkey business this one."

Gladys wrote in her journal, "Why did we have to pick these two years to come to Vietnam? Why didn't we choose the Year of the Tiger, or the Golden Gazelle, or some such glamorous and daring year.

"Everyone here shoots firecrackers to usher in the New Year. The noise is supposed to drive away all evil spirits. And, believe me, I'm about to go! But even Roger and Kathy are out shooting firecrackers. As the evening progresses, it gets worse and worse and at midnight everything goes. So I decided to write letters since there'll be no sleep tonight.

"The firecrackers have been going on for about two weeks and, in a way, it's kinda relaxing. You can't always tell the bombs from celebrating so I always say, 'Oh, its just a firecracker.' You won't believe how big some of them are. There's a law against any over 24 inches long. Our poor number ten–oops Kathy's number one–dog is a nervous wreck."

The Tet Offensive found us surrounded by war!

During the evening of January 30, 1968, the Tet celebrations engulfed Saigon. The VC and the Americans had called a truce. But at 3 a.m. on January 31, all hell broke out all over the city. Awakened by mortar explosions hitting Tan Son Nhut base, which is just four blocks away, Gladys quickly summed up the situation with, "That is more than firecrackers!"

Jumping out of bed, we checked on our children to be sure they were not frightened; then went to the balcony to see red-hot tracer bullets zipping past our house about 12 feet away. It would have been instant suicide had I stepped outside our gate. Our short block had a high wall at the dead end. The tracer bullets seemed to be coming from over the top of the wall; return fire came from the other end of the street, which fed, into a main street. Truly, the battlefield had moved in all around us.

We turned our radio to the Armed Forces station; it blared with urgent warnings to all Americans to stay in your quarters; if needed, a military escort would be sent to pick one up. The Viet Cong had launched their attack on Saigon.

Finally, we found ourselves with the war at our doorstep. I felt so helpless as I reprimanded myself for bringing my family into this situation. I found myself in constant prayer to God; He knows our situation; He is all-powerful; now God "please, please show us mercy!"

Across town, Howard and Mildred Horton, our co-workers, expressed it this way: "The battlefield has literally moved in all around us." Dennis and Toni Ruch, former missionaries now working for the U. S. Government, had been with them for a few days and their adopted son, Joseph, had a fever. Howard heard 'Little Joe' crying and got up to see if he could help them. Just as he opened his bedroom door and stepped onto the patio to go downstairs, a terrific explosion went off somewhere nearby. As he jumped back into their bedroom, another blast rattled the shutters.

Howard went on to say "Mildred is now awakened by the blasts. Our bedroom windows open to the back, which leads toward the river about a block away. The explosions came from somewhere in that block behind us, so we went downstairs which has no exposed windows.

"For 20 minutes or more, the heavy firing continued. Round after round was launched; also, we could hear muffled explosions toward downtown Saigon and elsewhere in the area. Although we had no idea just what was occurring, I am sure now that the VC mortar launchers had been set up somewhere in our block.

"Finally, machine-gun, rifle, and pistol fire opened up all around the block. After about two hours, things began to be quiet again and we went back upstairs to our bedroom.

"Just as we got upstairs, we heard a mortar round being fired; then small arms broke loose, and a bullet hit the outside of the house somewhere. We dove to the floor in the bedroom, and rather than cross the patio to return downstairs, I pulled our mattress into a corner shielded by the bathroom wall.

"We dozed a little off and on until morning; then we learned by radio that the VC had hit six targets in Saigon, including the U. S. Embassy. We had little difficulty complying with the radio instructions that all Americans stay inside.

"All day rifles, pistols, and machine guns could be heard before the VC could be rounded up. The general traffic could not go down our street. Then we saw police and soldiers marching captives to a point about a half-block from our house, where they were loaded into trucks and taken away.

"I found a spent bullet on our upstairs patio and another on the roof. Across the river a huge fire raged all day where the Vietnam soldiers burned several blocks of shacks where the VC had infiltrated to live with families. They first evacuated the families before starting the fires."

On our side of town, the mortar shells made an eerie whistle as they flew over our house on their way to Tan Son Nhut. Then we heard the explosions as mortars hit their targets. The Viet Cong had killed the guards on the bridge near the home of the Hortons. The VC marched up the street in front of the Hortons' place and occupied a French Cemetery about two blocks from their home. Later we heard rumors that for months the VC carried on mock funerals. Since the caskets being filled with weapons, ammunition, and mortars, the French Cemetery became the launching pad for mortars.

The shelling and small arms fire lasted the entire day. The noise of battle surrounded us and I felt engulfed by the war. As Gladys wrote in her journal, "What a day! It's the first time since we've been here that we never unlocked our gate. We've never heard so much shooting and plane activity. Right on our street! This is one time it doesn't pay to be so near Tan Son Nhut. The shooting is still going on; it's been a 'nervous' day. I made donuts this afternoon. All traffic has stopped on our street."

Gladys warned me to give special attention to our children.

All day I had been working on correspondence and lessons for my classes. By evening, feeling very depressed, I became very quiet. (This is my typical reaction to stress.) Gladys detecting my feelings, came into my study, closed the door, and quietly cautioned: "We need to have a little pow wow."

Her serious expression warned me to take notice. Several of our Vietnamese friends had shared stories of the cruelty many had experienced at the hands of the VC. With a chilling pathos Gladys continued: "We do not know how this is going to turn out. If the VC come into our home, I pray they will kill our children before they kill us. But if we survive, I do not want our children to be psychological cripples."

I came back with "What do you suggest?"

"We need to do like the fellas out in fox holes at this moment. They are constantly making the best of a bad situation. Somehow we need to put forth greater effort to reassure our kids of our love and how God is concerned about our situation. We need to keep them usefully occupied." To me she said, "Snap out of your quietness and quit using your study as a 'hidey-hole!'"

Then we started making plans on how we would approach Roger and Kathy. We went into the living room where the children were busy putting a jigsaw puzzle together. Roger said, "This puzzle is going to drive me crazy. It has a blue sky and water, which takes up half of the puzzle. On one side there is a tree with a barn but even that isn't going to be too easy."

Gladys started the conversation with "Roger, this is a good time for you to become a war correspondent. Take Dad's tape recorder. You can record the shelling and gun fire and report on what is happening around us just like a reporter on TV." This struck a favorable note. He quit the puzzle and immediately started setting up my tape recorder for his live sessions. (One of our prized possessions is the recording with the actual sounds you can hear from our place. You can even identify the weapons by their sound.)

I challenged Kathy with, "This is a good time for you to complete some of those Bible quarterlies someone sent us." I promised her a dollar for each completed quarterly. She was completing quarterlies far advanced for her age. What a surprise to me! I thought, "I hope I have enough money to pay up."

According to the *Pacific Stars and Stripes* of February 1, 1968, "The Viet Cong forces launched heavy attacks against Saigon on Wednesday. Guerrillas fought their way into the U. S. Embassy and occupied five floors of it for several hours. Other Reds invaded Saigon's Tan Son Nhut airport and battled American and Vietnamese troops and tanks." When I read about the attack on our Embassy, it reminded me of our own situation and vulnerability because of our closeness to Tan Son Nhut.

Across town as the Hortons prepared their mattresses to sleep downstairs in the kitchen with no exposed window, the mortars began firing again from very near their house. Howard said: "We could not tell the exact direction or distance. We heard the firing of two or three mortars. In three to five minutes, we heard two helicopter gun ships coming in low. A machine-gun began firing at the helicopters, and the pilots opened up with their powerful weapons. Both helicopters made two passes over their target with guns blazing full blast. They came over again; then silence: no shots fired from either side.

"Apparently they knocked out the mortar nest. With the neighborhood being quiet, we slept well without disturbance from the heavy shooting. Being awakened briefly twice, I heard scattered small arms fire, but nothing else except the comforting drone of the helicopters as they circled and searched and guarded."

Through all of this, Howard maintained his wonderful sense of humor. "After all," he said, "what chance has a stray bullet of hitting a man and woman flattened out on a tile floor under two mattresses in an inside room downstairs with no outside windows under a concrete slab ceiling? I lay so flat my trouser legs had creases on each side."

Howard's confident assurance provided us great comfort. Later he wrote: "Our Father's work is far more important than the coincidences of war. We are confident that He is able to cover us with His care while we seek to do His will and fulfill His purposes for us. Let us all pray for the day when the world can regain its senses and seek God's peace."

Back on our side of town, February 1st ushered in the second day our gate remained locked. Gunfire continued, but it stopped on our street in the afternoon. Still, Americans were not going to work. Jeeps mounted with machine guns escorted those in critical areas to their workstations. From reports we received, "The loss of lives is terrible and more expected before it is over."

Gladys wrote in her journal: "I made Kathy some doll clothes this afternoon and baked bread. We still are not able to get out with all the letters we've written. It may be a while yet."

The shelling and small arms fire went off and on for 38 hours. Then the American helicopters circled overhead. From our second floor-screened balcony, we could see the men firing the rockets. The explosions, with billows of black smoke gushing skyward, seemed so near; but we could not know for a while how close.

Roger continued his reporting with, "There are some big explosions nearby and Dad rushed upstairs to get some sense of how close they are." Then he reported, "Dad just came back and said that all he can see is clouds of black smoke."

On February 2nd, Gladys wrote in her diary, "Six more weeks of winter according to the groundhog; but I'm sure he was afraid to stick his head out of the hole to look for his shadow. Another tense day, although it is quieter around our house."

Our place became a refugee center.

Two friends, Bob and Chau Fairless, for whom I had performed their wedding ceremony, lived near the Cholon PX. The Viet Cong marched down their street shooting out windows. Bob's Vietnamese mother-in-law became concerned for his safety in case the VC made a house-to-house search.

From the time the shelling started, Bob and Chau slept on the landing of their stairway between floors because of their nearby water storage tank. Should anyone attempt to come in, Bob planned to crawl into the tank and breathe through a straw while the VC searched their home.

Bob's mother-in-law nervously watched for an opportunity for them to escape. During siesta time, the neighborhood seemed quiet. Chau's mother sent them on their way. They rode their motorcycle through all kinds of barricades to our place; they planned to stay with us until the immediate danger subsided.

On arriving at our place, Chau went upstairs and fell across a bed in shear exhaustion. But after resting for a short time, she felt a need to ride their motorcycle back to their home and get her mother. However, her mother decided to stay with an aunt.

Gradually, we received reports that others in our mission group were all right. Others came to live with us. We felt a mild sense of security, as a Vietnamese General owned our home; also, another General owned and occupied the house across the street. Because we lived on a dead end street, our place seemed more secure than many places at that time. The small area behind our house had a 12-foot high wall with broken glass on top with several rows of barbed wire above that. Also, our front yard provided protection with a smaller wall with broken glass embedded in concrete with barbed wire above it.

After being under siege for three days, Johnnie Everett, a serviceman, came by in an armed jeep with a large machine gun mounted on the back. Wearing a flak jacket with grenades attached, he rang the bell at our gate. Kathy looked out from our upstairs' balcony and said, "It's Johnnie."

As I opened the gate, he said, "I just came by to see if you were all okay. I thought you might be running low on food. I flew over your place a time or two to see what the situation looked like around your villa." As he shared his concerns for us, a feeling of gratitude welled up within me in thanksgiving to God for servicemen who really cared about our welfare.

Gene Conner, one of our American teachers in the international school, lived in a small village beyond Tan Son Nhut base. Being very concerned for his welfare for some time, but in the afternoon a military escort brought him in to our place. He had been in hiding because of the heavy shelling in his area; when the military action subsided, he went to a military post not far from where he lived. Our place seemed to be like a "refugee camp."

That night our electricity went off. Just what we needed to allay our fears–the dark! The fighting throughout the day had been heavy at the Cholon PX and An Quang Pagoda.

February 3rd found us still locked behind our gate. Without electricity, our refrigerated food began to spoil. Our neighborhood seemed quiet; no military action close by. Without a cold drink for two days, Roger did get brave and go to the end of our street and around the corner for ice; but no deliveries as yet. However, gratitude filled our hearts for water as most of the city had the water cut off; we had a well.

Our unique water system included a storage tank on the ground level, which we kept full with city water when available. We could pump the water to a storage area on the roof; this allowed water to circulate by gravity flow. Since water was contaminated, all water used for cooking or drinking had to be processed; Gladys spent additional time processing water for our family and guests.

Because of our quiet neighborhood, Conner decided to check on another American, Florence Vinyard. Florence, overjoyed to see someone, packed up her two babies — Vietnamese orphans — and came back to our house for the night. Our refugee center now numbered ten!

Many Americans and foreigners looked for ways to get out of Vietnam; however, all international flights had been cancelled coming in or going out from Saigon.

I kept busy with study and correspondence. However, I found myself reflecting on our situation. Gladys kept before her a Psalm, "This is the day the Lord has made; let us rejoice and be glad in it." It took real effort for me to rejoice. Yet, I could see the Lord's care surrounding us. We had everything we needed and I knew a host of people around the world kept praying for us. At every opportunity, I expressed my love to Gladys, the children, and our guests.

My prayer life became more intense. I could identify with David, who prayed: "O my righteous God. Give me relief from my distress; be merciful to me and hear my prayer. (Psalm 4:1. NIV)"

February 4th found us still behind locked gates with no electricity. Since this came on Sunday, we had a worship service at home. After the service, Conner took Florence and the babies home. Kathy went to stay with her overnight. Roger did sneak out and purchased a little ice—he paid about five times what we normally paid. Such a luxury did boost our morale.

Bob and Chau went over to her aunt's to check on her mother and brother. They found the VC had threatened her whole family because she married an American. They brought back Chau's brother to stay with us. Her mother would probably join us later. They lived in fear that their home would be burned.

Now I found myself in serious reflection. How grateful I felt for the life of Job. After Job reflected on a need for someone to present his case and not knowing where God could be located, he said: "But he knows the way that I take; when he has tested me, I will come forth as gold . . . . I have treasured the words of his mouth more than my daily bread. (Job 23:10,12b, NIV)"

Then when God spoke to Job, He said: "Who then is able to stand against me? Who has a claim against me that I must pay? Everything under heaven belongs to me. (Job 41:10b,11, NIV)" When Job replied to God, he said: "My ears had heard of you but now my eyes have seen you. Therefore I despise myself and repent in dust and ashes. (Job 42:5,6, NIV)" Surely, I needed to repent because God had taken care of us in a tremendous way.

February 5th began with Conner going for Kathy as well as a failed attempt at reaching the commissary because all the streets over toward Cholon had been blocked off.

When Gladys swept the driveway, she found a bullet right by the house. The conflict came nearer than we had thought!

The Vietnamese government allowed the markets to reopen for the morning hours. Most Vietnamese went to the market daily and prepared their meals from fresh produce. Our hearts went out to the people as the closed markets created a hardship for all of them. Chau and her brother went to the market for us and brought home the most delicious fruits and vegetables. This made us all rejoice; we truly felt grateful for Chau's efforts. Kathy got excited because Chau planned to cook dinner.

Later, Chau and her brother went to get their mother to stay with us because our area seemed to be safe. We prayed for them until they arrived back safely.

The electricity came on for about 30 minutes, just long enough to fill our water storage tank, which was getting low.

An Army plane flew over Saigon most of the afternoon dropping leaflets. Finally, one landed in our back yard and Chau read it for us. A Viet Cong leader had turned himself into the Saigon Government and he pleaded with all the VC to turn themselves in and not fight. Gladys responded with: "Oh, how we wish he will have some influence."

I went out to Tan Son Nhut to mail some letters, but I could not pick up our mail. I did obtain a copy of the Stars and Stripes and read about the protests in the States and some comments of Senator John Sparkman. Often when the Senator spoke, this gave the VC encouragement; sometimes they produced flyers from these negative comments and scattered them in neighborhoods. As Gladys put it: "We over here wish our Senators at home would keep quiet; they must encourage the enemy at times!" These protests created morale problems with our servicemen, who kept on serving in a most commendable way.

The bright spot in the day came as we enjoyed the Vietnamese dinner Chau and her mother prepared for us. We all agreed: "That

Vietnamese noodle soup is the best yet!" After dinner for some time, all the men played rook between news reports.

I came to a new appreciation for how letters build morale.

A real boost came to us on February 6th — our first mail in a week! Gladys reported in her journal: "We are all staying in. In fact, General Westmoreland has commanded all Americans to stay off the streets. He didn't have to tell me twice. I never would have gone across town for mail; only a fool would. But Gene Conner decided to try." Conner brought back the mail and groceries from the commissary. Like ravished wolves, we read every word in each letter over and over; somehow we felt we had made contact with the outside world.

We felt fortunate to have Chau living with us as she could go to the market every day. "But prices!" as Gladys put it. "Yesterday, Chau got a piece of fresh pork about the size of your fist and paid a fortune for it. I've thought about becoming a vegetarian. But the prices on veggies are right up there too."

Local news became available to us. We learned that over 600 VC had been killed in Gia Dinh, our suburb of town. So many dead VC pilled up in front of the gate into Tan Son Nhut, the military had to bring in a forklift to clear the bodies from the street.

Johnnie Everett came by again "wearing grenades," as Kathy described him. Also Captain Meinert came to check on us. Words cannot express the deep gratitude we felt for our servicemen. Johnnie brought us two packages from our families in the U.S. These packages gave a real morale boost to our children.

At this time, New York City reported being overwhelmed with garbage because of a workers' strike. This reminded us of our own waste. As Gladys put it, "We got to feeling so bad about New York City and their garbage that we got out in the street and burned piles of it. I only wish garbage had been all we had to worry about. Oh me!"

But our garbage had a surprise in it. Roger had discarded his fuseless firecrackers in the wastebasket. As I lit the fire, little explosions started popping. Everyone up and down the block came out on their balconies to see what precautions they should take with this latest firepower. As they looked down and saw my exasperation, spontaneous laughter came from up and down the block. At least they had a lighter moment at my expense.

The electricity did come back on in the afternoon and remained on during the evening. You could hear cheers up and down our street. The electricity allowed us to watch TV and get the latest war news.

On February 7th at 6 a.m., eight or ten mortar rounds seemed to be fired from very near our home. The VC must have been holed up nearby. Shortly afterward our street filled with armed Vietnamese soldiers. A jeep with a mounted machine gun drove in and parked right in front of our gate. As Gladys reported, "I stood on top of my desk at the window upstairs to see it all. They searched a while, then moved out and down to the next street." Then we heard some gunfire.

Because of the war, our school closed with an extended vacation; our children would have found this to be enjoyable under other circumstances. No mail today, in or out. Conner took Roger and Kathy to Tan Son Nhut to a movie in the afternoon. As Gladys put it: "This got them out of the house and the three or four blocks between here and there seems pretty safe now."

The bread lady and later the soup wagon came by for the first time in over a week.

After the early morning visit of the soldiers on our street, we enjoyed the rest of the day with quiet until the evening. Then the war seemed to intensify—we could hear bombings, mortars, and rockets. The news we received indicated the probability that more than 900 VC remained in the city.

*I began to feel for our parents and friends
as they received the war news.*

Knowing the evening news in the States included the gory details of the war in Saigon, I knew our parents, relatives, and friends must be worried. I started praying that they might be comforted even though we had no way of communicating with them.

February 8th found Americans still under a strict curfew—a 24-hour one! We wandered about how this affected our loyal maid, Chi Hai, as we knew nothing about her situation. Then her son, Canh, came out to tell us that his mother had gone out of town for Tet and had not been able to get back to Saigon. Gladys expressed her real feelings with: "Oh, how I need Chi Hai with this house full!"

Later in the morning, I went for groceries and picked up the mail. In our mail a cable from my Dad moved me to tears. It read: "We are concerned. Please let us know that you are all right!" Again, a sense of guilt came over me because we had no way of communicating except through regular mail. My parents and Gladys' Mother had not seen their grandchildren for two years. Our telephone had been out of order for several days. However, we exercised great caution and stayed near home. Again, we kept our gate locked all day. However, we had garbage pickup for the first time.

On February 9th we stayed in all day. Howard Horton and Dennis Ruch, who worked for USAID, got brave and came out during the morning. They took our Volkswagen bus to go out to the airport to pick up some things that Dennis had shipped down from Nha Trang.

Bob and Chau learned their home had been burned and they lost everything. Their coming to stay with us turned out to be a wise decision. During the Tet Offensive, reports indicated some ten thousand homes had been destroyed.

All day I worked on a tape to mail to Oklahoma Christian, who had granted me a leave of absence. I included some of Roger's work of January 31st as a war correspondent including the sounds of weapons being fired in our area.

What an empty feeling to experience another day without mail!

During the evening, we could hear intense warfare, but it seemed to be outside the city.

By February 10th we all experienced "cabin fever." Waiting is difficult when you do not know what the day may bring. Another sleepless night as the bombing and shelling seemed very near Saigon; also, we felt there to be considerable activity within the City because of loud shelling! We wondered how long this could continue.

During the day, two of my Vietnamese students in the leader-ship-training program, who lived in Saigon, came out to the house for help. One worked in a government sponsored refugee center and the other had eleven refugees staying in his home. They needed clothing; we provided help from things sent to us. They brought news of the happenings in their areas.

Ona Belknap's letter touched us beyond words.

A backlog of mail came through. What a morale builder! We read with the hunger of prisoners confined for 11 days. A letter from Ona Belknap touched us deeply. As mentioned earlier, her brother published **The Christian Chronicle.** She wrote: "Our Chronicle Editor has just xeroxed copies of all your last correspondence and is rushing some of it to the press today. Please, please keep us informed. We not only will stop the presses to let all those deeply concerned know about the situation there, but I have such a deep personal involvement, that we have tried to check into sources of direct communication–which of course was fruitless last week.

"I am afraid I have prayed more for your courage than I have for your physical welfare; for your faith and courage, I am sure, have been tested as few have of recent years. Last Saturday night I spent many hours praying for your emotional welfare under such stress . . . and am afraid mine was sadly lacking."

Ona's letter moved us deeply. Just knowing people kept praying for us strengthened us beyond measure.

We kept asking, "How long will this last?" But it was anybody's guess. Gladys started making plans to tutor our children. She baked bread, and it nearly all disappeared at the evening meal. She seemed to be showing signs of weariness as it takes a lot of food to feed ten people, and often more, three times a day. She continued to answer correspondence. I, too, worked on correspondence and started cleaning out some of my files and burning piles of waste just in case we got out and could not return. In the evening, I played a crazy card game with Kathy.

On February 11th we had worship in our home during the morning. Tran Van Can—my friend, translator, and confidant—and his son came out about noon to see how we managed under the circumstances. Their presence brought reassurance.

Our children endured this all patiently; our neighborhood seemed quiet, and Kathy decided she wanted to get out so we let her walk up around the corner for ice. We each kept a watch out for her until she returned.

Gladys wrote letters and prepared Valentines for several of our GI friends. She always looked for opportunities to give them encouragement.

On the morning of February 12th, Chi Hai, our maid, came to see us. Also, the General, who owned our house, sent his Lieutenant to collect the rent.

Later in the day, Nguyen Dan Bao, the preacher in Bien Hoa, risked his life in coming in to see us. He encouraged us to leave; he said, "If I could take my family out of Vietnam, I would; but we have no other place to go. My son is an officer in the Vietnamese military and he feels the war activity will go on for some time. Please take your family out if you can!"

Because of the unsettled situation in Vietnam, we started making plans to go to Bangkok to stay until we could determine if we would be able to continue our mission efforts.

From all reports we received, the military situation in Saigon could continue for some time. Because of the curfews and restrictions, I felt my work would be hampered; also, I felt deep concern for the welfare of my family.

One of the other missionary groups checked into the possibility of chartering a plane; they invited us to fly out with them. We decided to go if our family and the Howard Hortons could get ready in time.

I went to the government office and officially closed the American-Vietnamese School because most of our students had foreign parents, serving in Saigon in embassies, banks, or businesses. It became evident that these families were leaving Saigon as fast as they could; therefore, our enrollment would not be sufficient to pay expenses. Also, the teachers had a two-year contract with the provision of their return airfare to the States. Since the school account had enough funds for those desiring to leave, I personally visited each teacher and staff employee and gave the promised amount.

February 13th found us packing but still unsure what to do. Then came very disappointing news–the cancellation of the chartered flight to Bangkok. Five missionaries, who worked up country, had been killed; the sponsors of that missionary group put so much pressure on our government that they flew these families out on military planes. Air Vietnam started up flights again with bookings for weeks ahead. All foreigners were leaving Vietnam as fast as they could get out.

Two of the schoolteachers—Arlen Ewing and Dick DiNucci—came out to talk about our plans with the closing of the school. How good to see them for the first time in over two weeks. Arlen, as a most knowledgeable historian, kept me informed on happenings in nearby countries. Dick, with his insights from having served in the military, gave me insights on how the stricter curfews would affect my work. I taught Dick the gospel and will be forever grateful for his willingness to resign his commission and offer to help further our mission. What wonderful friends!

I applied for our exit visas. It is a tedious process to enter or leave a country when you are there for an extended time. I had to get clearance from the tax office. Also, shot records had to be current to get an exit visa; thankfully we had kept them up-to-date. We got more mail.

Prayers of friends and loved ones sustained us.

In the mail, we received encouraging letters from friends and loved ones indicating they prayed regularly for us. How encouraging to know that so many kept our name before the One who is able. One letter in particular came from a lady, Paula Limes, whom we had never met. She attended Helen Wright's ladies class at the Mayfair congregation in Oklahoma City. This class had more or less adopted Gladys by writing her every week and sending us gifts occasionally.

Paula's husband, Dr. Barney Limes, had received the newsletter from Oklahoma Christian which contained a reproduction of a letter

I had sent about the fighting in Saigon. Paula wrote: "When I finished reading your letter and could get the tears stopped–I prayed–Our God is alive and loves us–I have prayed for you before but never so earnestly or feeling so close to you or such a need to pray! These Scriptures came to mind:

"'When the righteous cry for help, the Lord hears and delivers them out of *all* their troubles.' I believe this and will continue to ask God to guide you and protect you.–'I sought the Lord and he answered me and delivered me from all my *fears*'–'Incline thy ear to me, rescue me speedily'–'The angel of the Lord encamps around those who fear him and delivers them.'

"I'd like to think that God has a special angel encamped around your house protecting you and your children and friends.

"'In face of all this, what is there left to say? If God is for us, who can be against us?–Can we not trust such a God to give us everything else that we need? Who can separate us from the love of Christ? Can trouble–pain– persecution–lack of clothes–food– danger to life–force of arms? No, in all these things we win an *overwhelming* victory.'

"I do not know your plans. I would like to help you. First, I'll pray. Then–you tell me how we can help . . . We are sincere in wanting to help you. This is not just a 'if you need help, let me know' and then you won't ask and I'll dismiss the idea. *Please* tell us what we can do and we'll try. Love, Paula Limes"

The tears flowed as I read Paula's letter. Somehow I felt her words had action behind them. Later, I came to learn how God answered her prayer for a guardian angel to protect us.

On February 14th Howard Horton came about noon; he had found a flight for us to Singapore to leave the next morning. Howard lived on the other side of the river from us, and he kept trying to find passage on any airline to any place out of Vietnam. When he went into the Pan Am office, a gentleman needed to turn in six tickets to Singapore because of being unable to get exit visas for his family. The Pan Am officials allowed Howard to take those six tickets.

Gladys wrote, "So the rest of the day has been pandemonium, believe me! Trying to move half way around the world and tie up loose ends with a strict curfew over most of the city is no easy thing."

We worked late into the night getting everything ready. Bob Fairless and Gene Conner gave us the help and support we needed. We packed some boxes of personal items, and Gene offered to mail them to us.

Being unsure about directions from our supporting church, I made arrangements with Bob to take over our house in case we could not return. Since they did not have a place to live, they gladly accepted our offer.

What a day February 15th turned out to be! Is it possible that we are on our way out of Vietnam? It reminded me of a sweat shirt we saw a GI wearing, it said, "I'm on my way to heaven; I've spent my time in hell!"

As we left our street, we could see how close the war came to us. Just over a block from where we lived three and four story apartment buildings had been leveled. The Viet Cong had set up a post in one of these. This explained what the rockets had been hitting when fired from the helicopters circling over our place. The explosions and the bellows of smoke came back to mind.

Gladys simply wrote, "Believe me, we got out of Saigon with our hides. The first time in over two weeks that I've been out on the streets. I had to get out to get to the airport. What a funny feeling to pass all the armed jeeps and tanks on the streets with rolls of barbed wire on the sides ready to block at any time."

Leaving Saigon left a hurt in my heart.

At the International Air Terminal, we joined Howard and Mildred Horton, checked in our luggage, and went through security. What a feeling of relief to be on board the plane. The military had secured an area for planes to come in and take off. As we took off, our plane seemed to go straight up. I looked down on the city with people I had come to love. I could see large blackened areas destroyed by the war. How thankful to be delivered from the war, but I felt a great heartache for those dear Vietnamese and GI friends left behind.

On arriving in Singapore, we stayed at an old English hotel, The Checkers. Overwhelmed by the quiet with no flares, no helicopters, no bombs or guns, no barb wire, and no high walls. And the cleanliness of the city, the beautiful parks, and the service at the hotel—all made us feel like we had arrived in heaven.

When we got settled in our room, Gladys simply fell across the bed in shear exhaustion. She had been such a stalwart companion, advisor, and gracious hostess to hundreds of guests, friend to the Vietnamese and servicemen, and teacher of God's word. For the past several days, she had dealt with being surrounded by the fighting and the noise of war with our home being used as a refugee center for many of our fellow missionaries. Truly, she needed some recovery time!

I made calls to our supporting congregation asking for instructions. We wanted to return to Saigon if the situation would allow us to continue our mission work. The elders asked me to call back in a couple of days for further consultation. They suggested we spend a few days recovering in Singapore.

Then I made a call to Dr. James O. Baird, the President of Oklahoma Christian. When he came on the line, emotion overcame me and I had difficulty getting words to come out. I did not think I could talk with our parents because of these feelings. I asked Dr. Baird to call our parents and tell them we made it out of Vietnam all right and that we would be in contact with them soon.

Dr. Baird expressed his gratitude for our safe deliverance. Then he said: "You are in the thoughts and prayers of the entire student body. Also, we just completed our Oklahoma Christian annual lectureship, and prayers were offered on your behalf during all of these sessions." With a tearful gratitude, I could only say, "God answered those prayers!"

Of course, our kids wanted to experience Singapore. I'm amazed at the resilience of children. We quietly left our room and went exploring the quaint shops. Roger and Kathy found a little bakery with the most tantalizing scents permeating the air and drawing us inside.

Then back to our hotel. Children under 12 had a separate dining room. Kathy seemed a bit reluctant to go there by herself, but she felt all right when Roger offered to eat with her; he gave up his place with the "adults." As Kathy got acquainted with the waiters and other children, she encouraged Roger to go back to the other dining room for future meals. According to Roger, one of the waiters gave her special attention.

We enjoyed the English influence during their mid-afternoon tea. The tea consisted of several kinds of cheese and meats, crackers, delicious pastries, and, of course, plenty of tea.

Our second day in Singapore found Gladys and Mildred Horton going downtown. Gladys reported, "First, we treated ourselves to the beauty shop. Then we walked all over downtown and shopped. Such beautiful! Big! Clean! Stores. I had just forgotten. The prices here are probably better than in the States."

While the ladies went out on the town, I took the kids to the park. The parks in Singapore are so attractive. Playful monkeys teased our children by slipping in and out from the trees. Visitors feed them so they constantly begged for food. If you happened to be eating something the monkey wanted, he just grabbed it right out of your hand.

As a family, we went to a large theater and saw the movie, *Camelot.* We enjoyed the beautiful music. How relaxing just to sit in a movie and be unconcerned about your surroundings.

Again, I called our supporting congregation, and the elders had made a decision. Because of the uncertainty of the situation and concern for our children, the elders asked us to return. In order for us to recover from being in a war zone, they encouraged us to take our time on our return. Thus, we spent extra time in Singapore while waiting for the money to be wired for our travel.

On Sunday, we went to church in Queenstown; it met in a storefront. Here we enjoyed the fellowship of a young congregation, made up of university students or young professionals in their twenties or early thirties. Henry Kong preached an inspiring lesson. The dynamics of this group impressed me so and I prayed that this group would grow up to provide future leadership for churches in Singapore.

Some of the members invited us out to a Chinese restaurant for Sunday lunch. With about 30 in our group, the waiter asked each of us what we wanted; he did not write anything down. Yet, he got every order right. I thought: "What a wonderful memory!"

We enjoyed the botanical gardens; here the monkeys peeked out from the trees and the kids enjoyed having them come up for peanuts. Next, we went to the Tiger Balm Gardens, which depicted the different stages of life after death; the good people enjoyed themselves but bad people suffered from torture–some being sawed in two in a most graphic way.

When our funds arrived, we completed our travel arrangements. Of course, we decided to do some final shopping; Roger and I found some bargains for car coats. We decided our Saigon clothes might not provide enough warmth when we arrived in the States.

Because of our close association with the Hortons, they took us to a classy dinner theater for our last evening together; here a beautiful Chinese star sang, "These boots were made for walking." To which, Kathy and Roger couldn't hold back the laughter. Then the Hortons shared their plans to stay in Singapore and Howard planned to commute to Saigon and keep the mission effort and orphan program moving forward.

Leaving our wonderful stay in Singapore, we flew to Bangkok, where we spent a few days. Our hotel had excellent accommodations. Being several floors up, our rooms gave us a view of this interesting city; however, Kathy found herself locked in her room with no way to get out. I called the desk and they sent up a bellhop to take care of the situation. After trying several things, the bellhop had to climb from the balcony of our room over to Kathy's balcony. Then he took the doorknob off and corrected the problem. After that, Kathy insisted she would not stay in that room; therefore, the management gave her a different one.

We visited several temples. How sad to see the people bowing down to Buddha, who cannot hear. Gladys viewed this with "How tragic to see people praying to gods who cannot give life!"

Being most anxious to get news from Saigon, we watched the TV news, which made us sad just to hear the tragic war happenings.

We enjoyed about five hours at the Floating Market. The little boat seemed to be traveling for miles. At one point, we got off at a place and watched a demonstration about how silk is made. Then Kathy rode an elephant. Kathy handled the elephant ride just fine until time to get down. The trainer climbed up on the elephant and patiently guided her down to the ground.

On Sunday, we went to church and ate lunch with a missionary family. Also, we met some OC graduates who lived in Thailand. Pittiya and Sutria Aryiapongse invited us to their home later in the day. Because Pittiya had to work, we visited with Sutria; she called another OC graduate we knew. Vatch came right over and we had a most enjoyable visit.

Later that evening Vatch and Pittiya came to our hotel. After visiting for some time, Pittiya indicated his family wanted us to come the next evening for dinner.

The next morning we went shopping downtown. Gladys got a star sapphire ring and some precious stones after much bargaining.

Pittiya picked us up and we went to his home. The Aryiapongse's had a large home; his father being a retired banker. The father showed us around their yard. He had a large collection of orchids and red-heart shaped anthurium. Every time Gladys would go "Ooo" or "Ahhh," Mr. Aryiapongse would reach over and cut it. When the call came for dinner, Gladys had an armful of flowers and he insisted she take them with us.

The Thai dinner lasted for almost three hours. Each course provided a surprise. All of us enjoyed the food. Every time Roger finished a course our host served him more.

On our way back to the hotel, Pittiya showed us Bangkok by night. What an adventuresome evening!

At the airport the next day, Pittiya and his father came to see us off. We flew to Hong Kong. Of course, our flight went over Vietnam, and we could look down and see the bomb craters.

On our arrival in Hong Kong, we about froze; Roger and I enjoyed our new coats. Thankfully we had heat in our hotel room; this being our first artificial heat in almost two years. We did some sightseeing and took a ferry over to the island. We purchased an oriental screen and a carved Chinese coffee table; we shipped these back by cheap ocean freight.

The local missionaries invited me to speak at their worship service. After worship, the Reeves invited us out to eat. In the afternoon, Paul Hui, an OC graduate, took us sightseeing and invited me to speak at his congregation's evening service.

Tom Tune, a long-time missionary in Hong Kong, offered to give us a tour. He had a boat ministry and took us to the docks to see his boat. Tom indicated that many of the Chinese live out their lives on their boats. While driving through the hills of Hong Kong, Tom drove fast; and being unaccustomed to cars driving on the left, we felt a bit uneasy.

The next day we got a call from Captain Crinkley, who had been with us in Saigon for a time. He invited us out to lunch at an outstanding French restaurant; then he showed us around Hong Kong. He took us to the Peninsula Hotel for afternoon tea. This is one of the grand hotels in the world. The exclusive shops had guards at the jewelry stores who limited the number of customers allowed in at one time.

The Peninsula had a large fountain in front but, because of the wind, it had been turned off. Captain Crinkley went up to the management and asked them to turn it on, which they did for our children. Then we enjoyed tea and the most delicious fancy pastries in this beautifully appointed hotel.

The next morning, because of heavy rain, we stayed in the hotel and rested. Then the Reeves and Paul Hui came to our hotel and we ate lunch together. After lunch Paul took us all over town. We visited a blind preacher, who, as a child, had been adopted by Elizabeth Bernard. Most of the people in his congregation were blind. He produced a weekly newsletter in Braille. He told us that the Braille duplicator had been given to him by a church in Duncan, Oklahoma; being from Oklahoma I found this to be very interesting. Bernard served as a single missionary for many years and had adopted several children she found wandering on the streets.

We flew from Hong Kong by way of Tokyo to Hawaii. Because we crossed the International Date Line, we left Hong Kong at 10 a.m. and arrived in Hawaii on the same day at the same time.

Hawaii breathed with fresh adventure. After getting settled in our hotel, Gladys and Kathy went shopping and got some new clothes. Because we had been in so many countries and exchanging money in each, Kathy decided to make some purchases. She asked the clerk, "Now how much is that in American money?" The clerk curtly replied, "Honey, this is America!" We laughed.

Next, I made a long distance call. I told the operator, "I'd like to make a call to the States." The operator replied, "Sir, this is the States." Then I said, "I'd like to make a call to the mainland." We both had a good laugh.

On our second day in Hawaii, we took an eight-hour bus tour of the Island. Our tour guide had a great sense of humor. Our tour included the Polynesian Village, pineapple and sugar cane plantations, and Pearl Harbor. Roger struck up a conversation with an elderly lady; she enjoyed his stories so much she bought his lunch. The bus driver gave Kathy a coconut he picked up so they both had a good day.

We flew to Los Angeles. I had a message at the terminal from a close friend, Wilson Meek. Because of our traumatic experiences in having to leave Saigon, he thought it necessary to warn us of plans being made for our arrival. He did us a real favor by helping prepare for an emotional homecoming. We spent the night at a hotel near the LA terminal.

When we arrived in Oklahoma City, friends and relatives jammed the terminal. What an emotional homecoming! We both had family members and a multitude of friends.

Ona Belknap had arranged for a private room at the terminal for us to be interviewed by journalists from newspapers and television. But Kathy spotted our dear friend, Ada Beam, who arranged for her Frosty to be brought into the airport. Kathy grabbed and hugged Frosty and thanked Ada for keeping her dog for the past two years.

After the interviews, family members went to the home of Gladys' brother, Dr. Irvin Hamburger. That evening everyone insisted that we go to the Central State Field House to see the Oklahoma Christian basketball team play. At half time, an official of OC read a statement about our presence and everyone jumped to their feet in a standing ovation. We were overwhelmed.

Those, who had lived in our home, had moved out. Joanne North, a close personal friend, and several other ladies had scrubbed and cleaned our place. For the first time in several months, we got to sleep in our own bed.

Several of our family members stayed over with various ones in Oklahoma City. The next morning we worshiped at our home congregation, The College Church of Christ. We spent the afternoon with family.

That evening we went to the Village Church of Christ, the congregation that had sponsored our orphan program.

After church, several invited us to go to the OC Field House. A surprise reception had been planned; when we walked into the Field House, everyone applauded and we felt like celebrities. Dr. James Baird, the President of Oklahoma Christian, gave a brief run-down of our work and traumatic experiences in getting out of Vietnam. Then he presented us with a sack of money. Everyone had given enough money to help us buy a new car.

Such love and support provided healing for our hearts. God helped us overcome the hurt experienced with the recall of Maurice and Marie Hall. Truly, God had provided healing and help in our time of need. I owe a great deal of gratitude to those who provided financial and personal encouragement. The Ansel Worley family stayed behind us every moment of the way. How grateful I am to 10th and Rockford, Brookfield, North Park, and a multitude of other congregations for making our work possible. We could not have survived without the love and support of our servicemen.

"Deliverance" is such a powerful word in the Scriptures. David said: "I sought the Lord, and he answered me; he delivered me from all my fears . . . A righteous man may have many troubles, but the Lord delivers him from them all. (Psalm 34:4,19, NIV)" God provided deliverance for us in such a powerful way. God truly delivered us from harm and fears. Praises be to our God!

After we had been home a few weeks, we received a letter from S/Sgt. Fred Hall, who had spent many evenings with our children watching TV; he wrote that he had been our guardian angel during the Tet offensive. He lived in a military billet about two blocks away. When the fighting started, he went up on the roof of his billet and could see clearly the entrance to our street. He had a machine gun pointed at that entrance in case he saw any questionable activity. He said, "I felt I was protecting your street." This reminded me of Paula Limes' letter indicating that she had been praying for a guardian angel to protect us.

Hall worked at the military mortuary; he indicated that wall-to-wall bodies filled the mortuary during the Tet offensive. How sad!

In spite of the discouraging war news, I found my heart still to be in Vietnam. After reporting to all the churches that had made our mission possible, I started praying for the Lord to open a door for our return to Vietnam.

Back to Vietnam in 1969

"Not that we are adequate in ourselves to consider anything
as coming from ourselves, but our adequacy is from God,
who also made us adequate as servants of a new covenant
... (2 Corinthians 3:5-6, NIV)"

Having left our hearts in Vietnam when we had to leave during
the Tet Offensive, we longed to return. From the time we left
in 1968, I kept writing and encouraging the Saigon church and many
people I wanted to bring to Christ. But because of the logistics and
costs of taking a family for a short time, we decided for me to return
alone. Also, our children had not fully recovered from the trauma
they endured during the Tet Offensive.

In addition, the Village Church of Christ had recruited a family to
replace us; therefore, I would be able to help alleviate some of their
fears. How I came to appreciate Dan, Lutrica, Teresa, and Jillena
Skaggs because of their commitment for taking the Gospel to the
Vietnamese. This trip would allow me the opportunity to introduce
and orient them to many people I loved and knew and taught. Since I
found visits in homes to be very productive, I would take Dan along
to help him experience this fruitful method and orient him on how
to locate homes with three or four slashes in the number; the first
number indicated the first street to turn on, the second number indicated the next alley, and so on; the last number being the house.

My plane stopped in Guam for refueling; then I spent that night in Taipei, Taiwan. When continuing with my flight, I had an overnight stopover in Hong Kong. I called Mrs. Paul Wong who now lived in Hong Kong and had four daughters, who had been students in our Christian school. She asked if she might come to my hotel with a studio family picture to send to her husband still working in Saigon. I invited her and she brought the picture and gave me an update on her family. My flight left for Vietnam early the next morning.

As I flew into Tan Son Nhut on April 25, I couldn't help but recall the situation when we left. How amazing to see how God had been at work in bringing healing to the Vietnamese situation. How comforting to see all of the military personnel guarding the terminal. Several people met me at the airport.

Dan and Lutricia Skaggs had an apartment, which former missionaries had occupied. Also, the Village congregation had another apartment in Saigon where I planned to live. Since my apartment had not been vacated, the Skaggs invited me to stay with them until it became available. Living in their home gave me a tremendous opportunity to get to know and appreciate this wonderful family.

My greatest disappointment came as I learned that the attendance at the Saigon congregation had dropped to about 12 Vietnamese for Sunday morning worship. During my first day in Vietnam, I spent most of it going to the homes of church members and former Bible students. The next day being Sunday, I enjoyed a reunion of the 36 in attendance. I remained convinced that the key to growth had to be in developing personal relationships when visiting in their homes and through individualized Bible studies.

As one of my first assignments, I called on Paul Wong, who owns a conglomerate made up of five corporations; he expressed appreciation for my bringing the family picture. He offered to provide me with a car and a driver for the summer. I declined since I had already worked out my transportation. I felt so sad for these families who felt it necessary to be split because of the uncertainties of Vietnam. Paul Wong indicated he would so like to have his family there but he didn't plan for the girls to come back for some time.

I knew I would miss Gladys and the children, but I didn't realize how quickly I would get homesick for them. Gladys always had a good sense of humor; somehow I missed that special sparkle. She really gave color to my world. She provided excellent advice when working with people. The Skaggs took me in and provided good emotional support.

When my apartment became available, I moved my few things to the fully furnished apartment. Wayne and Charlotte Briggs had worked full-time for several years with American military congregations. The Briggs lived on the ground floor in the same building; they treated me graciously. Charlotte offered her maid to do some of my laundry. Between the Briggs apartment on the ground floor and my third floor apartment, three prostitutes lived on the second floor—one American, one Vietnamese, and a Korean. The Briggs had warned me and even knew how much the American charged. When I wrote Gladys about this, I assured her I did not get this information first hand.

The Vietnamese orphanages were now closed.

After leaving Vietnam in 1968, the Village Church of Christ in cooperation with other congregations, who sponsored programs for orphans, made the decision to merge all the programs. Howard Horton served as the interim director. Later, the Village church recruited two missionary families—the Ron Stewarts and the Wayne Stephens—who studied the Vietnamese language and who were experts in childcare; together they provided direction for the orphanages.

Ron and Wayne worked diligently in reuniting several children with their parents, relatives, or mothers. Because of difficulties with Vietnamese orphanage directors and the war situation, they made the decision to get out of the orphanage business. This seemed to be a wise decision. They turned the Binh Trung orphanage facility over to the Vietnamese Government.

I had a sad reunion with a former student in the preacher-training program.

One of the great highlights of my return came from a surprise visit with Chau, one of the young men involved in the preacher-training program in 1967. He had his usual big smile, but he came hobbling in on a homemade cane. In addition, he had a very large scar over one eye that had not completely healed. He came hobbling up and said in broken English, "My teacher!" I became so emotional that I had difficulty keeping back the tears.

Chau explained, "When the war escalated after the Tet Offensive, the Vietnamese Government drafted me into the military. My wounds came from a battle in which my leg had been torn by a bullet and shrapnel had struck my eye and my side." Chau had been such a happy, carefree young man. His maturity amazed me; it seemed too fast for such a young man. He went on to say, "The last 13 months have been the most difficult time of my life!"

I am fearful that many Americans forget that the Vietnamese have suffered, too. Chau hoped to re-enter the preacher-training program after he completed his military obligation.

The next day Chau came for an extended visit. He showed me his wounds. He said, "I am thankful for the love of Jesus that I am not dead." He had been wounded in two different battles. Many in his unit were killed. He had scars all over his body.

Chau shared what he knew about the others in the preacher-training program. Most had been drafted. Chau knew that one had been killed. However, he said: "Three are dodging the draft and are in hiding in DaNang; one thinks it wrong for a Christian to kill." Later, we visited the family of one of the others in the training program. In the past, we had spent much time together in class, teaching in the marketplaces, and visiting in the military hospital. I planned to spend as much time with Chau as possible. I accompanied Chau to the ferry; I stood on the wharf as he left, he waved with his cane until he could no longer be seen.

Being a good Bible student, Chau also possessed the talents for becoming an outstanding speaker; I felt he had great potential. Another asset included his warm-friendly personality.

Chau's visit reminded me of the ongoing struggles the war brought on all Vietnamese. At night I could hear shelling out some distance. It seemed a little closer at times but I believed it to be outside the city. It reminded me of the tensions felt when we lived here before. There did not seem to be anything really frightening within Saigon.

Bob and Chau Fairless gave me special encouragement.

Bob and Chau Fairless befriended us during the Tet Offensive when we had to leave Saigon. Not knowing whether or not it would be possible to bring our family back into Vietnam, the Fairlesses offered to take over the rental of our house, if necessary, because their place had been destroyed during the offensive. Since I had performed their wedding ceremony, we enjoyed a very special relationship.

Chau's mother invited the Skaggs and me over for a Vietnamese feast. She had prepared Kathy's favorite noodle soup. I remembered how delicious it was from the time her mother prepared it during the Tet Offensive. Each course reminded me of some of the favorite feasts we had enjoyed in Saigon. Throughout the summer, Bob and Chau had me over for dinner or took me out. Chau's brother Phat encouraged me by his affectionate nature. Also, Bob and Chau had become the proud parents of a cute baby boy, John.

Bob and Chau expressed their pleasure for the way attendance had improved since my return; it grew each week. They encouraged me to return with "We believe there would be many Christians if you could just come and stay in Vietnam." However, I really wanted the church members to bond with the Skaggs. Dan started preaching more and more and, as we visited in homes, it soon became evident that their hearts had warmed up to him. The Vietnamese had a fascination for American children; from the beginning Teresa and Jillena won their hearts, too.

Visitation and Bible Studies kept my days full.

Soon, my schedule filled with special visits and with teaching individual and group Bible studies. One of my early visits took Tran

Van Can and me to the home of Dr. Chieu. Formerly, his two sons–William and Charles—attended our school. Dr. Chieu welcomed us with great warmth. We talked about the future of his two sons, who were very intelligent and possessed great potential. He indicated he wanted them to study in the States. In fact, he indicated he would like for them to live with us. I offered to try to help them find a place. Dr. Chieu attended church the following Sunday. I always introduced guests in the audience. When I introduced Dr. Chieu, I said that he had two very brilliant boys who once studied under Gladys, he turned around and beamed with a big smile that would have warmed Alaska.

I had many study sessions with Madam Cu, who is a cousin of Vice President Ky, and other members of her family. She belonged to an organization called Subud and believed it would make you better regardless of your religious persuasion.

She invited me to attend a meeting, which I did. They spent 15 to 30 minutes stretched out on a mat in complete silence. The purpose of this is for you to empty your mind so that you think of nothing. Exercises followed this and you then did whatever moved you. I heard one man yelling and speaking some gibberish. It reminded me of some of the religious tent meetings I attended when a boy. At least I learned enough to see some conflicts between this organization and New Testament Christianity that I could use when teaching those involved.

Nguyen Van Khanh became one of my most exciting Bible students.

Immediately, I engulfed myself in Bible studies with unfaithful Christians and many non-Christians whom I believed to be good prospects that I had known in the past. Since I had maintained a contact with them by mail, several met me at the church indicating a desire to begin Bible studies immediately. Since many spoke fluent English, I began studies with both individuals and groups.

One day Nguyen Van Khanh, a Vietnamese government worker, came to the church and asked if he might join one of these studies. Someone had given him an English New Testament, *Good News for*

Modern Man. He handed me his Bible. As I leafed through the pages of the Gospels, I noticed he had underscored unfamiliar English words; he had looked up these words in a Vietnamese/English dictionary; then he had written their meaning in very small notations in the margins. These notations filled each page. I asked questions about the life of Jesus. He knew the content of every parable and event in the life of Christ.

As I looked at his Bible, I asked: "What do you think of this man Jesus?"

His reply astounded me: "If all that is said about Him is true, He would have to be the Son of God."

Since he had not studied the book of Acts, I asked: "Would you like to know what people did to become Christians in the First Century?"

He replied, "Yes." This began a series of studies during which we became very close friends.

Khanh shared with me his earlier life in North Vietnam. He worked with the communists in driving out foreign domination. In time, he became disillusioned with the Communist party even though he supported their goals in the beginning. After the defeat of the French, he overheard conversations among some of the leaders, which disturbed him very much. He felt he would soon be losing the freedom, which so many had been seeking.

With the partitioning of Vietnam in 1954, he made the decision to take his wife and two small children to the South. He left behind many members of his immediate family that he would never see again. Also, limitations on baggage meant they took only what they could hand carry.

As we studied in Acts about the Good News as proclaimed by Peter on the Day of Pentecost, Khanh could relate back to the time when Peter denied the Lord three times. Khanh's amazement centered over Christ's selection of Peter to preach the first sermon and what Peter first proclaimed. Khanh showed awe at how Peter declared that forgiveness of sins is promised to those who believe in Jesus, who repent, and are baptized in His name.

Khanh asked, "What does it mean 'to repent'?"

I explained: "Repentance means to turn away from sin and change the direction of one's life by doing what is right."

On one visit to Khanh's home, I noticed the Buddhist altar dominated one corner of his living room. I kept thinking, "How will he respond to Jesus Christ?"

Khanh followed with interest in the Acts' account of how the Good News of Jesus Christ went out from Jerusalem and how people responded to the message by repentance and baptism. When we got to the account of Peter going to Cornelius, a non-Jew, Khanh read about this conversion with an emotional response.

Khanh said, "I feel very much like Cornelius. I am not a Jew. I have been studying the Scriptures and have come to believe in God. I have been praying that God would show me the way. I feel God has sent someone to tell me how I can be forgiven of my sins."

I asked: "Do you wish to accept Christ as your Savior and Lord as Cornelius did by being baptized into Jesus' name?"

He replied, "I need some time to think and pray about it?"

Khanh's wife came in and offered tea. As we drank our tea, we shared stories about our families. I excused myself and went back to my apartment.

The next day being Sunday, Khanh came to church with a bag that I knew contained his clothing for his baptism. Because our baptistry had not been filled, David and Ollie Weaver, civilians working in Vietnam, offered their water storage tank at their apartment. When we got there, the storage tank was small. I explained I could baptize him without getting into the tank. But his reply amazed me, "In the Bible, we read about Philip and the Eunuch both going down into the water." I said, "You are right." I squeezed in beside him in the tank.

After his baptism, while still in the water, he requested the privilege of praying. He offered a most moving petition to God. He said, "Father, I thank you for Jesus Christ and for making forgiveness possible and for the forgiveness I have received. God, please direct my life; I promise to use my life for your Son. Please help me win my family for You. In Jesus Name, Amen." This moving occasion made me feel this one event made my return visit worthwhile.

Khanh's prayer touched me deeply; this is the first and only time I ever had anyone offer a prayer while still in the water. In time, God answered his prayer as his wife and several of his children later accepted Christ as their Savior.

Later Khanh told me, "I've turned away from the worship of my ancestors because of the corruption within the leadership of the Buddhist church. The Buddhists have forgotten religion and entered politics. I am convinced that if the blind lead the blind, they will both fall into the ditch. It is so wonderful to know the light of Jesus Christ. Thanks so much for leading me out of darkness into the hope of eternal life in Christ."

The Vietnamese gave me much encouragement.

I became acquainted with Nguyen Dang Minh during the early days of our mission work. We first met under unusual circumstances when he had been asked to interpret for a Vietnamese who felt that my being the senior missionary meant I should be over all of the programs; he had a complaint about the discontinuance of an orphanage in his home. When I suggested that he should take his complaint to the missionary overseeing that home, he became almost hostile. At this point, Minh refused to interpret further. He politely asked to be excused; as he left, I followed him out of the room and got his name and address.

The next day I called on him, and we became good friends over a period of time. He had very high ideals and really demonstrated the Christian spirit. He was a talented Christian who served me well as a translator and interpreter. He had been trained by the military in the States to be a translator. He had a good knowledge of the Scriptures, which aided our work together. He translated and proofread a booklet, *Framework of Christianity,* which I had put together covering basic doctrines of the Christian faith. This proved to be a very useful tool for our mission team to use being printed in English and Vietnamese on facing pages.

During the summer, we exchanged visits and I enjoyed a Vietnamese dinner in his home. Minh's mother ate with us–which was most unusual–and so did his very attractive sister, Dung. His younger brother, Dinh, had to go to school. This wonderful family possessed the spirit that was so needed in a mission church. All the family seemed so unassuming, kind with pleasant smiles, friendly, so very intelligent, and completely trustworthy. Minh had an ambition to preach the Gospel.

Since I "batched," Minh even prepared a Vietnamese meal in my apartment. We enjoyed serious discussions about Vietnamese politics, religion, and the Scriptures. He attended the University while serving in the military. He offered to translate other materials for our mission.

Throughout the summer many Vietnamese had me in their homes for a feast with all the trimmings that always included nuoc mam, a potent fish sauce. I found myself getting acquainted again with chopsticks. All these occasions made my return most enjoyable and gave me much encouragement.

Y-Kim needed help and told about his tribal life.

Y-Kim, the Montagnard who once lived with us, came to Saigon to complete his paperwork in order to study in the Philippine Bible College. Wayne Briggs had agreed to sponsor Y-Kim in college. Y-Kim and I spent some time together reminiscing old times. One day he offered to go with me to do some shopping for my family; also, I offered to buy some things he could use while at college. We walked through the open market where the merchants had their wares spread out on the ground.

As we walked, looking at the merchandise, an older lady started following and talking to me; finally she took hold of my arm. Somewhat annoyed, I said, "Y-Kim, what does she want?"

He almost bent over in laughter as he replied, "She is inviting you to come live with her daughter. They have air conditioning. She lived with an American Major until he returned to the States. She thinks you would enjoy living in her home."

I said, "Please tell her I have a wife and children and I am not interested." Even with her continued insistence I walked on ignoring her pleas. Y-Kim teasingly said, "Are you going to pass up this good offer?"

The more we visited, the more I realized that Y-Kim was a true gold mine. Tran Van Can and I helped him visit government offices in order to get his paperwork required for him to study in the Philippines. The government bureaucracy had been stalling on his papers. Tran and I went to the Director of Mobilization. Because I had been there many times, they always ushered me in as someone important. In the office, we saw Lt. Anh, who had translated materials for me in the past; he ushered us into the Colonel's office. I told the Colonel my desire to help Y-Kim.

The Colonel gave us the red carpet treatment and called for Y-Kim's papers to be brought in. He personally checked them and found that Y-Kim had not signed some of the pages. He called for Y-Kim to be brought in; Y-Kim signed the papers and the Colonel asked him to come back the next day and indicated everything would be processed. Y-Kim expressed his gratitude with, "Brother Burcham, thanks! It would have taken weeks to clear that office if you hadn't helped me out."

Y-Kim told of some of the happenings in his village. His thrilling stories of his mountain people helped me understand a totally strange lifestyle. How the farmers in his village used "flash and burn" to clear an area for farming; when the soil wore out, they moved to a more fertile location. He described how they used elephants as beasts of burden. He told everything with picturesque descriptions and much humor.

As Y-Kim described life among the Montagnards, I realized he had lived in a world that I would never know. He made me feel humbly grateful for the blessings lavished upon all who live in the States. Yet, the Montagnards' life seemed so hard but simple–not complicated like ours; they had their tribal laws and customs that his people dared not break. Over and over Y-Kim expressed his love for Gladys, Roger, and Kathy. In describing his love for Roger, he said, "I wish I could go to school with Roger again."

I prayed for Y-Kim as he prepared to go to the Philippines; he had so much potential and I prayed that he would grow in his understanding of the Scriptures.

Love and support came from my home front.

During my time in Vietnam, we celebrated our 19th anniversary. Being away from Gladys, I realized more and more how much her love and companionship meant to me. On our anniversary I wrote: "Your love and dedication to Christ have been the cornerstone of our own love. It is Christ who has so filled our lives. May He continue to be the center of our lives. May He give us the wisdom, love, courage, and strength to lead and guide Kathy and Roger to a rich and abiding faith in Him."

Being away from the family, I felt strongly that I needed God's help in being a good Christian husband and father. I asked God for guidance to help me lead in our home so that we all mature in Christ and that we might utilize our lives to the greatest extent for His Glory.

Gladys has always encouraged me to do what I felt God wanted me to do. Throughout our marriage, she had always provided strength and support. During periods of transition or doubt, Gladys provided assurance, comfort, and understanding. She helped me keep my eyes focused on the Cross with the realization that I wanted to be in Heaven because she will be there.

Love is such a powerful force and I had experienced it from the whole family. I once read: "Some people confer their love with the idea that they are conferring a favor. But the real lover cannot ever get over the wonder that he is loved. Love is kept humble by the consciousness that it can never offer its loved one a gift which is good enough." This statement is so full of truth, and I felt no gift is good enough for Gladys.

Gladys, Roger, and Kathy kept the letters coming. Their teasing and sense of humor came through. They kept me informed about our acreage and the fruitfulness of our vegetable garden and the beauty of things in bloom. Of course, Roger reminded me of the labor involved.

When the servicemen sang, *"Cleanse Me"* at one of our worship services, it brought tears. I'm not sure I had really seen the words before.

"Search me, O Lord, and know my heart today,

Try me, O Savior, know my tho'ts, I pray;
See if there be some wicked way in me,
Cleanse me from ev'ry sin and set me free.
I praise Thee, Lord, for cleansing me of sin,
Fulfill Thy Word and make me pure within.
Fill me with FIRE, where once I burned with shame,
Grant my desire to magnify Thy name.
Lord, take my life and make it wholly Thine,
Fill my poor heart with Thy great love divine;
Take all my will, my passion, self and pride,
I now surrender, Lord in me abide."
Words by J. Ewin Orr

As the servicemen sang, the words really touched my heart. How I needed "the cleansing" of sin; I truly desired for God to "make me pure within." I wanted to be filled "with FIRE" in order to faithfully proclaim the Good News of a Savior. And I needed to be filled with God's love in order for my will to be wholly surrendered to His. This moved me to look at the Psalm, which this song is based on; it reads: "Search me, O God, and know my heart; test me and know my anxious thoughts. See if there is any offensive way in me, and lead me in the way everlasting. Psalm 139:23, 24, NIV" Therefore, my constant prayer to God included my desire for my family and me to live by the thoughts expressed in this hymn to ever live with faithful hearts for Him.

The servicemen continued to encourage the work among the Vietnamese.

The servicemen's congregation at Tan Son Nhut, where Gene Conner served as the minister, invited me to speak at their afternoon service. Charlotte Briggs, along with the Skaggs, took me; but the car had not been properly registered, and the MP's refused to admit us to the base. When I indicated that I had been invited to be the guest speaker at the Chapel, the guard apologized but with my press ID he gave me a temporary pass and I walked to the Chapel.

The hot afternoon and my rush to the Chapel made me perspire like an Oklahoma workhorse in August. My clothes looked like I had just had a dip in a pool. But to my surprise, Charlotte and the Skaggs greeted me! Seeing my startled look, they explained: "Charlotte took us to a different gate and the guard let us in."

Just before I started speaking, the electricity went off–no windows in the Chapel–and it got hotter by the minute. Because of a large group of servicemen, I cut the sermon short. I thought of Jim Reynolds' earlier advice "a good sermon does not have to be eternal." The men had a positive reaction; they listened very attentively. After the service, the men filed by and said they appreciated the lesson and wished they could have heard it all. Being wet with perspiration, they looked liked they had just been baptized.

Knowing how the servicemen encouraged the mission, Dan and Lutrica invited the GI's over for a fellowship at their home. Lutrica made some of the most delicious spaghetti and meatballs in a tasty sauce. She had a fruit Jell-O salad, tomatoes, cucumbers, cookies, and pop. The men really enjoyed it. The Skaggs closed with a devotional. To hear the married men pray for their own families helped me realize the sacrifice being made while away from their families for a whole year. I thought: "Surely I can make it for four months, but I'll not be away this long again from Gladys."

A seemingly hopeless situation for an injured serviceman moved me deeply.

I received a cablegram from a family in the United States. Their son had been injured and they had been unable to get any information about his condition. They gave his name, serial number, and his hospital location. I went out to the Long Binh base to see what I could learn. I checked at the administration building of the military hospital and they gave me his ward and bed number.

As I walked down the sidewalk looking for the building, a military doctor saw me and asked if he could help. "I'm looking for a patient by the name of Kenneth Reppart." He replied, "He's my patient; I'll take you to him."

Then with great seriousness he warned, "Ken received an injury to the head, lost an eye, and is hard to look at; we have not been able to do much for him; we are not sure he will survive; we're working to stabilize him. He comes in and out of a coma. But I want you to talk with him as if he understands every word you say. But do not make any reference to his injuries as we have not told him." I agreed, but I lacked emotional preparation to see one so severely injured. All of the men in his ward had experienced terrible wounds. Men with eyes missing, legs or arms missing; others horribly disfigured stared at me from every direction.

When we got to Ken's bed, the doctor told me that a bullet went through one eye, his nose, and so far he had no vision in the other eye. The injured eye, still in the socket, swiveled up; the other eye had so much swelling you couldn't see it. The doctor didn't know whether or not he would be blind; but I felt he might be. His head had been shaved and they had stitches everywhere. I didn't know whether or not he had brain surgery. He just lay there all exposed with tubes. His horribly disfigured face had lots of cuts.

While Ken lay motionless, I followed the doctor's suggestion and talked with him as if he understood every word. I explained my purpose in being in Vietnam and about the cable from his parents, who had a loving concern for him. But he made no indication he heard a word. I left that ward feeling so helpless and prayed earnestly for his recovery.

A day or two later the Skaggs and I visited him. He seemed to be slipping in and out of his coma. He talked a little. But we found him to be very depressed. He talked about some of his plans for the future.

But I could tell he had doubts about what the future held for him. He hoped to get married. However, even if he survived, I wondered what kind of care he would need for the rest of his life. The question that plagued me: "Will he find a wife who is willing to provide the kind of care he may need? This will be a challenge to any wife." However, I believed that only a loving relationship could make his life worth living. How sad to see one who had such great plans shattered by a bullet.

A week or so later, I went back to the hospital to see Ken. I stopped by the Long Binh Finance office where I knew Edna, who worked there. She asked, "What are you doing out here?"

"I came out to see a patient in the military hospital." Then I explained what I knew about Ken's situation. She asked: "May I go along?" I said, "Let's go." When we arrived at Ken's ward, the same military doctor greeted us and I introduced Edna. He explained: "Ken's condition remains critical but he is becoming more alert; he is being considered for transfer to a rehab center." I have never met anyone with a more caring attitude toward a patient than that shown by this doctor. He walked with us to Ken's bed. Again, he urged us to talk with Ken as if he could understand. We both talked to Ken for several minutes, but he did not respond.

As we left the hospital compound, we shared our feelings about Ken's situation. Edna expressed her feelings of compassion and said, "You know, I work just a few blocks from Ken's ward; I think I will go by and talk with him every day when I get off work." This she did.

The Skaggs, some of the church members, and Edna took communion to him on Sundays. He seemed very thankful for their consideration.

Ken had brain surgery. He still had slow reactions to conversation; still no eyesight in the one eye; the other eye had been removed. Because of his serious situation, he had not been evacuated for further surgery and rehabilitation. I wondered when this would occur!

In time, Ken started showing more awareness of people around him. He responded more and more to Edna's voice; she kept up her visits until the military made arrangements for Ken to be transferred to a hospital in Colorado for reconstructive surgery and rehabilitation. Edna kept the letters going to him in Colorado. Eventually they married.

I am convinced that the love and touch of Edna brought Ken back to reality. The healing power of love is truly amazing. Some 30 years later we met them in Washington, D. C. and Ken was still tall and handsome. The doctors did a marvelous job in reconstructive surgery; his artificial eye is unnoticeable. He had some limitations because of brain damage. Edna is one of my heroes because she played such a great part in Ken's recovery, continues to love and help Ken, provides income for the family, and works hard in parenting their two children.

What a sacrifice our servicemen make on behalf of our nation. How they need our prayers and love, especially those living with lifetime injuries!

A banker friend takes us to an exclusive supper club.

I wanted to introduce Dan to one of Saigon's wealthy bankers so I took him to meet Mr. Du Thi, General Manager of the Bank of Tokyo; in the past he had children in our school. Originally, Maurice Hall had introduced me to him. He invited us to an exclusive and expensive supper club, Maxims, and made it clear that Mrs. Skaggs should come along. This gave me a great opportunity to introduce the Skaggs to this man that I so wanted to bring to Christ.

During the dinner, the lively conversation centered around the latest I knew about Maurice and Marie Hall, whom he held in high regard. We had the most delicious food I had ever eaten. The superb service impressed us. The place is extra plush.

The colorful entertainment included performers from the Philippines who kept perfect rhythm as they danced back and forth between two large bamboo poles being clapped together and then extended.

The magician kept us on the edge of our seats when he threw knives at the center of the board; next he outlined his girl assistant with knives–they actually made her hair move. It was almost more than I could watch. I thought Lutrica Skaggs might faint. Then he swallowed fire.

We were all somewhat awed by the expensive cover charge our host paid for each person, which no missionary budget would allow. Ready for my birthday a couple of days away, I pretended this was my big celebration.

The Dan Skaggs are a great addition to our missionary force.

Dan and I visited in many homes. He immediately involved himself in Bible studies and language study.

During the summer, the Skaggs had several fellowships in their home for Christian servicemen and those attending the Saigon Church. Lutrica, with the help of Charlotte Briggs, prepared lots of food for these fellowships. They always concluded these fellowships with a devotion. Being a part of these wonderful occasions, I could see them building up the church in Vietnam and drawing many people together for a unified effort for Christ.

Family adjustments are difficult in any mission field, but especially in a country torn by war. I thanked God for the good adjustments the Skaggs made as they moved into the Vietnamese culture. I witnessed daily their hard work in bringing the light of Christ to a land that knew only the darkness of idolatry, sin, and the ravages of war.

Howard Horton, a former missionary, wrote a letter to the Skaggs; it is so full of sage advice: "You will soon get accustomed to the normal noises of war that at first seem so close. After a while you will begin to recognize the difference between the large bombers, the small arms, and the artillery that mean little for the city of Saigon.

"We thank God for your faith and pray that He will be with you in your new work in that country. We feel that the Vietnamese people have many very fine qualities and we know that you will come to love many of them even as we did . . .

"It is important that we always avoid the temptation to become impatient with those with whom we work. They have enjoyed so few of the blessings that we have enjoyed so bountifully in America that they many times act very selfishly. I was often tempted in Vietnam, as well as in Africa, to become angry when I could see such signs of childishness among the people that I was to teach. Eventually, I succeeded in remembering that it is their weaknesses that make it essential for us to go to them. This does not surprise us at all; however, when we remember, that it was our own weaknesses that brought Christ from heaven.

"We love you and pray that God will keep you and bless you and give you a happy and fruitful work in His Kingdom. May the Lord bless and keep you. Sincerely yours, Howard Horton." I, also, received much encouragement from Howard's letter because of its wisdom and love for the lost.

We used a local swimming pool for a baptism.

Dan Skaggs had been studying with Ngoc, the sister of Loan and Chau, who had been converted by Judy Colvin. Ngoc, very intelligent, majored in law at the university. Since our baptistry was not available, we went to a local swimming pool. Tran Van Can explained to the lady in charge of the pool what we wanted to do. He gave her a brief explanation of the place of baptism in becoming a Christian and wanted permission to use the pool.

She agreed and requested us to bless the pool. (I was not quite sure how this would be done.) She immediately asked everyone to clear the pool, which Tran had not requested. Tran decided to take advantage of the situation and explained what was taking place to all those standing around the pool. Everyone listened intently and watched as Dan baptized the young lady into Christ. Some probably heard and witnessed a little of Christianity for the first time.

When the pool owner told the swimmers they could return, many came up to Tran with all kinds of questions.

What is the future of the work in Vietnam?

Whether or not the cause of Christ will become a part of the culture in Vietnam will depend on the Vietnamese and the impact of our missionary force. Several times during the summer I had the opportunity to study with a young man, Phu, who served in the military at Quang Ngai. When in Saigon, he stayed overnight with me. This gave us the opportunity to have some serious Bible discussions.

Phu started a little group where he lived; the people there had never heard the simple New Testament message. He had a high of 38 in attendance and had baptized two. This young man is virtually a babe in Christ. He so needs more grounding in the Scriptures, but his zeal put me to shame! I'm afraid zeal is too often missing in our American churches. Phu helped me make some visits. Later, his brother, Que, and a friend came; we studied the Bible; and then went out to eat.

The future success of evangelism in Vietnam depends to a great extent on young men like Phu; this reminds me of what John Wesley once said, "Give me a hundred men who love God with all their hearts, and fear nothing but sin, and I will move the world."

Tran Van Can freely discussed the war situation. Tension seemed to be increasing again. I noticed more American MP's and Vietnamese soldiers along with policemen on every corner of the city. Because of increased security, the MP's stopped people almost constantly. Tran indicated he had talked with a person in high authority who indicated they were expecting another attack on Saigon. Cambodia recognized the new Viet Cong government in exile. Tran said that this gave sanction to the North Vietnamese and the Viet Cong who operated from that country. The Viet Cong had been building up large reserves of ammunition and manpower for this possible attack. Tran had great fear that the attacks may equal those during the Tet Offensive of last year.

As the word got out that I would soon be leaving, everyone seemed to feel obligated to entertain. The Vietnamese were so gracious. On my last Saturday before leaving the following Tuesday, I spent the day visiting in homes. Charlotte's maid, Dung, knew I liked Spring Roll; she prepared a large platter for noon and another for the evening. In the evening, three of my students came by and insisted I go with them to a Vietnamese restaurant for more Spring Roll and nouc mam. We came back to my apartment and had a marvelous Bible study. They would continue to study with Dan Skaggs; already I had him loaded with study appointments; Dan would soon see why I did not have too much time for them.

Throughout the summer, I felt rewarded by the number of people who came to the worship services. Attendance increased each week; and on my final Sunday, 66 people came for worship; some 20 people stood out on the balcony for the entire service. Many who had studied with me came and brought family members or friends.

How good to see one of those converted by Nguyen Van Ming in the prison ministry. He tried to make a living repairing typewriters. His progress impressed me. Ming served as such a faithful translator and worker; how good to see his attractive wife and son present.

One of the guests, Major Minh, Director of the Saigon Radio Station, which had been destroyed during the Tet Offensive, had played a major role in helping us get our original radio program. Tran Van Can and I had visited with him during the summer seeking to get a new radio time. Major Minh made gracious compliments after the service. He said, "I hope you will return to Vietnam very soon; and, when the new station is completed, I will help you get a radio program." He sent greetings to Gladys and the children.

James Hien came with his niece; he is an officer in the Bank of Tokyo and had studied with Maurice Hall. Dr. Le Van Can, a friend of Tran and knew Maurice Hall, came; he is a medical doctor who grew up in North Vietnam,.

Lt. Anh, who had translated for me at the Thong Nhut Gospel Meeting, came and interpreted my sermon. After the lesson, he said he would like to study with me further; since I would be leaving on Tuesday, I made an appointment to study with him at 7 p.m. on Monday. It seemed everyone wanted one more opportunity to visit with me; therefore, I had appointments at 5, 6, 7, 8, and 9 for my final evening in Vietnam. Throughout the summer I had studied with Mr. De, who had been attending worship services. Mrs. De came to the service with him; this being my first opportunity to meet her.

The father of Quan, who is Phil Carpenter's wife, came with two of Quan's sisters; he had tears in his eyes as he told me goodbye. Madam Cu's son, Them, came to bid me farewell. One of Nguyen Dan Bao's converts from Bien Hoa came and offered a testimonial of his life in Christ since leaving the Roman Catholic Church.

What an emotional and overwhelming response to their visits and gifts! That Sunday evening I went to the home of Mr. Ky and Mrs. Ha for a Vietnamese feast. Mrs. Ha, the principal of the school, came to our rescue when the school almost closed in 1967. Earlier in the summer Gladys sent their baby a cloth dog. They indicated he slept with it each night.

Throughout the summer this question plagued me: "What is the future of the work in Vietnam?" Individual and group Bible studies, plus visitation and correspondence, kept me busy throughout the summer and I so wanted to see more baptized into Christ; then I wanted the leadership school to be restarted. I prayed for all to be a part of the church of the future.

The dream of the Saigon congregation had long been for a permanent building. Therefore, Tran Van Can, Dan, and myself looked at several buildings. We, also, had others looking for a building; one of those was Mrs. Chanh, her husband is the Associate Minister of Education who had helped us get approval for a school. Mrs. Chanh confided that her husband really respected me and had strong appreciation for the Church of Christ. This gave me a glimmer of hope of winning the Chanhs to Christ.

But all buildings were too expensive and would require a large fund-raising effort in the States. We found one building that might be affordable but the owner wanted us to pay in an illegal way. We consulted a lawyer and he assured us the deal to be illegal in an effort to avoid taxes. Since it is illegal, I would have no part in such a deal.

In visiting with several familiar with the work in Vietnam, the Village elders decided that the unstable situation and the expense of a building made it unwise to purchase a permanent location at this time. Therefore, a permanent location for the church would have to wait for the future.

I remained firmly convinced that the prospects there for a very fine congregation still were very good. I met people every day that had a good feeling for the Church of Christ, and I believed all were serious. I think some seemed to be waiting to make a spiritual decision wanting to be sure the church was going to stabilize.

Because my future involved Gladys, I shared my struggles with her. That summer's experience gave me an opportunity to reflect on my own personal life and how I can best serve God. Somehow I felt needed in Vietnam because I love to study the Bible and delve into the Scriptures. I love to share the Good News with the lost. I found the Vietnamese to be receptive and strong congregations were a possibility. The big question concerned the war and, whether or not, we would be able to stay in that field. Too, I felt we could not permanently live in Vietnam until our children finished college. But if we were to work in Vietnam on a long-term basis, we would need to learn the language.

I kept asking the question: "How is our lost world going to be reached for Christ with the gospel in our generation?" I felt the answer to be only by men and women who love God with all their hearts and who love their neighbors as themselves. Only those with devotion and dedication that spring from an undying love will accomplish it. Those who are constrained by the love of Christ would count no sacrifice too great to make for Him. They would not count their lives dear to themselves. They would spend and be spent if only the lost might not perish for want of the gospel.

The biggest concern facing me: there were so many Christians concentrated in our area in the States that we almost stumble over each other. Because the mission spirit at Oklahoma Christian seemed so limited, I kept asking "Is it possible for us to inject a vision for foreign missions into the minds of the student body?" There would have to be a drastic reversal there in this regard for me to be really content.

Perhaps the Lord could use us in encouraging students to consider the mission field as a part of their lives. The questions that I raised with Gladys were: "Do you think it possible for us to change the mission climate at Oklahoma Christian? Can we influence students to consider missions as a part of their future? If so, how?" I really believed if we could put a vision of a lost world in the hearts of OC students, I could find great satisfaction and fulfillment in continuing to teach there. I felt this required a lot of prayer for both Gladys and me.

During the summer, I read through William Barkley's commentary on Romans. I particularly liked this paragraph which helped me put my meager efforts in perspective: "So long as we believe that everything depends on our efforts we are bound to be pessimists, for experience has taught the grim lesson that our own efforts can achieve very little. When we realize that it is not our effort but God's grace and power which matter, then we become optimists, because we are bound to believe that with God nothing is impossible . . .

A man may well hesitate to attempt a great task by himself; there is nothing which he need hesitate to attempt with God." (Barkley, William. *The Letter to the Romans*, The Westminster Press, page 69.)

What encouragement I received during the summer's work. In many ways, I found leaving to be very difficult; yet, I anxiously waited for the time to be with the family again. With this summer ended, would we be able to return for further mission efforts in Vietnam?

Vietnam–Here We Come Again, An Unbelievable Summer–1973

"I long to see you so that I may impart to you some spiritual gift to make you strong–that is, that you and I may be mutually encouraged by each other's faith. . . . I am not ashamed of the gospel, because it is the power of God for the salvation of everyone who believes: first for the Jew, then for the Gentile. For in the gospel a righteousness from God is revealed, a righteousness that is by faith from first to last, just as it is written: 'The righteous will live by faith.'
(Romans 1:11,12,16,17, NIV)"

Preparations for our return started immediately on my return in 1969.

When we decided to return to Vietnam in 1973, we recruited from Oklahoma Christian two students, Pat Peters and Gary Williams, to accompany us. During our preparations for this mission trip, we spent several months studying and orienting them to the work in Vietnam. However, we realized a different atmosphere awaited us because the American military planned to pull out at the beginning of the year before we arrived. The U. S. planned to leave only advisory teams.

223

We all took the 18 shots suggested; Gary and Pat took them without a word of complaint. What a good indication these fellas would be the kind of troopers to make our mission a success!

Our family situation weighed heavily in our prayers. We made arrangements for a Christian couple to live in our home. Lynn, the wife of the couple, had known Roger and Kathy for several years. Close to our family were Lynn's parents, Dr. James and Avanelle Baird, who served as the President and First Lady of Oklahoma Christian. Our children felt very comfortable with this arrangement.

To sweeten the pie, Gladys had a niece living in Hawaii, and we promised Kathy she could go there a couple of weeks before our return if she could save enough from the household budget. This also gave her the responsibility of managing household expenditures.

From our previous experience, we felt we needed to make additional preparation. We both worked diligently on Bible study. Gladys completed several Bible courses at OC. We both took a missions' principles course taught by Dr. Howard Norton, who served effectively for several years as a missionary to Brazil. We continued to read books on missions and the customs and culture of the Vietnamese. But above all, we constantly sought God's wisdom and direction.

Our preparation with Pat and Gary included a study of John, Romans, and the booklet, *"Framework of Christianity,"* which included basic doctrinal topics related to the Christian faith. Since the latter and the Bible Correspondence Course had been printed on facing pages in English and Vietnamese, this would provide Pat and Gary with printed support for Biblical teachings on salvation in Jesus Christ.

In addition, I edited a special edition of *The Christian Bible Teacher,* which was dedicated to teaching missions within the curriculum of the church Bible school. I called on present or former missionaries to write chapters for the various grade levels. Also, I edited a book on mission principles, which helped me to carefully examine current mission thought.

The Vietnamese encouraged us to return.

What wonderful encouragement we received to return to Vietnam by a national Christian, whom I had written about our desire to return. In reply, Madame Nguyen Van Cu, a cousin of Vice President Ky, wrote: "I enjoy your Bible classes very much and desire to see you return . . . Truly my son and I are deeply impressed by your letter. It is full of love, a true love that abides while everything else will pass away. We would also like to express to you our gratefulness for reminding us about God's Words; the Holy and precious words we never forget, even while eating, drinking, and sleeping. There are no words in our language to tell you–wonderful people in Christ–how much we grew to love and appreciate you." Over and over again we received letters encouraging us to return.

But a letter from Tran Van Can touched me deeply. From the earliest days of the work in Vietnam, he served in a commendable way our mission endeavors as a translator, interpreter, and social guide. Because of his former work with the U. S. Government, he knew many Vietnamese officials and had advised and guided me through many visits with them.

Tran wrote: "I have found great encouragement in working with you for Christ's sake. Since you came, your hard work has successfully drawn the people to Christ. This, indeed, is the result of your visits to Christian homes and church sympathizers; especially your hospitality and home Bible study sessions you have given to them. Everybody noticed that on the Sunday in 1969, when you gave your farewell sermon, the auditorium became so small that 20 attendants had to stand in the corridor . . .

"For these past several months, you have been out of my sight, but not out of my mind. I know you are really interested in the work for the growth of the Church of Christ in Vietnam. You are the first missionary who understands well my people and knows how to humbly win them to Christ . . .

"If I had to show you the development graphic of the Saigon Church, you will see the curve marking no progress. Try to arrange for your return the soonest possible . . . I pray the Lord Jesus Christ will guide your planning to come again to Vietnam to serve HIM.

My wife and children often speak of your nobility and zeal in serving Christ in Vietnam . . .

"The military situation here is really critical. If the VC succeeds in occupying more strategic provinces on the Vietnam-Cambodia border area, they might push ahead their offensives toward the Capital City. We hope this would not happen. Please pray for us that we will be strengthened and encouraged by the Spirit of God that we can face without fear no matter what comes to us but with full trust in our Almighty God. Signed: Tran Van Can." When I received Tran's letter, I felt we had made the right decision to return.

Jointly the Vietnamese and we made plans for our work.

In correspondence with the Saigon congregation, they developed a plan of work to be done on our return. They felt a primary need for stabilizing the work-included efforts in purchasing a permanent meeting place. With the military moving out of Vietnam, they felt this would force prices down and make more buildings available.

The congregation desired to begin a new radio program. I had developed a friendship with Major Minh, who was Program Director for the National Radio Channels. He had been most helpful in the past. In fact, he had given us free spot announcements to advertise our Bible Correspondence Course. I felt radio to be one of the most effective means for preaching the gospel to large numbers of Vietnamese. Because of Major Minh's helpfulness in the past, I felt we had a good chance for getting a new program.

In many ways, Saigon was developing into the melting pot of Asia; it had large numbers of Vietnamese, Chinese, French, Indian, Filipino, and Americans within its makeup. Certainly it will always be an important city in Vietnam. If the war ended and a stable government was formed, it would be one of the most influential cities in Southeast Asia. These factors increased our desire to be sure the Gospel was firmly planted in this great city.

Our major goal would be to evangelize–teaching the lost and strengthening the saved. During our previous work in Vietnam, I made many friends; I wanted to reach them before my friendship and influence waned. I had kept in touch with many of these by mail.

During our previous work, I learned the importance of visiting in their homes; therefore, we planned to visit in many homes.

A dream realized–we were on our way.

Gladys and I flew out of Oklahoma City on April 18, 1973; many came out to see us off. Since Gary Williams and Pat Peters flew out of a different city, we planned to meet them in Hong Kong.

In Honolulu, we met Gladys' niece and talked about Kathy's plans to join them later in the summer. Also, Howard and Mildred Horton made arrangements to spend some time with us. The Hortons, who had served as missionaries in Vietnam, took us to church and stayed up visiting with us until 4:30 a.m. The Hortons provided additional encouragement and counsel for our work in Saigon.

Strong emotions engulfed us as we arrived in Vietnam.

Gary and Pat met us in Hong Kong late at night. We left the next morning for Vietnam and arrived in Saigon at 12:30 noon on April 21. Several greeted us at the Vietnam International Air Terminal, including Tran Van Can, Duc and Bich Vo, Ruth Bao, and several Americans.

We wept with Ruth Bao as we learned the tragic news that their eldest son, just 21, had been killed at Quang Tri a month earlier and after the Cease Fire had gone into effect.

Gladys had not been in Saigon since leaving during the Tet Offensive, and four years had passed since my last work in Vietnam; therefore, our emotions seemed to be somewhat overwhelming.

Tran Van Can had made arrangements for us to rent an apartment in the same building where the church meets and Gary and Pat would stay in the church building, located on Suong Nguyet Anh Street; this good location was near the USAID headquarters where we would eat many of our meals. We had to make some final arrangements with the landlord and get a few items to set up housekeeping so we stayed in the Embassy Hotel downtown.

Gene and Nancy Conner diligently worked to keep alive the Vietnamese International School, which he successfully reopened after the Tet Offensive and faithfully directed for several years. They invited us to their place for dinner and insisted that Pat and Gary spend the night with them.

Our work begins in earnest.

On our first Sunday, we attended Bible classes. We had the great privilege of sitting in the class taught by Tran Van Can; he was a very capable teacher and had a splendid lesson. I preached at both the English and Vietnamese services. At the latter service, my sermon was translated but the rest of the worship was in Vietnamese. What a wonderful reunion with many old friends!

At last, the long-awaited-and-prayed-for return had arrived. I spent every available moment in visiting with old friends and following up on people I had once known.

That Sunday evening, the Conners had a fellowship in their home with 32 present. Of course, we had a lot of catching up to do to learn the whereabouts of many that we had known and loved in the past. The devotional included a period of singing led by Pat and Gary, who made an instant hit with all present. The fellowship, the food, and pop made this a terrific evening!

Our first week was filled with activities.

Our week started by orienting Gary and Pat to the downtown area. This orientation helped them to be more relaxed; it reassured them to see that life goes on pretty much as normal even though the war continued to be fought in many areas without the American military.

As we walked down one of the major streets, someone shouted "Oh, Mr. Burcham, so glad to see you." I introduced Pat and Gary and after some small talk we continued downtown. As we walked, Gary says, "Can you believe it? We are in a city of three million and someone recognizes 'Pa' on our first trip downtown."

Gladys and myself missed the American civilians and servicemen downtown. We ate lunch at the Floating Ship, one of the favorite places of our children.

In the late afternoon, Tran Van Can (we referred to him as Brother Can), who advised me on all matters, picked us up at the hotel to go visit with the landlord, who owned the place where the church met. The landlord had been most friendly to us for several years. He showed his excitement to see us again.

We rented adjoining rooms to the church. We had a large living room, a makeshift kitchen with a small refrigerator, a propane gas hotplate, and a large bedroom with bath. The kitchen did not have running water in the usual sense–the landlord's maid provided the running between the water storage tank and the large plastic container. We got processed drinking water from the Seventh Day Adventist Hospital.

Tran and I worked from early afternoon until late in going over the plans for our work, while Gladys wrote letters; she was an unbelievable communicator.

The next day we moved into our quarters, which would be home for the next four months. Ron and Jeanette Cotton, missionaries in Vietnam, came by to welcome us and loaned us some things to set up housekeeping; then took us out to eat.

We started each day with a devotion and Bible study. At this time, we shared impressions on the work and how we might encourage others. This proved to be a tremendous bonding time with Pat and Gary as they conducted or shared ideas and prayers during these devotionals.

By midweek, we got serious about setting up housekeeping. We exchanged money at the bank; then purchased groceries. Gladys shopped some in the afternoon and introduced Gary and Pat to "bargaining." I spent the afternoon with Tran and Vo Thanh Duc going over plans and what we might do to get evangelism on the move again.

After church, the Nguyen Dan Baos and the Vo Thanh Ducs stayed late just visiting. Since the church needed a permanent meeting place, we talked about what might be available for the money in the church building fund.

We decided to ask Mrs. Tran Van Can to begin a search for a building. Mrs. Tran knew several real estate agents personally. As soon as she found a place that had possibilities with the funds we

had available, she encouraged us to visit the building and evaluate the pros and cons of the location. In time, she located several
buildings.

Our visitation work begins.

With preliminary details out of the way, Gary, Pat, Tran, Gladys,
and I began visiting in Vietnamese homes. We visited in the homes
of Christians and non-Christians.

Taking Pat and Gary along on some of these visits and intro-
ducing them to people I've known proved to be a plus. Pat indicated
how meaningful this had been. He wrote: "Our visitation has been
most interesting. The Vietnamese people are friendly and very kind
to us wherever we go. We hear there is much anti-American feeling
in Vietnam, but we have only been given the best of treatment. In
almost every case, we get results from visiting someone's home.
Either they, or a member of their family, are present at our assembly
or in our classes. Wouldn't it be great if it worked so well in the
States!"

Canh, the son of our former maid, and his friend, Vinh, visited
us. What a delight to see them again! They wanted to continue their
study of the Scriptures so we introduced them to Pat and Gary.
Gladys had studied with them before we left Vietnam in 1968.

Later, we visited Sister Hao, a very aged Christian, who welcomed
us warmly. Her husband had died and Howard Horton had preached
his funeral. We enjoyed visiting with her son, Phong, a Christian and
a music professor at the University of Hue; being home for a visit,
we got to spend time with him. Phong is so very talented, and we
hoped to get him more involved in the work of the Lord.

Then we went to the hospital to visit Nguyen Van Khanh,
a former Buddhist. He is the great Christian gentleman that I
converted on my visit in 1969. He had made remarkable growth in
the knowledge of the Scriptures. He loved the Lord and desired to
use his life in service to Christ. Because of his lung cancer, he had
labored breathing. Being hospitalized for so long, he had almost no
energy; his doctors permitted him to go to church each Sunday so
that he could meet with fellow Christians, worship, and partake of

the Lord's Supper. I prayed for God to restore his health and give him more years to serve.

We visited Madam Cu, a Christian grandmother of seventeen grandchildren, and one who had encouraged us to return. Much of the afternoon was spent with people visiting with us.

We visited in a home preparing for a Buddhist funeral.

A Vietnamese family invited us to their home because the father had died suddenly. We went to pay our respects because of the loss of the husband and father. We had developed a close friendship with their children who had been in Gladys' classes in 1966-68. The girls demonstrated their happiness to see Gladys. Their father, a very wealthy Buddhist, had a huge home.

Several of the girls greeted us at the door and ushered us into their huge receiving room. They continued to show their love and affection for Gladys even on this very sad occasion. The girls, wearing sackcloth, ushered us to a table. Immediately a servant brought cokes and delicacies.

Being overwhelmed by our beautiful surroundings, we could not help but notice the tasteful way they displayed their wealth. Oriental tables, sideboards, chairs, and divans, decorated in black lacquer with mother of pearl inlay–all surrounded the large auditorium-size room. We enjoyed their large colorful vases and paintings placed in strategic places. In the center of the room, paper streamers hung from the ceiling over a large paper mansion, papier-mâché cars and things to be burned with the body. A group of paid mourners and musicians, playing oriental music, gave the room an eerie feeling. The pageantry of the occasion moved us deeply. After expressing our sympathy to the mother and the girls, we left feeling sorrow that this one died without Christ.

Love for those we had known encouraged us on many social occasions.

Each day seemed to be filled with a number of visitors to our apartment. Early on, the Vo Thanh Duc's invited several of us to a

Vietnamese feast. The delicious dinner concluded with homemade ice cream with a tasty mango topping.

Our second Sunday found 62 in worship. In addition, others came for the fellowship. The Vietnamese served a box lunch, which included fried chicken, a butter sandwich, cookies, fresh vegetables, and iced pop. To my knowledge, this was the first fellowship in which the Vietnamese planned and provided all the food.

Chi Hai, our former maid, came with some of her children. What a day filled with joy and reunions!

In the afternoon, we four went to Cholon for Bible study. This was mainly a Chinese work made up of several young people. Sponsored by the Village Church of Christ in Oklahoma City, Ron and Jeanette Cotton served as their missionaries. The young people stood and quoted together whole chapters of Scripture. Ron and Jeanette impressed us with their work. Also, the Cottons invited Pat and Gary to work with their young people on Sunday afternoons for the summer.

To begin the week, we started processing our immigration papers. Then Tran and I started making visits and conducting Bible studies.

While visiting in one home, a young Vietnamese girl brought in her baby that had an American father, who had abandoned her. She offered to give me the baby. What a sad commentary on war– everywhere we went we saw children who had American fathers. Most of these children were outcasts in their own society. I silently wondered, "What kind of a future awaits them?"

Lt. Nguyen Dang Minh invited all of us to his home for a Vietnamese dinner. During the evening, Lt. Minh showed slides he made when visiting us in the States. The Minhs proudly displayed their new baby–so delicate and pretty. We enjoyed another very memorable evening.

During the week, we went out to the Cong Hoa military hospital, which had over 2,200 patients and anticipated more. This was the hospital where we did some work in 1967-68. We went to see Phat, who was the brother-in-law of Bob Fairless. Bob, Chau, and Phat moved in with us during the Tet Offensive and took over our house when we had to leave. Phat, a helicopter pilot, had been a VC prisoner for over 18 months and was recovering from Malaria.

We continued to make visits to Christians and missionaries. Ron and Jeanette took us to the home of Nguyen Van Hieu, a Christian who served in the military. He had translated all the Maurice Tisdel charts into Vietnamese. His most artistic work provided a great tool for us. In addition, I felt Hieu learned a great deal from this special work.

Pat and Gary were overwhelmed with students for Bible study.

From the beginning, Pat and Gary immersed themselves in the work. We ran an advertisement for a free English-conversation Bible class using the book of John. To their amazement, they had over 200 students enroll! Of course, many of these would drop out; but we hoped that many would stay long enough to really examine the claims of Christ and what He can do for one's life. The students ranged in age from15 to 61. We used Vietnamese Bibles , which contained both Vietnamese and English in parallel columns. When classes began, each student would be given a free copy of the Bible along with an insert, which provided an introduction to the Scriptures.

Gary and Pat had so much personality. Everyone enjoyed their pleasant smiles and enthusiasm. Being excellent song leaders, they spent time in teaching their students some songs.

Pat Peters summarized their mission efforts: "By far our biggest undertaking has been in the classes we have started. A newspaper ad was published advertising a class wherein people could practice their English as well as learn Bible. It is free, so that is an added attraction. The response to the class was almost too much. From the 200 who pre-enrolled, we have just over 100 now attending regularly.

"We do let them practice their English, but we mostly teach Bible. Many are coming for no other reason than to learn about our Christian religion. The interest shown us by people we are teaching is certainly encouraging. Many want to learn more and more and are asking a great number of questions indicating that their interest is more than passive. We hope to start some individual studies soon from this experience. We are observing several whom we feel are good prospects, and we pray that our work with them will bear good fruit. Each of us teaches two classes a day, six days a week. Each class group meets three times a week."

After one of his class sessions, Pat came in and said: "Pa, I need some advice."

Thinking him to be having a real problem in the class, I said: "What's the problem?"

He replied: "I have these students that have these habits and I don't know what to do."

Seeing my puzzled look, he laughingly said "I have two Catholic nuns in my Bible class. They keep inviting me over to the foundling home where they care for children who have American fathers."

Pat asked "Do you think it wise for me to go?" I told him I thought it would be a good idea.

When he visited the home, they kept bringing different children for him to see and made Pat feel they wanted him to choose one to take back to America.

Visitation in homes continued to fill our days.

We visited three families of military men, who had been trained at Wichita Falls, Texas; they received some teaching from the Tenth and Broad congregation. Before leaving for Vietnam, I had mailed these men a letter telling them of our return visit. All had received the letter and this caused us to be warmly received.

Locating an address in Vietnam was not easy unless you had precise directions, but we located two of the servicemen, converted in Wichita Falls; both men served in the Air Force and had great potential. Captain Nguyen Si Le introduced us to his father-in-law and one of his twin sons. After this visit, the father-in-law attended regularly on Sundays. We met several of the family members of Lt. Le Van Son; they, too, visited our services; we had hopes of reaching them.

Before leaving the States, a friend asked us to call on Dr. and Mrs. T. T. Lo; we wrote them about our coming visit. When I called them, they expressed their desire to meet us. He served as a very important official in the Chinese Agricultural Mission to Vietnam. The Taiwan Government sponsored him.

Dr. Lo had worked in Vietnam from 1964 until 1968 and had just returned to be in charge of agricultural research; his specialties include sugar cane production and diseases, increasing the output of pond fish production, and the development of a strain of pork capable of reaching the market sooner. In addition, he provided instructions for farmers about new strains of seed; how to fertilize; how to combat plant diseases. His work would be a major factor in the future economy of Vietnam as this potential could greatly increase the production of large quantities of badly needed foodstuffs.

Mrs. Lo invited us to dinner at their home. They picked us up. It is difficult to describe the artistry involved in a truly Chinese dinner. Mrs. Lo served the extremely delicious food in courses. We had crab, duck with vegetables, beef with vegetables, pork ribs, shrimp with snow peas, soup, fried rice, sweet potatoes, and watermelon. Gladys and Mrs. Lo struck it off so well that their friendship led to regular English Bible studies.

Trying to make the rounds as soon as possible, we gave priority to visit in homes where I had maintained a relationship by letter. The Vietnamese graciously received us and with each visit served either hot tea or cokes with ice. Because of the many homes visited on a daily basis, at the end of each day we felt like a teakettle–full and ready to blow.

On our third Sunday, Pat Peters preached at the English service. I taught the Bible class. I had a Bible study with Do Van Khuyen, who had studied at the FAA in Oklahoma City, and had an important position being in charge of air traffic control at Tan Son Nhut. After the service, so many came to our apartment that we could not eat until 1:30 p.m. After we ate, we continued to receive visitors until evening. Then Tran and his son Loc came with a bag of live crabs. He showed Gladys how to cook them by dropping the live crabs into boiling water.

On our fourth Sunday, Gary preached at the English service. He had an excellent sermon and did a fine job presenting it. Pat led the singing. The Vietnamese really enjoyed the talents of Pat and Gary; in every way, they proved themselves to be tremendous assets to our mission efforts. I presented the lesson at the Vietnamese translated service.

Visitation and studies continued to keep us busy. One visit to Dang Vu Tiem, who speaks English quite well, really inspired us. Mr. Tiem, born in Hanoi, spent some 20 years as Vietnam's ambassador to the Philippines. He told us: "My son has been accepted into Medical School in the States in some place called 'Oklahoma.'" When I told him that we lived in Oklahoma, he gave us a Russian bear hug!

Both Gladys and Pat had a brief illness–probably from fatigue, since we had been on the go ever since we arrived.

I spent many hours with the Vietnamese Christians on an individual basis to find out what each felt about where he could best serve to further the cause of Christ. Gradually, the Vietnamese developed a program of work.

From a psychological point of view, I believed the logical time to inaugurate the program of work would be at the time we moved into the new building if one became available that we could afford. Prior to that time, I would be giving instruction, encouragement, and suggestions. Rebuilding was a slow process; yet, I could see a new spirit developing among individual members; and I believed in time this would affect the collective body. But before I did anything else, I felt I had to do something for Nguyen Van Khanh, whom I taught and baptized.

Nguyen Van Khanh's cancer troubled me!

From the time I left Vietnam in 1969, I continued to correspond with Nguyen Van Khanh and encouraged him in his new walk with Christ. However, Khanh developed lung cancer, which deeply saddened me. On our return, we visited Khanh in a Vietnamese hospital. My emotions almost overcame me to see my dear friend again with his labored breathing and his difficulty in talking. He had been under treatment for several months. Khanh indicated he had gotten permission from his doctor to leave the hospital each week to attend worship even though he felt short of breath and felt weak.

With sadness, he told me that his wife remained a Buddhist. Before we left, we prayed and I simply asked God to heal him.

After leaving, I made the determination to visit the Saigon Adventist Hospital, which had the reputation for being one of the best. There I met Dr. Newbold, who specialized in lung and respiratory diseases. Being on a brief loan from his hospital in Korea, Dr. Newbold agreed to run tests on Khanh and asked that we get his x-rays.

When Dr. Newbold examined Khanh, he told him that he either had TB in its final stages or a tumor or a combination of the two. Dr. Newbold said: "Your only hope for recovery is to have surgery immediately. Otherwise, you will only have a few weeks to live." At first Khanh seemed reluctant because so many Vietnamese do not survive surgery in their hospitals. I tried to reassure Him; we prayed for wisdom in deciding what to do.

Later, we went back to the hospital where they made several tests. Dr. Newbold indicated that an opening in his schedule would permit him to do the surgery; he instructed us to make a deposit at the finance office. I had already told Khanh that Christian friends in America would cover the expense. The cashier told us what the deposit would be.

The tears started rolling down the cheeks of Khanh. He looked up at me and said, "I am not worth that much money. There is no way I can pay you back."

I told him, "You are worth more than that to the Lord and the Lord needs you to work for Him."

On the appointed day for him to check in, I took Khanh to the hospital along with his wife and daughter, who had become a Christian since my last visit to Vietnam. One of his sons currently studied the Bible; in all Khanh had seven living children. We prayed before leaving him behind.

Next morning, several of us arrived at 7 for the scheduled surgery. Khanh's wife had intended to come. However, her daughter explained, "My mother has to work because my sister is ill and unable to fill in for her." Mrs. Khanh prepared and sold her famous duck soup at a stall in the Central Market in downtown Saigon. She had many customers; she felt obligated to fill their regular orders.

We had a prayer session with the family before they took Khanh in for surgery at 8:30. Then we continued in a prayer vigil throughout the day.

Mrs. Khanh arrived about 11 a.m. Being very anxious about word on the progress of the surgery, I told her, "The last report indicated the surgery is going well." She turned to me with tears in her eyes and said, "I want to thank you for your help. Every member of our family must work to earn enough to live on. I prepare duck soup early each morning and sell it at the Central Market. Since my daughter became ill, I had to prepare the soup and sell it before I could come." By this time she was crying so much that I bowed my head and asked one of the Vietnamese Christians present to console her.

The surgery lasted until about 2 p.m.

After the surgery, Dr. Newbold reported: "I had to remove the center lobe of his lung. I believe the cancer is fully contained in this lobe. The cancer had enlarged to the point where he was not getting sufficient oxygen. In time, his lung will expand and he can live a normal life." We had a prayer of thanksgiving.

Christians and Khanh's wife and family visited him in the hospital on a daily basis. One day Mrs. Khanh told me, "I now understand what my husband has been telling me about the love of Jesus and how His followers love each other. When my husband returns home, I want to study the Bible."

With his successful surgery, he regained strength day by day. When he had the stitches removed, a new x-ray indicated the healing to be almost complete and his lung had expanded as desired. Khanh prayed, "I thank you God that I can now breathe with ease." Within a few days, he returned to work for the first time in months. My prayer, "Thank you God for saving the life of this fine Christian man."

Just nineteen days after his surgery, Khanh made a most moving presentation to the church. He said, "Obviously, I'm not completely recovered. I need to rest, but I'm eager to go to church because I miss you very much. Secondly, the essential and important cause which urges me to go is to talk with you, after the Lord's Supper, about the blessings I have just received from God, our Father.

"I have been a victim of cancer since May, 1972. Immediately I went to see the Vietnamese doctors at the Hong Bang Hospital (a government hospital). They told me that it was not a tumor but a small lesion. After ten months treatment as an outpatient and two months as an in-patient, I did not feel better. Instead, I felt worse than I had ever been. I lost weight and felt fast tired when I had to speak.

"From a small spot, the tumor grew bigger to a diameter of four centimeters. Again I asked the doctors about surgery; again they answered me shortly 'Not necessary.' Truly, they were unable to make such an operation. They were not sincere to recognize their weakness in the surgical field.

"My wife and my children felt it was hopeless, but their troubled feelings did not disappoint me. I kept on praying to God for His help. I know that 'My help comes from the Lord who made heaven and earth' (Psalm 121:2) and 'Call to me and I will answer you, and will tell you great and hidden things which you have not known' (Jeremiah 35:3).

"Sometimes God seems to delay in answering our prayers, but it is good to know that His delay does not mean that He refuses our requests. Abraham had to wait many long years before the birth of Isaac, after he had the promise of God to give him a son. It was the same with Joseph. He had to suffer terrible challenges. He had to stay firm in his long waiting and to overcome hard missions, who were beyond the ability of a human being before he reached to a high and powerful position in Egypt, (see Genesis 41:1), even though God had shown him wonderful things in his dreams when he was still a boy of seventeen years old.

"Some other Scriptures give me hope when I trust in the Lord: 'Is anything too hard for the Lord?' (Genesis 18:14); 'with God nothing will be impossible.' (Luke 1:37); 'When I am afraid, I put my trust in Thee.' (Psalm 56:3); 'My God will supply every need of yours according to his riches in glory in Christ Jesus.' (Philippians 4:19)

"After many days and nights, after many weeks and months, my prayers have finally received God's answer. God's help has been with Mr. and Mrs. Ralph S. Burcham when they came back to Vietnam last April. Brother Burcham and Brother Tran came to see me at the Hong Bang Hospital. I told them about the temporary treatment without effect and the lack of conscience of the Vietnamese doctors. With no hesitation, Brother Burcham made a quick decision to let me be treated by an American doctor; but I did hesitate because I knew the bills for the treatment would be too expensive, and the money is from the collection of an unknown American brother whom I have never met. Brother Burcham and Brother Tran comforted me then they left.

"On Sunday, May 13, as usual I got out of the Hong Bang Hospital to attend the Communion at the church. After the worshiping hour, Brother Burcham told me to be ready to meet Doctor Newbold at the Saigon Adventist Hospital at three o'clock the next afternoon. We were in the doctor's office at the appointed time.

"After a careful examination about my health and x-ray pictures of my lungs I took along with me, Doctor Newbold said, 'The best way we need to do right now is to cut that tumor out of your lung. Don't delay. The surgery may be difficult, but do not be afraid. About eight or ten days after the operation, you will get out of the hospital safe and sound.'

"I looked at Brother Burcham asking his opinion. He nodded his head. I found a consent in his eyes. Two days later, we went back to the Saigon Adventist Hospital. Brother Burcham had to deposit at the accounting desk a check for an advanced payment. The total was much more, but Brother Burcham did not want to let me know how much. How kind he is.

"The surgery happened the next morning at 8:30 a.m. When the nurses carried me on a wheeled bed from the ward to the operation room, I saw the Burchams, several of my Christian friends, and my daughter.

"Very often most of the patients feel afraid when they are moved to the operation room. I was quite different. I did not feel any trouble that morning because I knew all my brothers and sisters would pray for me during all the time of the surgery. I also knew that God was with me that time because 'Where two or three are gathered in my name, there am I in the midst of them.' (Matthew 18:20)

"The surgery was delicate and ended at about two o'clock in the afternoon.

"One morning after feeling my pulse, Doctor Newbold said, 'I believe there is a God who blesses you. The new x-ray picture we took yesterday shows a good and complete lung expansion. You are allowed to leave the hospital tomorrow, and in two weeks you are to come back for a re-examination.'

"A great emotion ran over my body. I said, 'Doctor Newbold, I never will forget your devoted treatment. Please, receive sincere thanks from me and from my American Brothers and Sisters who were there that day to follow your operation. Two weeks later we will meet together, won't we? I am a Christian. May God's blessings be upon you and your family! That is the only word I want to confess to you now.

"A smile appeared on the doctor's lips. 'You don't need me anymore,' he said. 'After tomorrow, I'll go back to Korea. Doctor Pritel will take care of you.'

"My heart beat fast. I began to sweat as I was having a hot fever. Tears of happiness ran down on my checks. I thought it was really a blessing of God. If the Burchams had been late to come back to Vietnam, or if I had not obeyed his suggestion, we would not meet Doctor Newbold and everything would become worse now.

"Dear Brothers and Sisters, I want to thank you very much for your prayers. Only Christians, as you are, know how happy and grateful I am when I have received the blessings from God, our merciful Father in Heaven."

What a joy to unite a family in Christ!

When Khanh returned home, Mrs. Khanh requested a Bible study. I had developed a booklet with basic Christian doctrine, called *"The Framework of Christianity."* It contained both Vietnamese and English on a facing page. Also, I used the Scriptures about Christ along with Isaiah 53. At the conclusion of this series of studies she said, "I'm ready to be a Christian."

As we gathered together on a Sunday evening for her baptism, Mrs. Khanh seemed overwhelmed at the number of Vietnamese and American Christians present for this great event in her life.

The next time I visited in the home of the Khanhs, to my amazement, the Buddhist altar had been removed. I praised God for His providence that worked out events in their lives in order for this family to become united in Christ. Again this affirmed for me that "God moves in a mysterious way, His wonders to perform."

An historic event occurred in the Saigon congregation.

Many of us had been praying for a church building. Then the owners of the building two doors down from our rented facility indicated a desire to sell. The location on Suong Nguyet Anh Street was so good because it was just off a main thoroughfare. The buildings up and down the tree-lined street had been maintained in excellent condition. Because of limited traffic, it was a quiet street.

The Vietnamese building committee met with the owner and through negotiations came to a price within our building fund.

Then on June 7, 1973, a true historic moment came into the life of the Saigon church when the Vietnamese Christians signed the official papers with the owners of the building at 9 Suong Nguyet Anh. Upon the completion of the transaction, the owner of the property turned over the keys.

God truly answered the prayers of many because the Vietnamese Christians had dreamed of owning a building almost from the beginning of the church. Many American servicemen contributed to the building fund during those years; my sponsoring congregation, the Brookfield Church of Christ in Rockford, Illinois, had held these funds, along with interest, in trust. These funds completely paid for the building.

The Vietnamese decided to pay for the remodeling and repainting out of their contributions. They also paid the legal fees for completing the transaction. Immediately, they started the construction of their first permanent baptistery. The rental fees paid in the past could now be used in developing the local work. This began a new era for the Saigon Church of Christ.

Upon our arrival in Vietnam, Gary noted the general attitude of the congregation and how this gradually became more positive. "When we arrived this summer, it was apparent that the church was suffering a period of depression. Now it is equally certain that we are witnessing the beginning of a new era of work for the church. With the final possession of a new building and the growing involvement and interest that is being demonstrated among the Christians here, the Lord's work seems sure to continue and increase. The improved health of many of the Christians and the growing responsibilities that the Lord is opening up to us every day make us certain that the He has answered many prayers." In writing home, Gary made this appeal: "Let's continue to pray for the growth of our brothers in this tragically war-torn country."

Over and over again, the Vietnamese Christians expressed their deep gratitude to all who had made this building possible. They prayed that this building would be used as a tool to bring honor to God, the Father of our Lord Jesus Christ. Immediately, the members began planning an open house and a lectureship.

As the various committees started making plans for the open house and the lectureship, God opened my eyes to the way He had been working in the lives of these men. I bowed my head in thanksgiving to God for allowing me to see the rewards of all who had made this moment possible through many personal sacrifices, heartaches, and tears.

The Saigon church had a memorable open house.

In answer to many prayers and with the help of hundreds of churches and Christians who gave so generously, the Vietnamese had a grand opening and reception for their new building on July 1, 1973.

For years servicemen and civilians in Vietnam contributed to the purchase of a permanent property. From the purchase on June 7 until the open house, the brethren and a contractor remodeled and redecorated the building on the inside and out.

The building had two floors and a storage area in the rear. In addition, a small-enclosed area in front provided parking for Honda motorcycles and bicycles. The first floor would be used for a reading room and office during the week. On Sunday, it would be used for classes. The second floor provided an auditorium for worship and Bible study.

The open house ceremony started with Tran Van Can and me cutting the ribbon together. This short ceremony took place in the auditorium. Tran expressed appreciation on behalf of the Vietnamese to all who had a part in making the building possible. Over and over again they expressed their gratitude for the sacrifice of many who helped this permanent facility become a reality.

About 300 guests came. Each guest received a Vietnamese Bible with a special insert that contained an "Introduction to the Bible" and a copy of "Framework of Christianity," which contains some of the Scripture locations of major doctrinal concepts of Christianity. Dr. and Mrs. Chang came; he had served as the Minister of Education and had helped us get accreditation for the American-Vietnamese International School during our first mission efforts in Saigon.

The reading room contained a library made available through work funds sent to the College Church of Christ in Oklahoma City. It contained a very fine collection of books in English, Vietnamese, and Chinese. Our fellowship wrote many of the commentaries and books. The Vietnamese hungered for knowledge in every realm. English had become very popular and the reading room would attract many who wanted to learn about religion in America. Tran would conduct special studies there during weekdays.

What a humbling experience for me as I had prayed for a building for almost 10 years! I began the spring wondering if a building could ever become a reality. Praise God for generous hearts that made it possible. God answered many prayers in providing this facility and may it ever be used as a tool to honor His Son.

The first Vietnam lectureship held.

The lectureship-workshop would provide an opportunity to strengthen the leadership throughout churches in Vietnam from Quang Ngai in the north and to Cantho in the south. Several Vietnamese Christians in the military requested a leave to attend.

The workshop provided for planning sessions, classes, discussions, devotions, and lectures. The fellowship would be strengthening to all. Tran Van Can completed the sound tape for a filmstrip on "How We Got the Bible"; this would be shown.

The evening lectures provided for very basic instruction: The Need for the Gospel; What Is the Gospel; Love Is the Spirit of the Gospel; The Significance of the Resurrection; How Through the Atonement God Is Able to Extend His Grace; How Man Is to Respond to the Gospel; How the Church Enables One to be Faithful; How God Wants the Gospel Spread to All the Earth; and The Victory that Is in Christ Alone.

Classes included: A Textual Study of Romans; The Scriptural Organization of the Church; How to Reach Buddhists and Other Religious Groups; a series on planning and conducting worship with sessions on prayer, singing, the Lord's Supper, preaching, and giving; how to help new converts to be faithful; a series on basic Christian doctrine; and a class on the inspiration of the Scriptures.

This first workshop, planned by the Vietnamese, turned out to be a wonderful time of reunion, fellowship, study, and planning sessions, which lasted for ten days. All the classes were conducted in Vietnamese, except the translated class on Romans that I taught.

My class on Romans had about 30 plus each day. The well-attended evening sessions included several non-members present on a regular basis.

What a wonderful time of reunion. Le Nho, who was in the military, came down from DaNang. He attended the preacher-training program for several months that I conducted in 1967-68. He was a talented speaker and presented one of the inspiring evening lectures. When he got out of the military, he hoped to preach and teach full time.

Nguyen Van Hieu obtained a military leave. He presented one of the evening lectures and taught a class during the week on "Using the Maurice Tisdel Charts." His most thrilling moment came when his brother, who served in the Special Forces, came and decided to become a Christian. Hieu demonstrated his joy as he baptized his brother into Christ.

Quan Phat Cao obtained a military leave; he, too, presented a lecture on "How to Help New Converts Remain Faithful." His carefully organized lesson contained extremely good illustrations. When he got out of the service, he desired to preach the gospel in the Delta area of Vietnam. He had been exploring the possibilities for starting a work in that area. I prayed that God would help him achieve his desire to preach the Good News.

Lt. Tran Trong Su got a partial leave from the Navy. He, too, desired to preach the Gospel. He felt he needed further training when he got out of the military.

Other speakers included Vo Thanh Duc, Bui Nguyen, Tran Van Can, Nguyen Van Thuong, Nguyen Dan Bao, and Nguyen Van Khanh.

Tran worked diligently throughout the lectureship by keeping everything moving. After a busy week, I asked: "Are you exhausted?" He replied, "No. I am very happy; everyone is most eager to go to work for the Lord."

The afternoon sessions included periods of discussion centered on the various work areas of the church. Several leaders of the churches attended these sessions. I really believed they saw their potential for the first time. I prayed they would be able to carry out their plans. They all had lively participation in the session on "how to improve the worship service." At the next worship service, it became evident that their planning made a big difference for a more meaningful experience. They had the best-organized worship I had ever experienced in Vietnam. The inspiring song service made worship so meaningful; the service had a good pace without being extremely long.

Yes, I could see that the Vietnamese congregation had reached a new level of maturity. I thanked God for His loving patience in helping all to grow. I prayed that all would continue to grow in this Christ-like Spirit.

Helping a man injured in a helicopter accident.

In addition to their Bible classes, Pat and Gary accepted the challenge to help a man, Phan Van Dat, who had multiple handicaps. They referred to him as Mr. Dat. On our visit with his father, the three of us tried to encourage him to be more faithful.

At one time, Mr. Dat served as a brilliant soldier, who spoke fluent English. An American Colonel developed such a love for him that he planned to sponsor him for American citizenship. I read the many citations and honors he had received from the U. S. Government; his awards included the bronze star. All looked very well for this soldier until the day that he got drunk and fell about sixty feet from a helicopter as it took off.

After the accident, Mr. Dat remained in a coma for three months. His injuries included breaks to both legs and one arm. He walked with a severe limp and his arm remained very stiff and unusable.

At times, Mr. Dat's mind seemed like a three-year old child; at other times, he seemed almost normal. We had an EEG made and found that he had some brain damage. We planned to have further tests made to determine if surgery would alleviate this problem. An American orthopedic surgeon examined him. Another American doctor, who examined him earlier, told us he suffered mentally which resulted from lack of daily exercise and neglect by his family.

Pat and Gary decided to take turns and work with Mr. Dat at least an hour a day. When they took on the challenge, Pat and Gary decided they wanted to know as much as possible about his home life. After getting acquainted with Mr. Dat, Pat summarized the problems in two areas: " the home environment and the lack of physical activity.

"Burcham had long been acquainted with this family and, after meeting Dat, he arranged to have him examined by Dr. Arnold, a well-respected physician. Dr. Arnold began running periodic tests to see how much of Dat's condition could be improved. The doctor immediately noted that Dat needed more exercise, so we tried to have one of us visit and walk with him for about an hour every day. We were hopeful that his limp would soon disappear as he strengthened his legs. We do not yet know just how far Dat's physical improvement will go, but each of us feels that we may be able to share with him the hope we have in Christ."

I made the decision to return to the Vietnamese Military Hospital.

In 1967, I made regular visits to the Vietnamese military hospitals. This gave the students in my leadership-training program a practicum to learn about working with severely injured patients. Therefore, I had a desire to return to see if we could still do something.

In recognition of the annual Armed Forces Day, the Special Forces of Vietnam pay tribute to their wounded. I visited with Brigadier General Do Ka Giai, Commander and Chief of the Special Forces; he invited us to give a special program for the wounded in two military hospitals. He asked us to explain about our mission and give a message to the men.

Captain Vu Vin Thung, an aide to General Giai, set a date for us to give small gifts and Bibles to 260 of the wounded in the Special Forces. Some Vietnamese and Americans got together and planned the event. They decided to give each man a bag of gifts. Several got together and prepared the bags.

Each patient would receive a loaf of French bread, a can of condensed milk, a towel, a brush and toothpaste, a bar of soap, a Bible with an insert explaining the location of key passages, and the first lesson of the Bible correspondence course. These seemed unusual gifts to me, but we found them to be highly appreciated. The Vietnamese Christians had special plastic bags made with the name and address of the church imprinted on each and included a boxed statement: "Jesus Christ is the way, the truth, and the life." Below this, they had imprinted "The churches of Christ salute you. (Romans 16:16)"

On the appointed day, Captain Vu Vin Thung came to escort us to the first hospital. At the hospital, Brigadier General Giai received us and introduced some of his aides. They served hot tea, and then escorted us in military style to a hospital auditorium. There we found 110 wounded servicemen clad in their pajamas waiting for our arrival.

After a great deal of military pomp and ceremony, the General introduced us. I explained about our mission, which was translated. Then Vo Thanh Duc preached a short sermon. From the beginning of his message until its conclusion, he had the audience in his hands.

Then I presented the Brigadier General with a copy of the Bible with a statement placed on the inside cover of our appreciation for his role in making our visit possible.

The Christian brethren handed out the bags of gifts to each serviceman personally. Many expressed appreciation in English; all seemed happy to be remembered.

At the conclusion of the service, the General stepped up to the mike and presented me with a plate embossed with the symbol of the Special Forces, the date, and appreciation for our benevolent work among the military.

After the presentations at this hospital, a five-jeep military escort whisked us across town to the Cong Hoa Military Hospital. Because these patients were confined to their beds, we felt it necessary for us to be divided into two groups. The 150 patients were scattered throughout different wards in this sprawling military hospital complex. The General and several of his aides went with us as we personally visited each of these patients.

Some of the patients' injuries made it difficult to look on. We saw two men who had just been brought in from a helicopter crash. Because both suffered horrible burns, their face and hands had black charred material over them. One managed to say "Cam On," which is "Thank you" in Vietnamese. As he squeezed out these words, the skin looked as though it would crack from his slight movement.

We walked down aisle after aisle of amputees. Some new patients had just come in. Many had a terror-stricken look in their eyes. I could only imagine what they must be thinking, "what on earth is going to happen to me?" In an underdeveloped country like Vietnam, I wondered if they would live out their lives as a burden to their families, to themselves, and to society. What a price these men had paid for the cause of freedom!

As we rushed from ward to ward, down long corridor after corridor, and aisle after aisle, I began to feel ill from this mass of suffering humanity. Many patients had bedsores. I found the stench of blood, bandages, medicines, and human waste to be overwhelming in the heavy tropical air. None of the wards had air conditioning. Everywhere we went the patients had to put up with flies and mosquitoes because the open windows did not have screens. Because of the understaffed hospital, each patient needed a family member to care for him or her; otherwise, they would often be neglected.

I found myself offering up prayers everywhere we went. I knew that God loved each one and wanted a relationship with each but how will they come to know the Good News of a Savior. Gratitude built up in my heart that for one brief moment God's Word had been placed in the hands of 260. But this was just a drop in the bucket for the total number in the hospitals. We soon learned that many of these did enroll in the Bible Correspondence Course.

Pat Peters and Gary Williams make a half-time assessment of their work.

I asked Pat and Gary to keep a journal of their daily activities and impressions in order to inform those supporting them. I found these two young men to be very insightful concerning mission work. Here are abbreviated excerpts from their reports after the first seven weeks.

Pat wrote: "The summer of 1973 will long be remembered as a growing experience for me. But more than that, it will also be looked upon as a time for growth in the church in Vietnam. Our program is far from complete, but we have had such a fine beginning that I feel that I must share some of our excitement with you. We are grateful for the trust and support that you, as fellow Christians, have given us, and we are doing our best to represent well Christ and His Church.

"Gary Williams and I are taking part in this activity as an experiment in the mission field. It is hoped that giving college students a chance to work in the mission field will prompt more interest for us as future teachers and preachers to encourage our congregations to put forth an added effort in this area of our Lord's work. We know that many would like for us to come back convinced that we would spend our lives in some foreign country teaching about Jesus. I am not sure this will happen, but I am certain that wherever we will spend our energies we will be more equipped to **'give reason for the hope that is in us.'**

"ChoLon is the Chinese section of Saigon. Ron Cotton and His wife are doing a fine work over there. We try to go to their young people's meeting every Sunday afternoon. Most of our efforts in that area have simply been in leading and teaching songs to them. We are doing whatever we can to encourage this group.

"Then to round out our work here, we have taken part several times in the morning worship. Gary and I have both spoken for the English service and have led singing on several occasions. The group is pretty small, but with the withdrawal of American troops that might be expected. We are grateful for the opportunities to work any way we are able.

"This summer is also giving us a fantastic chance to meet some very interesting people. Many of the Vietnamese that we know are refugees from the north. In 1954, the Communists gave a certain amount of time for people to leave North Vietnam before they closed off the roads.

"There were about 3 million who wanted to go south, but because of the Red Tape, (excuse the pun) only about a million could come. Such interesting stories can be told about the days before the Communists came. We have heard much about the beauty of the cities of Hanoi and Haiphong. It is very sad.

"Other stories, of course, about the war are real thrillers. There is one couple here that hid in their home for two days during the 1968 Tet Offensive and finally made a run for safety on a Honda. Two days later their house was burned because of fighting in that part of town. Many of the stories are worthy of a good novel or exciting movie.

"I would like to say just a word about the relationships that we (the Burchams, Gary, and I) have established. I feel very lucky in being here with such great people. We all get along so very well. I guess it all comes down to the reason we are here. Sharing Christ means giving of one's self and when you are giving yourself; it is impossible to be self-centered. I have been blessed by being able to work with three people that really want to give of themselves. This whole experience is being made more valuable by this loving spirit that is so alive in our team."

Gary wrote: "The first seven weeks of our work here have passed amazingly fast! The sights, sounds, and smells of Saigon have become more natural each day and have merged for us to see a rather charming culture. We have quickly seen how Christ can revive hope and love in all men and we are greatly encouraged by the big steps the church here is making towards stronger growth. There is much good news to share!

"We are very fortunate in our housing and food arrangements. Although Asia seems to move rather slowly at times, we were quickly able to obtain an extremely convenient apartment for a very good price. It is located downtown, which puts us close to the major shops, markets, and restaurants, and is in the same building as the church meeting place. 'Going to church' is now a trip of about twenty feet for the Burchams and is no commitment at all for Pat and myself, for we sleep in the back of the one-room auditorium.

"When Pat and I are not busy teaching classes, we try to spend some time with individual students. We are developing a good friendship with several high school and college students of our own age; in addition to our large group classes, we now study weekly with some of them in groups of two or three. Pat and I plan to devote more time, also, to visiting those who began our classes and have not come for a while. As we are becoming more familiar with the people, we are trying to arrange as many of these smaller Bible studies as we can."

"All of us are quite excited about the completion of transactions for buying the new two-story building in which to worship. There are many good things about this new step. By investing its money in this way, the Saigon church can now begin to manage and expand the budget toward filling other needs. The Vietnamese brethren are now no longer dependent upon the English-speaking brethren. The new building is located only two doors away from the old; so the church is quite blessed in that it will not lose its local identity by moving.

"The congregation is also excited and busy concerning the preparations for its first Lectureship-Workshop. Planned by the men of the church, the program calls for a continuous schedule of classes, discussion groups, and fellowship periods.

"The main goals of this week are (1) to involve as many of the capable men as possible in study and teaching, (2) to help strengthen the church in faith and Biblical knowledge and stimulate everyone toward more Bible study, (3) to promote more church unity and involvement among the Christians, (4) to openly outline a program of future work, challenging the congregation to utilize its new building and its growing zeal to the fullest; and (5) to help all understand more about the church and its functions. All of these are certainly strong needs here. The Workshop is planned late enough so that high school and college students will be free to attend during their vacation, yet early enough to provide an effective springboard of activity for the beginning of the work at the new building.

"We have been given a chance to work with the Special Forces in Vietnam. The suffering of the many soldiers is tremendous. On our visits to the hospital, we saw the seemingly endless train of long rooms filled with amputees, paralysis victims, and all those with crushed limbs and dreams, we were wordlessly aware of the smallness of what any one of us might consider our problems. Most of us have probably never seen such intense suffering.

"On our visit to those hospitalized in the Special Forces, we presented small gifts and Bibles to 260 such men. We pray that we can comfort as many as possible."

Since this represented the first half of the summer, I looked forward to the final impressions of Pat and Gary. It is amazing what these two fellows accomplished in such a short time.

Lighter moments gave us relief from our long days of work.

The military had warned us to avoid large crowds. So the four of us talked about the importance of observing this warning. Shortly after we arrived, the Vietnamese celebrated Buddha's birthday. As we went walking one evening, we could see a parade in progress on the main street ahead of us. We kept walking but the floats really caught our fascination. The tremendous sized floats had colorful decorations with large moving objects with neon lights. Most floats had beautiful girls and some had monks who looked just like monks!

We thought we would just watch but we got caught up in the crowd headed towards a shrine dedicated to a Buddhist monk who had poured gasoline over himself and set himself on fire in 1966. We watched the ceremony for a time. As the crowd started dispersing, Gladys reminded me: "You set a good example for the boys today by avoiding a large crowd!" I thought, "Your sins will find you out particularly if you have a good wife."

Our apartment, joined next to the church building, seemed to make everyone feel at home and they just walked through whenever. Many people walked in and out of our apartment most every day. One day after several had walked through, Pat said: "I feel like we live in the bus station!" We all got a good laugh. Pat had a way of making us forget our lack of privacy. But how blessed we felt to have so many friends.

We ate most of our meals together, but occasionally we would go out on our own. Pat and Gary found a restaurant that advertised "an American Steak." Of course, they had to try it. They came back all excited about this great place to get an American steak. We went. The dinner consisted of a steak, on top of that a nice slice of ham, and on top of that a fried egg. We decided that some GI had given them the recipe for an American steak. Also, the good food helped our budget.

Our apartment being near the USAID headquarters, we ate several meals in their cafeteria. Gary had a hard time meeting a scheduled time. Usually, we would go without him and he would join us later. We got excellent service but the waitresses always asked about Gary. When Gary arrived, all the waitresses would stand back and giggle and he would look embarrassed.

When they wanted pizza, we would go to Dolce Vita downtown. With the Americans gone, they had too many waiters. Usually, we had a waiter standing behind each of our chairs. As Gary said, "I'm afraid to put my fork down because someone will grab my plate before I'm finished." Over and over again, we felt thankful these guys had a good sense of humor.

While still reading after we had gone to bed, Pat and Gary knocked and came into our bedroom. Gary had three eggs and he proceeded to demonstrate his expertise in juggling. He moved closer and closer to our bed until juggling right over Gladys. Then in her sharpest tone she said: "Gary, get back right now! I've never known a juggler who didn't keep at it until something dropped."

He moved back but kept juggling; then one of the eggs went crashing to the floor. To which Gladys responded, "You can thank your lucky stars that didn't break on me. Now clean it up!"

Another night we heard a terrific noise in the church building where Pat and Gary slept. From the crashing noises, it sounded like a fight in progress. However, two rats decided to make their appearance in the boys' room and they gave chase. Finally, Gary killed them. Being proud of Gary's bravery, Pat made him kneel and dubbed him "Sir Gary, the Rat Killer." Since Pat did not have a sword for the dubbing, he used one of Gladys' spatulas.

Mice could be seen running around our apartment most every night. Gladys shopped diligently for a mousetrap as she could remember her earlier rabies shots. When she found one, I set it for her and she got five the first day in our living room. The second day she caught two. Even though the mouse population seemed to be on the decline, we kept the trap set until we caught a lizard. The lizards are our friends because they catch mosquitoes. This put us in a dilemma. Which is worse: mosquitoes? Or mice?

Each of the boys shopped for souvenirs to take home. Pat purchased three Ao Dias–beautiful floor-length silk dresses with slits from the waist to the shoes with silk trousers worn underneath. Gladys said: "Pat, how much did you pay for those?" When he responded, Gladys said: "That's a lot of money." To which Pat replied, "When you go to France, you might as well see Paris." This became a saying we use to this day.

I had a tailor make me a suit. When we went to pick it up, we spent some time looking around the shop. Pat came in and said, "Be careful when you go out, there are three pick pockets outside." This warning put us on the alert. Sure enough, when we went out one child grabbed one hand and the other grabbed my other hand. While the third child went for my billfold, Gladys came to my rescue. Her umbrella had a sharp point. She waved it at the young boy and yelled: "Do you want me to make you into a shish ke-bob?" All three scattered.

Throughout the summer, we enjoyed dinner in many homes. Dr. T. T. Lo and his wife had us over many times. Near the end of the summer, we took Dr. and Mrs. Lo, Pat, and Gary to the Dong

Khanh Hotel for a 9-course dinner. When they served the fried rice, we had a large amount left. Dr. Lo said, "Why don't you ask for a doggy bag?" While leaving, the waiter brought the fried rice in a plastic bag. Pat carried it and, just before we got to the elevator, the bottom of the bag gave way and this pile of fried rice fell to the floor. Pat stood there aghast holding the empty bag but Dr. Lo saved the day and laughed out loud. Dr. Lo called for the waiter who brought someone out to clean it up.

Susan Lau and her mother invited us over for an especially delicious Chinese dinner. The Laus had been very close to us since our first time in Vietnam. They were quite wealthy and owned the Capitol Hotel, which the military used as a billet; also, at one time, they owned a conglomerate, which included a large shipping firm that transported products up and down the Mekong River. We could recall the sad occasion when someone kidnapped Mr. Lau and they never heard from him again.

Bob and Chau Fairless invited us to celebrate their wedding anniversary at a nine-course dinner at the Dong Khanh hotel in Cholon. They often expressed thanks for performing their wedding ceremony.

Close to my birthday, Bich and Vo Thanh Duc took us for a picnic at the Zoo. Duc took me for a canoe ride and showed me how to paddle in such a way to keep the canoe going round and round.

More conversions help us see God at work.

As our Bible studies progressed, more and more started accepting Christ as their Lord and Savior. This growth caused rejoicing among the entire congregation. Not only did we rejoice for a growth in numbers within the church, but also we rejoiced because of the saving of lost souls.

Gladys studied for several weeks with Mrs. Phan Thi Viet; they studied three days each week. Gladys drove out to their home on the outskirts of Saigon. Mrs. Viet asked if her brother might study with them also, which he did for several weeks. Being both good students, they studied between sessions and wrote out many questions that came up during their private studies. During the studies one morning, Gladys heard big booms out in the countryside. This brought back memories of the booms during the Tet Offensive; but neither of the students seemed concerned so she just dismissed it as a regular event.

As a result of these studies, Mrs. Viet put on Christ in baptism. The Viets had one little girl. The mother said, "Now I hope that my little girl will grow up to be a Christian." At her baptism, when she came up out of the water, she said, "I am so happy." Mrs. Viet's husband had been baptized in the States.

Her husband's family owned several rice paddies and a farm with over 2,000 chickens, which made them well to do in Vietnam. Also, they grew mangoes, papaya, avocados, bananas, pineapple, and other fruit as well. They also had a large pond stocked with fish.

Her brother, Phan Viet Cuong, decided to put Christ on in baptism. Since Mrs. Viet had a part in bringing her brother to Christ, we called her our modern "Andrew." She found her brother's baptism to be deeply moving. Since both husband and wife and her brother had accepted Christ, we believed they had a better opportunity for remaining faithful.

Another baptism made us very happy when Nguyen Van Hieu baptized his brother, Phan Van Thuan, into Christ. Hieu had been a Christian for several years and had grown tremendously as he had prepared artistically designed charts explaining various aspects of Christian doctrine. Both of them showed their joy at this life-changing occasion.

Gary shares final impressions of the summer.

At the end of our four months, I asked Pat Peters and Gary Williams to give their final assessment of their mission activities. Here is Gary Williams' summary of his final impressions of the summer.

"'How do I begin to tell the story of how great a love can be?' So begins a favorite American song of the Vietnamese youth, and so also, with a little misplacing of context might we well explain our thoughts as we search for a way to summarize the four months of work in Vietnam. It is indeed a job. But since love is what made this trip feasible, let's remind ourselves that is also the only height from which any of the Lord's work may be properly viewed. Certainly if all the actions and all of the money which has been spent cannot be interpreted as the speech of the universal language of love, then the power of all of our efforts has been lost. And if the Burchams, Pat, and myself ever tried to recall the progress and the change that the Lord has brought to Vietnam without an equal emphasis on His love in the hearts of those of you who provided financial help, then we might do well to inspect our noisy gongs and clanging cymbals. Within this 'lovely' atmosphere, then, let me share some last reflections.

"The many opportunities to teach have continued to multiply as quickly as have our hopes. The church here is growing, and more and more of our time is spent in private Bible studies. Time is going much too fast, though, in many ways. If life is a vapor, our brief stay in Saigon has been but the rainbow of that vapor. My, but what bright colors we've seen!

"Patrick Peters–now affectionately called 'Petrick'–and the Burcham have written you much about our work here.

"Ralph Burcham is a man who can show more love in his dissatisfaction than most can communicate through praise. Refusing to speak in terms of weaknesses whenever good things can be found, he has, like Christ, a tremendous capacity for finding the best in anyone. His wife and he are no doubt fine examples of lives dedicated to spreading the love of Jesus. Are they paragons of sacrifice? I don't think so. As they themselves have well quoted, 'It is not sacrifice to do what you want to do.' Pat and I watched their love for the Vietnamese spread like salve to soothe many an embittered heart this summer . . .

"So be certain that your love has been accepted. The Good News of Christ stands in bold contrast to the common Eastern religions, and those who truly understand and accept it are joyously emancipated from what would have otherwise been a dark life of guilt and superstition.

"In the face of their country's sorrows, many Vietnamese are accepting this news for what it is–the best hope for any man's life.

And thus, as is always true, our increased understanding brings us the blessing of added responsibility–for can anything quite so strongly demand our search for love as our refreshed knowledge of His need? Let us continue to try to understand and aid these brothers from whom so much has been taken, so that, to the prayers and hopes of those whom we may never meet on earth, we will always add our own."

Gary always requested others to pray for his many students.

The Vietnam I will always remember by Patrick Peters.

Pat wrote: "It is hard to realize that almost four months have passed since we stepped off the plane into the Vietnamese sunshine for the first time. So many experiences have conglomerated to give us a new look at this 'third world' that it seems almost impossible for all of this to have taken place. Nevertheless, it is true that these busy weeks have passed.

"And now the summer ends. What can we possibly say that would describe adequately the things that have happened? Exciting? Educational? Spiritually uplifting? It is true that the summer has been all of these, but it has been so much more.

"Even if you are a statistics watcher (and I'm afraid we all are), you would be pleased at the fruit that is beginning to show itself. Baptisms are always a highlight, and there have been many of them. Also, there seems to be a new spirit of movement in the Vietnamese congregation. The combination of new members being added to the Lord's Body; and the obtaining of a new building, as the first permanent home of the congregation, has brought forth the realization of the active life that is available to those who are dedicated to God's work. I really feel as if a new hunger to teach the word of God has come to the Saigon congregation. I will talk mainly of the work of Gary Williams and myself.

"Still, by far, our number one project is the Bible classes that Gary and I are teaching. We started by teaching the Gospel of John in order to give our students a good idea of the character and person-ality of the man Jesus. Now that the summer is drawing to an end we have finished that study and have turned to a Bible Correspondence Course to carry us through until we leave. Actually, the whole course has worked together very well. Now that the students know Jesus, we are able to go into more depth about the whole realm of Christianity with them, and this works in very naturally with the correspondence course.

"Our classes have leveled off in attendance with about twelve or so in each class, with the exception of Gary's evening session which has as many as twenty-five. Although this is much reduced from the original numbers that we had, we are not too disappointed. We suspected that the number of people might fall as time went on. However, we are happy to observe that those remaining in class have, for the most part, shown more than just passing interest. We feel that there is a closeness developing among the students and even bridging the teacher-student gap. This feeling has enabled us to set up many individual studies with them. It is from these studies that we see the fruit being harvested.

"We must admit that we have had our disappointments. We sometimes think that a person is showing a real interest in the Bible, when suddenly we can see that the interest is really only in having a friend from America or an English Language tutor. Even with unfruitful times, though, we cannot help but rejoice in the interest that some of the students have shown. Because of them, our summer has been worthwhile.

"Some students are now leading a new life in Christ. Others are now realizing that they must either accept Jesus or reject him. This Christianity is a new element in the lives of many people, and as Christ always does, He is showing His power in the lives of those who follow Him. Many of these students have heard the truth of Christ for the first time this summer. We are very grateful to be the ones who brought these teachings to them.

"The Church in Saigon is now more alive and active. With the Spirit of God working among the Vietnamese congregation the way it is, we feel certain of their continued growth. Nine baptisms occurred during our last three days. Most of those are the result of the Vietnamese teaching their friends and families. This type of growth shows that the congregation can carry on without Americans ruling over them–a good sign to be sure.

"Each Sunday afternoon, we have been attending the worship service in Cho Lon, the Chinese section of Saigon. Ron and Jeanette Cotton have been working there for the past four years and have established quite a good young people's group. The Cottons are on furlough in the States so we are doing our part to fill in while they are gone. Gary and I have each given a lesson and also led them in many a song. They do so love to sing. It is a joy for us to be with the Cho Lon group. Before we leave Saigon both Gary and I will probably have a chance to bring them another lesson. They are so receptive to our lessons that we enjoy teaching them. It is a real pleasure to show them some more of the life-giving gospel.

"Sunday mornings have turned out to be yet another time for us to teach class. It was suggested that while we are here we could lead a class for the young people. We agreed, only to discover that it would be impractical to try to teach only one class and cover such a wide range of already established Biblical knowledge. Therefore, we divided the class into two groups–one American and one Vietnamese. The thought was that in the American section we could go at a faster pace because of the lack of a language barrier. Gary worked with the Vietnamese and I with the Americans. When many of the English-speaking children returned to the Philippines, we decided to divide the Vietnamese into two groups because they had grown beyond a workable size.

"Another project that occupied us this summer is the exercise program that we have been trying with Mr. Dat. Dat is the one who fell from a helicopter and was so badly injured. The doctors told us that the main thing he needed was to walk, so walk we did! At first we walked nearly every day with him but we gradually changed to about three times a week. Dat has developed a tremendous attitude about his recovery, and walks every day by himself. Although he still does not walk as quickly or easily as most people, it is plain that he is getting around much better. His mind is still lacking in many ways. The doctors tell us that it may improve but will definitely not deteriorate any more than it already has. We can see a dramatic difference in his actions, and even more important, in his attitudes. No longer does he doubt himself, but instead he is sure that he will someday be able to work and carry on his life like other people.

"Many tests have been run to find just what the whole problem is. We know that there was a certain amount of brain damage, but we did not know how much. We just learned that the brain had the fresh blood flow cut off. His body has naturally healed itself as much as it could (marvelous things, our bodies) by re-routing the blood into and out of his brain. The situation now is at a point that it will not get any worse and may improve with time. Even with that good news, though, we still have a problem. It is a must for his family to accept him back as a part of them. They have been treating him terribly, and therefore making it all the more difficult for him to recover. We will continue to pray for him.

"We have had many good experiences just going places and doing things in a recreational way with our students. I never knew there would be this sort of activity for us here. Gary and I went with one of our Chinese students one day to a skating rink. We were sore the next day from such a wild time. I would have a difficult time describing the way things were, but I can tell you that a cement floor and tie-on type skates are a little different than what we have in the good ole USA. Other activities included swimming, a movie (Vietnamese style), and a lot of time for just talking. All of these things just add to our impressions of our great experience this summer.

"Of course, many times it seemed impossible to see ahead, and, at such times, we found ourselves confused or even bewildered. But we know that we have planted the seed of truth of Jesus in the hearts of many people. Now let us pray and watch for the increase.

"It has been a rich experience for all of us. We are grateful to all the people that helped make the whole thing possible. But most of all we thank God for His guidance and help through this time. We have become all the more aware of the way Christ can work in the hearts of men, and of the power He gives us to work beyond our own capabilities. It is a grand thing to see Christianity functioning, as it should. This one fact shines out through the summer– CHRISTIANITY WORKS!

"In closing, I would like to say just a word about our general impressions of this country. Vietnam is a beautiful place. We are very lucky to be here working for our Lord. We have felt no danger in this adventure. I know that many of you have wondered just how safe we really are, and I can assure you that we are as safe as we would be in the United States. However, the days of peace in Saigon may be limited. We know that it may be several months, or even a year, but there will be more military trouble here. The enemy is building his force in readiness for an attack. It is, therefore, not us that you should be praying for, as much as it is for the people in the Vietnamese congregation. They may have some difficult times ahead, and therefore need our prayers and encouragement. The people, the climate, and the culture—all have given us a new and refreshing look at ourselves.

"Praise God for our freedom. His hand has truly granted America an added measure of His grace.

"I also want to add a word of thanks to the Burchams for their counsel and support. I have come to love them dearly and appreciate the wisdom they have gained as obedient children of God. Also, I thank Gary for his help. Together we have uncovered a world of experiences and discovered much about ourselves. Gary has been a real Brother to me, and I thank him for that.

"Pray for those that are in foreign countries teaching about God and His Son. Pray for all work, in and out of the United States, that is contributing to the Kingdom. But now remember the Vietnamese Brethren and what troubles they face. Pray for them."

Pat Peters and Gary Williams truly gave of themselves every day for each week in Vietnam. I cannot imagine anyone accomplishing more than they did. They built relationships with the Vietnamese and truly taught that salvation is for everyone who accepts Jesus Christ as Lord and Savior. I was so thankful God led us to these two fine young men, who truly gave of themselves twenty-four hours a day, seven days a week. After weeks of work, Pat and Gary were rewarded to see Mr. Dat walking by himself. What a tribute to the power of God working through Pat and Gary!

God be praised for the life of Pat and Gary and the way they gave of themselves for the cause of Christ in a very troubled land. God empowered all of us far beyond our abilities. God gave us endurance and encouragement throughout the summer. He, also, gave us a spirit of unity as we attempted to follow Christ Jesus. All of us prayed that our efforts brought glory to God and His Son.

A Vietnamese shares why this was an unforgettable summer.

I asked Tran Van Can, the minister of the Saigon Church of Christ, to give his impressions of the happenings in the congregation. He wrote:

"The summer of 1973 came and passed away leaving the Saigon Church of Christ with a series of historic records. When you turn on these records, you shall first hear resounding these words: 'Welcome to the Burchams!' 'Welcome to Pat Peters!' ' Welcome to Gary Williams!'

"As one of the closest collaborators of the Burchams during this summer, I played the role of recorder to broadcast the wonderful things they did.

"On April 21, the Burchams, Pat Peters, and Gary Williams, arrived in Tan Son Nhut International Airport. A number of Vietnamese and American Christians were ready to receive them. After exchanges of warmest greetings and joyful chats, we left the airport passengers' hall.

"The following day was Sunday. Burcham preached, and Pat Peters led the singing in the morning worship which was followed by a reception party organized by the Vietnamese brethren to welcome the Burchams, their long-known missionaries, Pat Peters, and Gary Williams, two students from Oklahoma Christian who were sent for mission apprenticeship work with the Saigon Church of Christ.

"Burcham began his mission work with visiting the Vietnamese brethren, writing letters greeting the students who were best friends of the International Mission; those taught by the 10th and Broad Congregation in Wichita Falls, Texas; and the students, while studying in the States, who visited the Pen Woods family in Oklahoma City. So to say the least, in the first week the Burchams were busy with a crowded schedule: visits, greetings, preaching, letter writing, and receptions.

"In response to his letters, a number of students paid visits to him and had individual Bible study sessions with him.

"Pat Peters and Gary Williams too were busy with their Conversational English Bible study classes for non-Christian students every day. These resulted in several baptisms.

"The most striking thing Burcham did this summer was to help the Saigon Church conclude the purchase of a fine building for its permanent meeting place. The members of the church here had so long wished for this purchase. They all, therefore, feel very much indebted to the churches and brethren in the States for the funds contributed for this purpose.

"The building consists of a ground floor and one upper floor. The upper floor is used for the auditorium, whereas the ground floor is divided into two rooms. One is furnished for a reading room, and the other for an office. The back kitchen is transformed into a book storage area in which a very beautiful baptistry has been constructed.

"The opening day of this new building began on July 1 with a public reception party which was followed by a week of lectureship-workshop for members and friends of the church on the initiative of Burcham. This lectureship-workshop week brought great encouragement to the attendants to the point that a number of them volunteered to participate in various programs of action set forth during the lectureship-workshop.

"Another remarkable job the Burchams did was to relieve the war wounded who were given medical care at hospitals. On an agreement with Brigadier General Do Ke Giai, Commander-in-Chief of the Rangers, a church delegation headed by Burcham made an official visit to the Tran Ngoc Minh Military Hospital. On our arrival, the Colonel Director of the hospital in his office greeted us. About 15 minutes later the Brigadier came. After shaking hands and a brief introduction of the delegation by the Colonel to the Brigadier General and his staff, we left for the meeting hall of the hospital where many wounded rangers were ready to receive us.

"After the Director of the hospital had presented the delegation and expressed thanks to the delegation, an Evangelist of the church took the chair and declared the Gospel of Christ to the audience. Then a Bible and a kit of gifts were distributed to each Ranger. After that, we went to the Cong Hoa military hospital where the same gifts were presented to the crippled and blind Rangers.

"Among other benevolent deeds performed by the Burchams is the case of Nguyen Van Khanh, who underwent lung surgery and was restored to his normal health.

"Then Mrs. Khanh, a fervent Buddhist, seeing this benevolent deed in favor of her husband, said that she felt deeply impressed with Christian love in the Burchams and that she was willing to study Christianity. After some Bible study sessions with Burcham, she made up her mind to accept Jesus and receive baptism.

"A number of other members of the church and unbelievers enjoyed the same kind of help from the Burchams.

"On the spiritual realm, Burcham helped the Saigon congregation set up everything in order scripturally. He also financed the printing of several religious books and pamphlets including *Nichol's Pocket Bible Encyclopedia*; all of these have been translated into Vietnamese.

"The printing cost for these publications amounted to nearly one million piastres.

"The Burchams did other odd jobs which were very helpful to the church and to individual Christians. This resulted in nine baptisms by him.

"Dear brethren, I believe that the above records provide you enough information on the great work the Burchams did for the Vietnam Church of Christ during their 1973 summer mission efforts in Saigon.

"Now let me close this report with my expression of hearty thanks and deepest appreciation to the Burchams, Pat Peters, and Gary Williams for all that they did to help build the Vietnam Church of Christ in Saigon. I also feel grateful to all the Churches of Christ and Christians in the States for their financial contributions to the mission work that was achieved by the Burchams during the summer of 1973. This is an unforgettable summer for all the Vietnamese brethren here and me. Sincerely in Christian Service and Love, Tran Van Can, Minister"

The Vietnam effort viewed from our woman missionary..

Gladys expressed in her journal some of the events about the summer that made it unusual: "Here we are in our last week in Saigon, and we are having problems just wandering what needs are the most urgent. Night seems to come too soon each day with jobs left undone.

"I had my last study with Mr. Cuong on Monday. He had requested that on the last day I give him a summary and explanation of the entire New Testament. Now how do you do that in one hour? I tried and left him some books to study. Before I left their home, Mrs. Viet, her husband, Mr. Nhat, and Mr. Cuong presented me with a beautiful gift.

"The gifts are getting embarrassing. Two families have given us something that they hand carried from Hanoi in 1954. One is a family heirloom that has been in the family for three generations. We couldn't turn it down but felt bad about taking it. Another brought two small plates, and this friend spent time apologizing because she couldn't give me something valuable. The plates are over fifty years old and represent the best of Chinese art. And she wanted to give me something valuable!

"We had no trouble getting our exit visas. After spending all summer getting an extension of stay then taking only six days to acquire exit visas, how do you suppose we felt? Ralph has a good story about that concerning a handful of papers he had to take to the police station to get notarized. As Brother Tran says, 'That's just customary.'

"We stay busy but Pat and Gary do have their diversions. We were all four downtown the other night; and when we were ready to come home, Gary said, 'Pat, I'll run you a race home with you taking the pedicab.' You should have seen those two scoot. Ralph and I took a taxi and Gary beat us home. Don't know how anyone could pedal that fast. The last time I looked at the pedicab driver, he was wiping the sweat from his neck and face. But it was such worthwhile fun that the boys paid him well–200 piastres. I told them the driver probably didn't even work the next day.

"Every mission field has its talent. You know that Paul was a tent maker; well, we have our roofers here.

"We live on the first floor of a four-story building with a flat roof. Adjoining our building is a two story house and above that a slanted tile roof. Gary purchased a one-string fiddle. He decided to have Pat take his picture on the tile roof, posing as "Fiddler on the Roof."

"After taking the picture, Gary had the problem of getting back up on the roof of the taller building. He jumped and jumped trying to grasp the wall above him; then he could hear some of the tile crack. Finally, Pat put down a garden hose and pulled Gary up to the roof.

"Their problem: what to do about the cracked tile! They were afraid to tell Ralph so they went searching for tile and cement to repair the crack. In fact, the homeowners never knew they got some new shingles! Gary probably should never have invested in that coconut one-string instrument. But everyone needs some culture!

"When the boys started their classes, Tran told them of the five types of students that had enrolled; he warned them to be careful. He classed them as Viet Cong, Government agents, loose girls, anti-Americans, and pro-Americans. The boys were never able really to distinguish some, but you can guess the ones who weren't hard to spot! But now that their classes are over, I believe they would say that the majority were the 'good guys.'

"The summer has been great. We have had much joy in seeing students give their lives to Christ. Much seed has been planted, and we believe that 'God is able.'

"What an enriching experience in taking the Gospel to the Vietnamese. We four have grown to love each other very much."

Vietnam–What does the future hold?

The question that I kept pondering during spare moments: "What does the future hold for the Vietnamese people I have come to love?" I kept thinking of what one of my dear friends said when I posed this question to him. Nguyen Dang Minh said, "It depends entirely on American policy."

At first, this gave me comfort because America has a long history of staying by its friends. Then I recalled the protests on the streets back home, a Congress divided over this issue, the American troops that had moved out earlier in the year, and the U. S. cuts in spending on Vietnam.

Yet, after the American troops returned home, the South Vietnamese military won some major battles on their own. However, the North Vietnamese received both financial aid and materiels from China and Russia. Will the South Vietnamese be able to withstand the better support of the Communist North?

Over and over the Vietnamese, who had once lived in the North, shared with me stories indicating the Communists to be masters of terror. Truly the Vietnamese people have been terrorized and victimized for over 30 years.

South Vietnam had become a political football and the Vietnamese people fear–after all the years of blood, sweat, and tears–they would be sold out to the Communists. They have paid, and continue to pay, a very high price in their struggle for freedom. There have been hundreds of thousands of casualties and deaths in that war. Men, women, and children would live out their lives with permanent disabilities–blind, crippled, or horribly disfigured.

The evils of war affect every aspect of a society. Corruption remained rampant in Vietnam; but before we become too critical, let us not forget the thousands of Vietnamese women, enticed by the American GI's money, who gave themselves to prostitution. At one time according to the statistics kept by one serviceman's office, the VD rate exceeded several thousand new cases each month.

Probably one of the most heart wrenching sights in Saigon was to walk down one of the lanes and see the child who had a foreign father. One time I saw a group of children at play and in their midst a little boy played who had bright red hair, freckles, and blue eyes in the middle of Vietnamese children with black hair and dark brown eyes. It broke my heart to see this red-haired lad's failure to be accepted by the group. While being bullied, I could see this child was an outcast from the telltale expression of his sad blue eyes and wrinkled brow. Though I am sure he had encountered this over and over again, the ridicule struck the notes of his sensitive heart, and with bowed head and tears streaming down his cheeks, he ran back to the sanctity of the little shack where he must have lived. Though I never saw his mother, I am sure that she, too, suffered from the glaring stares of her fellow countrymen.

Pat Peters had in his Bible class a Nun who worked at an orphanage. She persuaded Pat to visit the orphanage, where scores of children lived. She tried to persuade Pat to adopt one of the children. I can just visualize Pat's astonished look of disbelief. Many unwed mothers gave their children away; yet many others lived in orphanages in Vietnam. What does the future hold for those unwed mothers and the children with deserted fathers?

When I looked at all the problems facing the Vietnamese, I kept asking, "Is there no hope?"

But I am thankful that God continues to work in Vietnam!

Though corruption, immorality, and idolatry remained rampant in Vietnam, I am thankful God's love still works here.

As Christians, we sought to see the spiritual dimension of a situation where we could bring God, His Word, and His Church into the picture. While a loving God did not willingly design the suffering of men, yet amid the unavoidable consequences of man's rebellion, God often overrules so that men may come to a realization of their need for Him and thus turn bitter retribution into opportunities for men to seek God.

Let us always be thankful and grateful for the American Christian servicemen who started the mission in Vietnam. They were the ones who sent out the call for others to come to Vietnam. Maurice and Marie Hall heeded that call and inspired many others to participate in the proclamation of the Good News of a Savior to the Vietnamese.

My family and I served the cause of Christ in Vietnam from August 1966, until the Tet Offensive of 1968, when we had to leave because of the war in Saigon. In the summer of 1969, I returned to Vietnam for additional follow-up work and to assist a new missionary family. My wife and I along with Pat and Gary returned to Saigon in April 1973, and served until mid-August.

As we looked back, we see that God was at work there. Because of the upheaval in society that war brings, many of the Vietnamese had abandoned ancient traditions, such as ancestry worship. Many saw the emptiness of idol worship. Everyone seemed to be searching for meaning to life and longing for some assurance of what lies beyond the grave.

The Vietnamese have inquisitive minds that longed for knowledge of our world and other religions. Truly God prepared this people for the reception of His Good News of salvation and eternal life available to all who accept and live for Christ.

Through God's work in Vietnam that summer, twenty souls were brought into a right relationship by the acceptance of Christ through repentance and baptism. In addition, a number of unfaithful members returned to their first love.

Pat Peters, Gary Williams, Gladys, and I conducted many individual and group Bible studies. We firmly believed that the seed had been planted in hearts that would eventually bring additional fruit for the Lord.

We felt the Saigon congregation was better organized for its great mission in Vietnam. Until elders and deacons could be appointed, the congregation would operate through the men's business meeting. Committees were selected for various areas of work; however, each committee had no authority within itself and would be responsible to all the men. The legal authorization for the church with the Vietnamese Government now carried only the names of nationals.

The men of the congregation selected Vo Thanh Duc to serve as their regular evangelist. Duc's unusual capabilities would serve the congregation well. He was extremely well read, an effective writer and preacher, and graduated with highest honors from the Philippine Bible College. In addition, he was a most capable song leader. He had a very dedicated wife, who served as a Bible schoolteacher; and they had three lovely children.

Tran Van Can faithfully served the congregation for a number of years. He served on a full-time basis as a personal evangelist. He spent much time visiting in homes to encourage the members and taught home Bible studies. He would supervise the Reading Room at the church. In addition, he promoted the Bible Correspondence Course and supervised the grading and follow-up work.

Nguyen Dan Bao, also a graduate from the Philippine Bible College, was another dedicated worker. He did effective mission work at Bien Hoa but had to leave that effort when the servicemen moved out and he lost his support. Even though he worked full-time in one of Saigon's banks, he spent time teaching home Bible studies and classes at the church.

The English-speaking people moved to another location. This would allow the Vietnamese leadership to develop in a more natural way.

As already indicated, a permanent building was purchased and completely redecorated. The reading room on the ground floor contained a very fine reference library in English; also, it had copies of commentaries and other books that had been translated into Vietnamese. The Vietnamese had the right to be proud of their new building.

The church purchased a new Honda motorcycle to be used by the church in its visitation program and for transportation to home Bible studies.

Several books and tracts were translated and printed in Vietnamese. More were to be printed as funds became available.

As a part of our outreach to the people, our benevolent work included the provisions for medical care for many. Certainly physical life for many was improved or prolonged through this special medical aid.

Hundreds of families now had their first copy of the Word of God. This program of giving Bibles was to continue as long as funds became available. When a radio program started in the provinces, free Bibles would be made available to those who took the Bible Correspondence Course. Each Bible contained a special insert that was an introduction to the Bible with a challenge to read it and an outline with Scripture references for the major doctrines of Christianity. It also had the address of the Saigon church and offered a free Bible Correspondence Course.

Yes, everywhere we turned we could see God at work. Through the generous contributions of hundreds of churches and Christians, this work became possible. God's Son had been and would continue to be proclaimed. Our prayer was that God would save this land from slavery, atheism, further bloodshed, and death.

We helped the Vietnamese catch a vision of their potential.

In visiting with Vietnamese about using their talents for the Lord, I encouraged Vo Thanh Duc to do more preaching and writing. He wrote two very fine tracts based on the needs of the people in this war-torn country.

His first tract was entitled *"The Vietnamese and God."* He developed this tract around the common beliefs among the people concerning their general belief in a supreme being or beings. Then he pointed out the characteristics of the true and living God. His approach reminded me very much of Paul's discussion of "the unknown God" in Athens in the First Century.

He entitled his second tract "Liberation." He said, "There are not many of us who do not feel deeply the need of liberation or salvation. We feel this need because we have within ourselves conflicts that we find impossible to bring into harmony. We praise *love* but we are filled with *hatred*. We love *purity*; but if we are honest with ourselves, we will not be proud of our 'purity.' We want to *transcend*, but we are degraded.

"The weaknesses and decay of the body we temporarily accept as established fact for which we are not responsible. But spiritual depression keeps us constantly restless and frustrated. For we know we are responsible for this fall. We, therefore, condemn and despise ourselves. Since we know that we are guilty and contemptible, all of us try to make for ourselves a facade, a mask, and want to be known by this facade or mask. We, at the same time, are fearful that people may discover our real person behind this artificial cover. On the other hand, we do our best to escape from this tragic conflict. Tragically, the more we try the more we sharply and despairingly feel the unconquerable power which gives us no chance to transcend ourselves and to do what we know we ought. From this sense of helplessness and despair, we acutely feel the need of deliverance . . .

"Liberation, therefore, has the concern of man and especially of religion." Then Duc showed how Jesus Christ helps man out of this dilemma. His extremely well written tract would serve the church in a good way.

Tran Van Can possessed intellectual qualities that would inspire many in the Reading Room. My prayer was that God would use these men in preaching, radio ministry, and in writing effective materials that would address the needs of the Vietnamese people.

What a sad farewell to our beloved Vietnamese church family.

Sunday, August 12, found us up early packing and making final arrangements. For our final worship service, the auditorium had a capacity crowd. So many good-byes and tears challenged our emotions. We tried to reassure everyone that in two years we would be coming back if the Lord allowed.

Duc and Bich took us out for lunch. From the moment we got back to our apartment, many more came to say good-bye. Even the taxi driver Gladys had used all summer came all dressed up to wish us well.

Gladys, Pat, Gary, and I had given of ourselves spiritually, physically, and emotionally to the effort to reach souls for Christ. All of us felt completely drained. We received so many gifts that it became embarrassing. Gladys had to go downtown to purchase an extra suitcase just for the gifts.

Then Pat and Gary came in with a big wrapped box and said, "This is for you." When Gladys went to pick it up it weighed so much, she almost dropped it. She said: "I'm sorry there is not room for one more thing." To which, both boys bent over with laughter. Inside the wrapped box, they had placed some bricks. How good to have a brief moment of levity at just the right moment.

When time came for us to head to the airport, the Captain, we had come to love from the military hospital, escorted us with his jeep out to the airport. Several of the Christians obtained passes and climbed into a flat bed truck to follow us.

After piling out of the truck, they held a devotion that touched us deeply. Our flight had been delayed for two hours, but after several more hugs and tears, we excused ourselves to go through customs.

Gladys went ahead of me. As Security checked her carry on, he picked up her camera and said: "Lady, is this a radio?"

I could hear her frustration with her "Yes."

With a somewhat amused look, he replied: "Lady, it looks like a camera to me."

Then he pulled out my shaving kit, which she was carrying, opened it and took out a jar of salt that I used for gargling. With a somewhat stern expression, asked, "Lady, what is this?"

By this time, Gladys flushed as she said, "It is salt."

He replied, "Lady, do you know what it looks like?"

Meekly, she replied: "It just looks like salt to me."

Seemingly exasperated, he responded, "Lady, this looks like cocaine!"

To this she replied, "Why don't you just taste it!" He laughed and let us on through. After this, we all felt a sense of relief.

Then I had to go to the bathroom; I paid the attendant, a lady, one of my last coins. When I went to zip up my trousers, the zipper stuck and I tried and tried to get it to work. Being in the bathroom so long, Gladys sent Gary in to see if I had a problem.

He didn't have a coin and had to do some tall talking to get the attendant to let him go in. When I told Gary my problem, I said: "Take these trousers out to Gladys and see if she can fix this zipper."

Gary obeyed. He paraded the trousers as he went through the large international waiting room and plopped them in Gladys' lap. Gladys worked and worked on the zipper to no avail. She had a safety pin and gave it to Gary and said "take this back to Pa." By this time, Pat and Gary were having a heyday of laughter.

The attendant insisted they pay. Then Gary gave her my trousers and asked her to take them in. At this, she let them both come to my rescue.

Finally, it came time to board our plane for Bangkok. We enjoyed our smooth flight out of Saigon in contrast to our flight out during the Tet Offensive.

I prayed for God to allow us to return to Saigon in 1975.

Weighing heavily on my heart: "Would we be able to return in 1975?" Only God knew what the future held for Vietnam.

There was stepped-up fighting all across the country. The Communists had control of large areas of the countryside. In addition, the North Vietnamese moved in large numbers of women into South Vietnam to live with Communist soldiers for procreation. Atheistic Communism used its citizens to accomplish its purposes as any other animal might be used. They willingly used any means to bring about a desired end, as they subscribed to no real moral standards.

The Communists take the weaknesses of human nature, and the deviations from morality, and fashion them into a flexible standard. They had done as some did in Isaiah's time. They called good evil and evil good; they put light for darkness and darkness for light. (Isaiah 5:20-21) The Communists started bringing into the South large quantities of war materiels and more sophisticated equipment.

Deterrents to Communism are freedom and the message of Christ. The most significant impact on a society comes by changing the heart of men and women one at a time into the likeness of Christ. Christ frees men and women from slavery to self and passions; Communism enslaves the heart, body, mind, and soul.

In a very real sense, the future of Vietnam was in the hands of Christians. What resources would we be willing to give in the battle for souls? Would Communism or Christianity control Vietnam?

As I reflected on how God had worked so mightily with the four of us, I offered a prayer of thanksgiving and prayed that God would allow us to return in two years. God blessed our feeble efforts beyond my wildest imagination. Souls now belonged to Christ. Many received copies of God's Word and spent hours studying it. Several enjoyed better health because of aid given. The church was better organization and members enjoyed their own building. The opportunities to further the work gave me a new vision of the possibilities. But the credit and the glory belonged to the God who gives endurance and encouragement through His Son, His Word, and His Holy Spirit. Our team enjoyed a spirit of unity, which God gives to those following Christ Jesus.

The Tragedy of South Vietnam

" . . . I thank my God through Jesus Christ for all of you, because your faith is being reported all over the world. God, whom I serve with my whole heart in preaching the gospel of his Son, is my witness how constantly I remember you in my prayers at all times; and I pray that now at last by God's will the way may be opened for me to come to you."
(Romans 1:8-10,NIV)

Most of 1974 and the early part of 1975 kept us in prayer and plans for returning to Vietnam. Planning occupied our time for a four-month evangelistic campaign. We recruited four Bible majors from Oklahoma Christian to join us in the work–Tim Denton, Joe Gray, Jeff Hasseltine, and Gary Williams. We studied diligently in our preparation for four months of missionary activity. Funds raised, shots taken, passports received, and applications for visas waited for final approval.

We kept up correspondence with our brethren and friends in Vietnam. The members of the Saigon congregation continued to make strides in building up the members, in developing the Bible school, and in outreach activities. After the adoption of a campaign strategy, both American and Vietnamese Christians worked hard in preparation for this period of evangelism.

In February, 1975, Vo Thanh Duc, the Saigon minister, wrote about those plans; he concluded by saying: "Please work harder for the cause of Christ here . . . The political future of our country is in total darkness. We may have very little time to work for the Lord. Please help us to do what we can while we have the opportunity."

As Christians, we sought to see the spiritual dimension of a situation where we could bring God, His Word, and His Church into the picture. While a loving God did not willingly design the suffering of men, yet amid the unavoidable consequences of man's rebellion, He often overruled so that men may come to a realization of their need for Him and, thus, turns bitter retribution into opportunities for men to seek God.

As we look back, we see that God had been at work in Vietnam in a powerful way. Because of the upheaval in society that war brings, many of the Vietnamese had abandoned some of the ancient traditions, such as the religion of ancestors. Slowly, many saw the emptiness of idol worship. Consequently, we found opportunities with those searching for meaning to life and longing for assurance of what lies beyond the grave. The Vietnamese possess intelligent and inquisitive minds that longed for knowledge of our world and other religions. Truly God had opened the minds of this people for the reception of His Good News of salvation and eternal life available to all who accept and live for Christ.

The Vietnamese Christians worked hard in promoting the Bible Correspondence Course under the direction of Tran Van Can. He reported, "There are over 2,500 active students." In addition, the Vietnamese had translated a new 20-lesson Bible Correspondence Course and other materials that would be printed before the campaign.

From our past experiences in Vietnam, our eyes were not blind to sins' destructive nature. Though corruption, immorality, and idolatry remained rampant in Vietnam, God continued to work there.

Since our last work in Vietnam in 1973, the Saigon congregation worked on improving its organization for its great mission. Until elders and deacons could be appointed, the congregation continued to operate effectively through the men's business meeting. The men selected Vo Thanh Duc to serve as their regular evangelist; he had earned his degree from the Philippine Bible College.

Tran Van Can faithfully served the congregation for a number of years; he served as a full-time personal evangelist, made visits to homes to encourage and teach, supervised the reading room, and promoted the Bible correspondence course. Nguyen Dan Bao, also a graduate of the Philippine Bible College, served as a very dedicated worker; God blessed Bao and his wife Ruth with talents to work with children and youth. Bao started the congregation in Bien Hoa.

God led me to many Vietnamese for whom I developed a close relationship and had a part in leading many to accept Jesus Christ as their Savior. Each added a special dimension to my life.

Many lived in North Vietnam until 1954. They voted with their feet by becoming refugees and leaving behind most of their possessions. But South Vietnam became a political football and I found the Vietnamese people to be fearful–after all the years of blood, sweat, and tears–they would be sold out to the communists. The Vietnamese had suffered hundreds of thousands of casualties and deaths from this war. Men, women, and children will live out their lives with permanent disabilities–blind, crippled, or horribly disfigured.

Because of Bibles distributed to students in our Bible classes and to Special Forces Soldiers, while hospitalized, hundreds of families had their first copy of the Word of God. From our early experiences, we knew that just giving a Bible to be almost meaningless unless they had a guide. Therefore, we included a copy of "Introduction to the Bible" to help the reader to know something of the book's organization and how to find key passages.

Yes, God continued to work in Vietnam. God's Son had been and would continue to be proclaimed. Our fervent prayer continued to be that God would save this land from slavery, atheism, further bloodshed, and death.

By late 1974 and early 1975, all personal reports from Vietnam and from the media–television, magazines, and newspapers–indicated stepped up fighting all across the country.

I felt the war in Vietnam had ended for Americans but not so for the Vietnamese. This year alone there were over three times the number of casualties and deaths than Americans suffered during all the years of our involvement. Refugees streamed into temporary camps leaving most of their earthly goods behind for the communists to loot. Could anything be done to alleviate the tragedy experienced by these refugees? What about the war wounded?

According to the September 30, 1974, issue of the *U. S. News and World Report*, the number killed by the war that year alone would exceed 158,000. It was too late to help these.

In addition to those killed, the war wounded poured into military hospitals in great numbers. The above article pointed out that over 31,000 war-wounded remained in hospitals. From visits we made in 1973, this meant that wards and corridors were jammed with suffering humanity.

Yet, the Lord works in every nation preparing people for the gospel; but God did not cause this suffering; yet, He uses what man causes to bring people to Him. The door seemed to be open for us to teach the gospel to the victims of that war.

What about the war victims?
What is being done and what needed to be done?

American Christians provided two men with wheel chairs. This was just the beginning as I had seen wards of paraplegics filled with men who would never again walk. Some of those could gain some mobility with the aid of a wheel chair. Scores of patients needed wheel chairs but could not be provided for lack of funds.

The degree of paralysis differed for each man. With proper surgery and therapy, many might regain partial use of their limbs. All of these men had one thing in common–time that weighed heavily with little to do. Bibles, Bible Correspondence Courses, and Christian literature had been provided to some.

Into this vacuum, many were able to read the Bible for the first time in their lives as we gave away thousands of Bibles and copies of the Bible Correspondence Course. Even some of the orderlies who worked with patients had enrolled and completed that course. Through the generosity of American Christians and servicemen, thousands of Bibles were put into the hands of those who had time to read and study God's Word.

A man is not helped very much if only given physical aid, but the emphasis of our Vietnamese brethren was to provide spiritual help. During the past few months, 12 had been baptized into Christ, which demonstrated the effectiveness of that work in hospitals.

The Vietnamese Christians supplied clothing and mats for refugees and families of the war wounded. One Christian in Nashville had collected and shipped large quantities of good used clothing. Vietnamese Christians in refugee camps near Saigon distributed that.

In every way, our plans seemed to be moving forward for a four-month evangelistic campaign for the coming summer.

My big concern: "Because the communists had stepped up their campaign, should we go?"

By late 1974, the communists were in control of large areas of the countryside. The question foremost in my mind: "Was it possible for the communists to take control of all of South Vietnam?" When the Americans pulled out, they left large quantities of equipment and war materiels with the Vietnamese. Because of the anti-war demonstrations and the weariness from huge losses suffered by Americans, funding had been drastically cut. The South Vietnamese had won some major battles after the American pullout; however, without funding for bullets and ammo there seemed little hope for their long-range success. China and Russia continued to pump funding and supplies into North Vietnam.

President Ford asked Congress for nearly $1 billion in emergency military and economic aid for South Vietnam. He also requested clear authority to use U. S. military forces to evacuate Americans and endangered South Vietnamese, if necessary. Members of Congress, however, reacted strongly against Ford's military aid requests.

Ford requested humanitarian aid to "ease the misery and pain of the monumental human crisis which has befallen the people of Vietnam." Ford also asked for a "prompt revision of the law to cover those Vietnamese to whom we have a special obligation and whose lives may be endangered, should the worst come to pass." The best estimates indicated about 200,000 South Vietnamese fell into this category.

The communists became more aggressive as they learned the American Congress would no longer provide economic and military aid to the South Vietnamese Government. With North Vietnam's war capabilities increasing with greater economic and military aid from the communist block, the South panicked with the realization they could not hold all of their territory with the superior power of the communist forces.

Tran Van Can wrote: "The economic condition here is collapsing terribly . . . The possibility of a general offensive is predicted . . . The military situation is really critical . . . If the VC succeed in occupying some strategic provinces on the Vietnam-Cambodia border, they might push ahead their offensives toward the Capital City.

"We don't know what the will of God is on our plan for His work in a country at war. The danger of destruction is near to us every minute, every hour, and every day . . . We know only one thing: that is to fulfill our duty in the state where we are called towards the lost souls of our Lord."

As the war-clouds darkened, Tran wrote: "Please kindly remember us in your daily prayers that in all circumstances we may stand faithful to Christ and will have no fear of giving up our lives for Christ's sake."

As the communist forces increased their pressure on the northern provinces, refugees started moving southward to escape the enslavement of their bodies, minds, and souls. Many of the South Vietnamese had experienced communism first hand prior to 1954 when they lived in the North. For those who once lived in the North, the fears of a communist take-over recalled their previous experiences with this inhumane and godless form of government; most had left everything behind to start a new life in the South.

While the communists seemed to be increasing their efforts in the South, we decided it necessary to re-evaluate our plans to go. Then our Vietnamese Christians started sending us letters asking for our help in a different way.

As the communists swept across South Vietnam and the northern provinces began to fall, it became clear on the evening news that opposition for further aid might be stymied in the Congress. Therefore, our Christian friends made an urgent appeal for help for the masses of refugees crowding into Saigon. They needed help in providing spiritual and physical aid to all of these refugees.

Appeals for help went out to our many Christian friends!

The tragedy in Vietnam seemed to increase day by day. Truly, Vietnam had become a sea of suffering humanity. The communists had driven millions from their homes; the refugees had no place to live, and no means of sustaining their livelihood. Into this dilemma the Christians of the Saigon Church determined to become a mission of mercy for the refugees pouring into the city.

Tran Van Can, the minister of personal work, described the work by church members to help the refugees pouring into Saigon trying to escape the bondage of communist slavery. He described the morale of the refugees: "They are panic-stricken, fearful, down-spirited, and losing confidence . . . The people show their fear concerning the coming offensive in Saigon. In my opinion, based on the information obtained from the escapees from fallen areas, when the offensive comes to Saigon, it shall be the doomsday for the Saigonese. You will not have a chance to come and see your friends and dear brethren in South Vietnam. We shall surely quit this cursed earthly home."

Tran's letter moved me deeply. Yet, it brought encouragement because, in spite of the impending doom that hung over their heads, the Vietnamese Christians made the decision to do what they could to be God's light in a dark world of pain and death. They established a camp to care for up to 100 refugee families.

Bill Estep, a Christian on a special assignment to Vietnam by the U. S. Government, wrote: "If this effort to help refugees is to be successful, it must be fast and we can use every dime you can get from the people at home. As the refugees arrive in Saigon, they are hungry, homeless, penniless, and jobless–with no jobs to be found. They need help now. It breaks my heart to see a group of little boys, not much older than my five-year old granddaughter, sleeping on the sidewalk in front of my apartment complex. There is plenty of volunteer help on this end. We need rice to feed the refugees."

On behalf of this effort by Vietnamese Christians, Vo Thanh Duc wrote: "Please help the brethren in the U. S. to see that this might well be the last opportunity for them to help Vietnam. I do believe that the communists will take over South Vietnam very soon. Perhaps, before any funds can arrive. There is no time to be lost."

In early March, I wrote to Bill about our plans to return with a series of questions for his assessment: "Your help is really needed in evaluating the situation there. As you know, it would be a poor stewardship of funds if we arrived in Saigon unable to do any mission work . . . We were scheduled to leave on April 19 and would arrive in Saigon on Monday, April 21. Do you feel the present situation in Saigon will reduce the number of students who will study with us? How will the Vietnam Government's compulsory conscription of men affect our numbers?"

Bill replied: "The present situation will affect the number of students who will study with you. The police for use in the army are presently picking up men. I believe all able bodied men will be fighting before long."

Another question: "How has the loss of several provinces affected the morale of the people?"

To which Bill replied: "I'll try to answer this one from the military side. The morale of the Vietnamese officers I work with is to fight for freedom. I know they are discouraged by the setback they have experienced but they have the guts to fight to the finish. The civilian side is looking to the U. S. for aid. They hear of aid being supplied North Vietnam by China and you know this must be very discouraging."

Then we got an official request from our fellow Christians in Vietnam; they did not feel it wise for us to return. Bill Estep wrote: "It is very discouraging to see the defeat of a wonderful and brave nation of people that I have come to love very much.

"Vo Thanh Duc (who was the minister of the Saigon Church) loves you very deeply and has planned for most a year as to how he can spend most of his time with you while you are here. He is very concerned about you and the groups' safety. He feels that if he must die, he doesn't want you to die with him. The Christians here are very wonderful people."

Estep included a letter from the congregation, which read: "This is coming to you while South Vietnam is passing through the darkest hours in her history. On behalf of the Christians in this part of the world, may we ask that you will specially pray for our country?

"As you may know, thousands of innocent and defenseless civilians, including women and children, have been killed recently while millions of others are mentally and physically suffering in countless refugee centers. They have lost everything, including lives of their loved ones. They are living in terror, in agony, and in want. In the name of Christ, we would like to ask that you would open your hearts generously to help relieve the pain and suffering of these victims." As I read their appeal, tears flowed and I felt I had to do something.

Then in late March, I received this letter from Vo Thanh Duc: "Brother and Sister Burcham, I know that you are very anxious to come. I know your courage, your devotion, and your love. However, I do believe that you would be more helpful to Vietnam by being there rather than here under the present situation. Nevertheless, the decision is yours to make. I do pray that you will make the right one."

Therefore, we decided not to return to Vietnam; but we determined to assist the Vietnamese Christians in raising funds to alleviate the terrible conditions of the refugees. The Vietnamese Christians set a goal of caring for 100 refugee families. They obtained volunteers, which included doctors and nurses, to assist in this work. With their benevolent work, they developed plans for evangelism. I agreed to try to raise funds for food, clothing, and medicine to relieve the suffering of the thousands of panic-stricken refugees flooding into Saigon.

I thanked God for their desire to serve in spite of the impending doom that hung over their heads. A sense of gratitude and appreciation welled up within me because the Vietnamese Christians did what they could to be God's light in a dark world of war, pain, and death.

We received many letters from Christians asking us to increase our prayers on their behalf. Most felt the Church of Christ faced its final hour in Vietnam as the communist forces moved in on Saigon.

Being deeply moved by their pleas for help in preventing the greatest bloodbath of the war, I prayed for direction on what I could do.

Why fear communism?

The communists were masters of terror. The communists murdered, kidnapped, and terrorized thousands of South Vietnamese. All who once lived in the North lived with the threat of reprisals if the communists gained control of the South.

I remember conversations with Nguyen Van Khanh and Tran Van Can about what they had experienced under communism before they fled the North in 1954. I felt deeply touched by the way Tran could see the parallel with why he fled from Hanoi and the present situation: "South Vietnam is my last refuge–there is no place for me to go. When the communists move into your area, there is *no place to hide.* Now we must take our stand here in the South." The North Vietnamese communists threatened that when they take over the South the first to be executed would be those who left the North in 1954. How I prayed that this would never happen.

Almost before the ink dried on the 1954 Geneva Treaty, the communists from the North started infiltrating the South and helped in organizing the Viet Cong. The Viet Cong murdered and terrorized thousands of South Vietnamese. Some rural Vietnamese were "executed" for teaching neighbors to read and write. Along with a number of women and children, the Viet Cong terrorists by 1966 had killed more than 60,000 provincial, district, and local government officials and workers, noncombatants all.

Other thousands were kidnapped to unknown fates. Pauline Lau and her daughter Susan, members of the Saigon church, could give personal testimony to the anguish that came when their husband and father had been kidnapped to an unknown fate. The VC kidnapped Mr. Lau in early 1967; the VC sent them an exorbitant ransom note for which they could not pay, and he had not been heard from since. At one time the Lau's possessed great wealth; they owned a shipping company and a hotel that the military used as a billet. Yet, they did not have enough to pay the ransom. I sought the help of the CIA but no one discovered anything about Mr. Lau.

The VC burned down whole villages and hamlets, making homeless refugees of hundreds of thousands of humble, peace-loving rural folk. They attacked camps set up for refugees. Schools and medical dispensaries were put to the communist torch since these represented symbols of hope and progress. After 1970, over a half million Vietnamese–men, women, and children–were killed.

Why all this terror? Why all this suffering? Why all of these heartless killings of men, women, and children? Godless, atheistic men produced this. When the communists control a people, they lose all personal rights. The individual belongs to the State and could be used by the State in whatever way it deemed important.

Communism represents more than a form of government; it is a religion. That religion must be rigidly followed. In practice, no other religion is allowed. The individual did not have the right to openly believe in God because communists do not believe in God. The individual cannot read the Bible because the communists considered the Bible to be foreign propaganda. They forbid free public assemblies because the communists do not allow any dissent.

For most Americans, it is difficult to fully appreciate the bondage of a people under communism. Yet, the South Vietnamese learned through years of struggle against communism that when the VC entered a hamlet or a village there was "no place to hide," just as Tran Van Can said. Consequently, the people became refugees and left everything behind in order to escape this enslavement. This was the reason Tran Van Can, Nguyen Van Khanh, and their families chose to flee Hanoi in 1954.

Vo Thanh Duc's assessment moved me deeply: "According to eye witnesses, the suffering of the war victims is beyond all power of human description. And, for lack of space and time, I cannot share with you what I have read and heard. But the descriptions haunt me day and night . . .

"I am writing this letter while my spirit is greatly disturbed. Brother and Sister Burcham, let me speak up what is disturbing me. South Vietnam might be lost and very soon! It is predicted that by April there will be a ceasefire, a coalition government will be formed, and an exodus will be granted to those who choose not to live with the communists. Where can we go? Who would receive the immigrants? What could we do when this happens?

"Please pray for us and do something in advance to help us if this comes true. There is no time to be lost and all must be done most discreetly because those who attempt to leave and cannot will have no chance to survive when the communists take over. . . . Do not believe those pacifists in your country who say that the communists will love the people. This is a lie! A most wicked lie!

"Brother and Sister Burcham, please take this seriously. The prediction is not just an unfounded fear. This is made by well-informed sources. This is a matter of life and death for many Christians here . . . Please get in touch with your Senators and other VIPs to see what they could do to help the Christians to have a settlement in any non-communist country. *WE PREFER A JUNGLE, A FOREST, AN ISLAND, A WILDERNESS, OR A SEA COAST* to a prosperous territory with the communists. Will you please work hard so that the United States Government will accept some Vietnamese as political immigrants? . . .

"Saigon is full of refugees from all over the country. We may have to move to Saigon in the very near future. People in our area have been in a state of readiness to leave their houses. Those who have vehicles keep them in good condition so that they can be used at any time, particularly during the night.

"Truckloads of refugees with their belongings have been passing our house daily for weeks. We pray daily for our safety; we sleep in peace, however. I am confident in God's protection . . . Please pray for us and help us as we have requested you. We will do our best and leave the rest to the Lord . . .

"If the communists take over, I believe the first thing they will do is to kill off all possible reactionists based on what happened at Hue in 1968. From past experience of their sister socialist countries, Christian leaders are the hardest to tame. If they do not get rid of them in the first place when people are too terrified to have any reaction, they will have problems with them in the future. Later on they will have to put them in prison; they will have to torture them and to feed them in prison. To torture the Christians, in the Marxist view, is unproductive labor; and, worse, to feed them is a waste of the people's product. So, the best thing to do is to kill them at the most appropriate time." Truly the Vietnamese Christians desired above everything to be delivered from this monster.

Then a few days later, I got this letter from Duc: "It is impossible to leave the country by normal procedures. Please get in touch with some influential personalities who could bring some pressure on the American Embassy in Vietnam to be more flexible in granting visas.

"As you know, General Frederick C. Weyand has suggested that the U. S. Government would help a number of Vietnamese leave the country in order to escape from communist revenge. Please follow this closely and try to include our names in the list. I am going to mail you pictures of our family and necessary papers for passports.

"The whole country is in despair as Thieu decided to remain as President. I think that a coup d'etat would take place very soon and I am fearful that this would not be for the good of the country. I hope that Thieu would resign.

"We have moved to the city. I am going to see if I could give my children up for adoption in order that they might leave the country. Then, if we could go abroad, we will be reunited. And if Bich and I could not, then they would live.

"However, so long as God keeps us alive in this country, we would like to do the best we can for the less fortunate people. Please work hard to raise the money for refugees' relief as suggested in my previous letter.

"Thank you for your decision not to come. Otherwise, I would have great fear for your lives. All schools have terminated their school term one month earlier than usual . . ."

Preparing Christians to live under communism!

In another letter, Duc described how he had dreamed of a peaceful country in which he and others could freely proclaim the Good News of Jesus Christ. Now, he faced the reality that the communists might soon take over the entire nation. He indicated that he had worked on sermons to prepare the mind and the heart of the Christians for the persecution that might fall on them. Duc wrote: "I have completed the selection of Scriptures which are in two parts–one is for the spiritual edification of the Christians under persecution; the other is for the propagation of the faith. In addition to this, we will distribute individual books of the New Testament among members of the church to be safeguarded under communism . . ."

Duc gave instructions on how to form the underground church based on the experience of Christians in other communist countries because public assemblies would be forbidden.

Duc encouraged Christians to memorize Scriptures or to hide the Scriptures in hard-to-find places because the communists would take their Bibles and destroy them. My heart chilled as I read these words of Duc: "If the communists take over, those of us present leaders would not be able to do much even if we would not be killed. We will be watched closely."

When I got this letter, I could not hold back the tears because I felt that time was running out for the Christians that I had known and brought to Christ. I could sense the final desperation Duc felt by his willingness to put up their three children for adoption in order that they might live.

Tran Van Can pointed out the Vietnam crisis in these words: "The situation is now hanging in the balance. Whether Vietnam (?)–Almost all Vietnamese people are actually obsessed with this question."

When considering the tense situation in Vietnam, Tran's unselfishness, as reflected in his request for prayer, moved me deeply: "Please kindly remember us in your daily prayers that in all circumstances we may stand faithful to Christ and will have no fear of giving up our lives for Christ's sake."

Despite decades of war and countless predictions of doom, the opportunity for both foreign and Vietnamese Christians to work for the extension of Christ's church in Vietnam continued. If ever there were a people who needed to hear the announcement of God's saving grace, it was the Vietnamese. If ever there were a people who needed the presence of God, working, healing, and reconciling them to one another and to God, it was the Vietnamese. They needed the church in their midst! I wrote to several churches and friends: "Let us not forget that, if the communists take over, there will be ***no place to hide for our Vietnamese Christians."***

Each of those appeals brought heartache because of my fear of what would happen to all of those with whom I loved, or worked, or taught the Good News of Christ, or witnessed their growth in their faith and service.

I prayed diligently for God to bless my feeble efforts and give me wisdom and guidance. Immediately, I began putting together a plan to help my friends. During my restlessness at night, I tried to dream of ways to do something.

Since I taught at Oklahoma Christian, I asked for permission to plead with the student body to do something to help prevent another great bloodbath in Vietnam. As I spoke about how time might be running out for the Christians in this war-torn country, I read letters from Vietnamese Christians who made such moving appeals for help. A noticeable hush fell over the chapel service. I asked them not to forget the mass executions at Hue in 1968 when hundreds of men, women, and children suffered torture and executions, and some even buried alive in trenches! I asked "What about the massacre of American missionaries at Ban Me Thuot?"

I made a plea for the students to pray, to write to their congressmen, to appeal to our State Department and urge our leaders to make provisions for those who desired to leave South Vietnam if a coalition government was formed.

In addition, I pointed out the benevolent work the Vietnamese Christians provided for the masses pouring into Saigon. I suggested the students write their home churches and start fund-raising efforts for food, medicine, clothing, and Bibles.

At the end of the chapel service, the students engulfed me and wanted to help. Then I met with student leaders and suggested the following appeals be made to our governmental leaders: (1) seek a country, perhaps the United States, who will accept the Vietnamese as political immigrants; (2) put pressure on the Vietnamese government to assist those wanting to leave with passports; and (3) provide transportation to get the people to the country of refuge.

As a result, the student body worked liked an oiled machine and wrote letters to every Senator, Representative, and to the State

Department. In addition, I sent news articles about this situation to all of our brotherhood newspapers.

As the end of March approached, I asked the elders of the College Church of Christ in Oklahoma City to allow me to raise funds. They agreed to become the overseeing congregation for funds raised.

The elders asked me to raise funds based on the following priorities: (1) assistance to Christian families who are in need; (2) provide help to Christians leaving Vietnam if this becomes possible; and (3) provide care for refugee families.

In addition, many congregations and individuals had already contributed to our personal funds for travel and living expenses for four months of work in Vietnam; therefore, I asked each one for permission to use these funds for this benevolent purpose. If this was not agreeable, I promised to refund their contributions.

While in worship during the last three Sundays in April, I prayed silently for those I had come to love. Tears flowed. I had difficulty keeping my emotions from turning to sobs. I silently prayed over and over again "God, please, please help my friends in Vietnam!"

Funds started pouring in to the College church to aid the Vietnamese.

The tragedy of Vietnam seemed to be building daily.

Vietnam is the real tragedy of the 20th Century. From the moment we arrived in Vietnam in 1966, we hoped this conflict would give this nation peace. The protests in the States seemed to be more and more organized. Most servicemen we knew looked on Jane Fonda as a traitor to the nation. As we came to know the Vietnamese more intimately, they shared with us how the Viet Cong took advantage of such protests.

Earlier, when the Vietnamese prepared for their election, Senator Sparkman made the statement that "Thieu was just a puppet of the United States." Our maid brought a flyer passed out in her neighborhood showing how the Viet Cong used this as a propaganda piece. These protests and such statements from our congressmen intensified the Viet Cong activity throughout Vietnam.

Some years later, we came to understand more clearly how the North Vietnamese had been encouraged by these protests and the actions of Congress, which weakened our resolve to win this war. Stanley Karnow interviewed North Vietnamese General Vo Nguyen Giap, who said: "We were not strong enough to drive out a half-million American troops, but that wasn't our aim. Our intention was to break the will of the American government to continue the war."

I often wandered how many deaths could be attributed to those protests!

From the moment we arrived in Vietnam, the American servicemen told us victory over the communists was possible provided the military were given authority to pursue the enemy across the border from Vietnam into Cambodia or Laos. The Viet Cong made military strikes in the South and then would dash across the border into the sanctuaries of those countries. The North Vietnamese and Viet Cong received their supplies from the north in a network of roads in those countries and river traffic on the Mekong River. Our servicemen told us over and over they needed to cut off those military supply routes.

I searched for the difference in attitudes in the States between the Vietnam War and World War II. Having reached adulthood during World War II, I could remember a nation united in purpose with clear direction to win the war. Newspapers and magazines published stories supporting every effort being made. Newsreels at the movies made you proud to be an American. No one doubted that Hitler and his war machine to be the enemy. "Tokyo Rose" became the symbol of disgust. What made the difference?

I came to the conclusion it had to be the media. The Freedom of Information Act did not exist during World War II. The mail of our servicemen was censored in order to prevent the enemy from getting any details about troop movement or projected assaults. I remember seeing letters with heavy black marks covering what might be considered sensitive material. The media recognized that military plans had to be kept secret from Japan and Germany.

The media in Vietnam considered it a scoop to be able to broadcast military plans in detail or about any defeats and casualties suffered by our troops. In the military briefings I attended, every newsman wanted to know about future engagements. This mania of "keeping the public informed" allowed Hanoi to react and inflict unwarranted heavy casualties on our troops.

During World War II, the media always presented an upbeat picture in defeat as well as in victory. Our defeats and our victories made you proud to be an American. On the other hand, the media in Vietnam could always find something derogatory to say in our defeats but primarily in our victories, such as during the Tet Offensive. Having been in Vietnam during the first fifteen days of the Tet Offensive, I remained amazed at the negatives being reported by the media in the States.

During the Vietnam War, tactical maneuvers seemed to be prescribed by Congress, not by our generals. Hands of the generals remained tied and their voices muffled. Perhaps it would be more accurate to say that the tactics seemed to be prescribed by protesters on the street and Congress listened.

In August, 1974, Rowland Evans, and Robert Novak summarized the dilemma facing this nation in an article entitled *"Vietnam Aid Cut Dangerous."* Their article stated: "Although top strategists here (Washington) still disagree on the Communist timetable for the next, massive countrywide offensive against South Vietnam, the remorseless political-military warfare now being waged by Hanoi's invaders is having devastating effects with cruelly perfected new tactics.

"Despite the success of these tactics, Congress is showing ever more reluctance to finance Saigon's defense, as witness the immense reduction in both military and economic aid requests from the Ford administration. When final action is completed, both will probably be slashed by close to 50 percent . . . This means precisely what it implies–a 50 percent 'decrease in the capabilities' of South Vietnam's army.

"What makes these threatened congressional cutbacks so perilous is the steadily increasing aid to Hanoi from both China and the Soviet Union.

"As for military help, U. S. officials believe that there is now enough ammunition in Communist hands to sustain an offensive at the ferocity levels of the spring 1972 Communist offensive for fully 18 straight months.

"Directly matching this combat potential is the alarming fact that Hanoi has now infiltrated 160,000 fresh combat troops into the south since the January 28, 1973 ceasefire.

"Statistics now available here tell the story. In the Sonha district of coastal Quangnai province, 130 homes of new settlers were burned to the ground in late spring to discredit Saigon's power. The inhabitants were then 'encouraged' to move west into regions 'liberated' by Hanoi where the Communists suffer grievous shortages of manual labor, farm workers and pack carriers.

"One month later, in the Donglo resettlement center, 200 homes were destroyed, 100 civilians killed and 15 wounded.

"To the north in Quangnam province–near the port city of Danang–the invaders forcibly uprooted more than 10,000 civilians settled there two years ago and moved them west to 'liberated' areas as virtual slave labor . . .

"Vastly aiding the Communists, of course, is the absence today of U. S. air power and the fact that Hanoi's troops are more muscular and better-trained . . ."

Vo Thanh Duc gave a first-hand report on the situation. He wrote, "When the news of the loss of Ban Me Thuot, an important province in the highlands northeast of Saigon, sent a shock wave over South Vietnam in the middle of March, 1975, I was shaken to the core. For quite some time, I believed that the defeat of South Vietnam by the communists was a matter of time. However, I did not think that it could be that early.

"On that day the loss of Ban Me Thout was made public, I got together with some friends to make our own assessment of the event. We put together rumors and information each of us had collected relative to the future of our country. I got out of this meeting feeling several years older than when I went in. That evening, I wrote to a professor at Oklahoma Christian who previously served as a missionary to Vietnam, Ralph Burcham. I told Ralph that the defeat of South Vietnam was imminent and urged him to put pressure on the United States Government to work out an exodus from Vietnam for those who chose not to live under communism.

"While South Vietnam had not recovered from the loss of Ban Me Thuot, the 'strategic retreat' from Pleiku and Knontum in the latter part of March erupted like a volcano gushing out its destructive lava to the whole country. As the soldiers were moving southward, civilians were terror-stricken. They followed the convoy on foot, by cars and by whatever means of transportation was available. As the larger mass expanded, the terror became more intensified and the panic uncontrollable.

"Waves of humans rolled under the showers of bullets and rockets. Men, women, and children fell down never to rise again. Here, the human wall behind him pushed a husband forward before he could cover the face of his wife who just fell down. There, a mother was trodden to death when she reached down to pick up her child. On the roadside, a baby was at the breast of its dying mother.

"The waves of humans moved on. Men, women, and children were demoralized and dehumanized by terror, agony, and exhaustion. The exceptional acts done among them were unobserved! The heroes among them died with no song and no recognition! Within a matter of days, the stream of refugees flowed into the streets of Saigon, carrying with them horror stories they had witnessed.

"When April came, it became obvious that the only hope of South Vietnam was the defense of its capital, Saigon. A new defense line was soon drawn from Tay Ninh to Phan Rang. All entrances into Saigon were carefully screened. Roadblocks were set up on the streets. Refugee centers were located out of the city to block possible infiltration of the enemies.

"Since my family and I lived about five miles from the border of Saigon, these ominous developments posed a threat to our safety. We moved into Saigon in the first week of April. I kept in close touch with a few American friends who were still in the city. These friends kept me informed of the American plan for the evacuation of Vietnamese civilians.

"Even though no way of escape was in sight, my friends in Saigon and in the United States kept my hope alive. My American friends in Saigon spared nothing to work for my departure. Fellow Christians in the United States fervently prayed for me and other Christians at public gatherings and in private. I read letters from

Christians in the United States at our worship services and we all thanked God for our brethren. The thousands of miles between the United States and Vietnam did not keep us from having a deep sense of Christian fellowship."

When Congress refused to continue aid to Vietnam following the American departure, South Vietnam had a fine fighting machine, and could have held their own indefinitely. However, when America withdrew complete support, there was no way the South Vietnamese could stand up to the Viet Cong, the North Vietnamese, China, and the Soviet Union. The South Vietnamese army may have been brave, but they were not foolish enough to stay and be slaughtered.

Even though the South Vietnamese had been successful at first after the pull-out of American military in 1973. Now, when the American Congress cut military and economic aid to Vietnam, this provided a sure death for the South Vietnamese Government.

What a tragedy to see the waste of human life and dollars by the protestors and the American Congress.

As the month of April seemed to vaporize, I became more depressed and prayed fervently throughout each day for my Vietnamese friends. As I reviewed the situation, it seemed impossible for any of my Vietnamese Christians and friends to escape communist bondage. My big question: "Will I ever see and be able to work with any of my friends again?"

The Triumph of
Some South Vietnamese

"Blessed is the man who perseveres under trial. . . . .
(James 1:12a, NIV)"

The news indicated the U. S. to airlift some Vietnamese orphans.

As the situation in Vietnam worsened, I prayed that something could be done for the people I had come to love. Then the State Department's Agency for International Development announced that some 2,000 Vietnamese orphans would be flown from the threatened city of Saigon to the United States in an airlift. At the start of the airlift on April 4, a plane with 326 persons—including orphans, aircraft personnel, and care takers—crashed with some 190 casualties. I grieved for those who almost made it to safety.

This airlift gave me hope that some of the orphans I had helped would make it out but it made me wander what would happen to all of my friends. After this fateful flight, two to three military planes shuttled between Saigon and Clark Air Base in the Philippines each day with their human cargoes.

By April 12, a fleet of C-141s crowded the air base ready to step up the airlift operation. Busloads of Vietnamese civilians were discreetly transported into the air base at Tan Son Nhut. At first, these missions took place during curfew hours to keep the public from knowing the nature of the flights. But in a matter of hours, the ongoing evacuation became common knowledge.

Crowds began to cluster around the American Embassy and other government agencies in Saigon. The few Americans who remained in the city suddenly became angels of liberty to the Vietnamese. Every American represented a chance of escape. Affection, money, and proposals for marriage were frequently offered to these Americans in exchange for exits from Vietnam.

By April 21, the airlift operated around the clock. The processing center at the Defense Attaché Office in Tan Son Nhut was packed with people. Among the privileged crowd were Vietnamese government officials, employees of the American Government and private enterprise, and those who had family relations with American citizens.

None of our Vietnamese Christians fell into any of these categories. There seemed to be no hope for any of them to be evacuated.

Then Bill Estep, who worshiped at the Saigon congregation and worked for the DAO as a technician, could not bear the thought of leaving this besieged city before attempting to help some of these Christians to safety. Bill gave of himself freely at the risk of being left behind. He worked fearlessly and tirelessly looking for a way to get as many as possible out of Vietnam. I waited breathlessly for news concerning whether any of the people I knew made it to freedom.

Vo Thanh Duc described how Bill tried to help: "Bill did not have much sleep in those last days. I saw him a few times early in the morning before the exhaustion on his countenance set in. In silence, I gave thanks to God for a friend who placed the safety of others above his own personal safety and good health."

With many provinces under communist control, they started putting greater pressure on Saigon. Bill Estep wrote: "Ralph, do what you can to get them out from that side. Time is running out . . . We will do what we can, but I can't assess that effort yet . . . I only wish I had the wisdom of King Solomon for just a few days."

While the elders at the College church were in session on Tuesday, April 22, a call came from Bill Estep in Saigon. He reported that several Vietnamese Christians were being considered for processing to leave.

Estep's question to the elders: "If I can get some of the Christians out, will you guarantee their financial support on their arrival in the States?" The elders agreed to be responsible for them.

Estep indicated all Americans were being evacuated. He felt that our government would help those Vietnamese who had worked closely with Americans.

The news reports indicated the fighting was fierce and refugees were pouring into the safe zone of Saigon. The Vietnamese began to panic in their efforts to get out of Saigon; chaos ensued around the U. S. Embassy for those seeking help to leave. The drone of the helicopters could be heard as people were airlifted from the Embassy to the Tan Son Nhut airbase, where people were loaded on planes for refugee centers outside of Vietnam. Also, refugees were airlifted to American ships stationed offshore. In addition, many were trying to get out to sea by boats and ships with the hope they might be rescued.

On April 24, Bill went to work as usual. When he arrived at the office, his boss told him to get ready to leave Saigon in the evening. While Bill was filled with despair, his boss asked him if he had anyone he wanted to take out of Vietnam with him. He indicated those he desired to help and his boss gave permission for him to go get those people and make final arrangements for leaving.

Vo Thanh Duc described it this way: "About 11 o'clock, I went to see Mac LeDoux at his home. When I arrived, I was surprised to see Bill Estep and Mac coming down the stairway to greet me. Both men looked grave and tense. They told me that they had been trying to reach me all morning. They told me to go home, get my family, and meet them at a place near the entrance into Tan Son Nhut airport. My family and I would leave Saigon that afternoon."

When Duc went to get his family, he and Bich's seven-year old son Albert had gone with a relative and could not be found. Duc returned to Bill Estep and explained the situation. Bill warned that time was running out and any delay might jeopardize the chance of all getting out. He told Duc and Bich that they must decide whether or not to leave with their other two children or all stay behind. He reminded Duc that Albert would be living with relatives, and that Duc, himself, might be placed in a situation where he would be unable to help his family. Mac agreed to try to locate Albert.

Duc described their feelings: "Never before did time move forward so torturously and so painfully as the hours in which I was waiting for my seven-year-old son. It was April 24, 1975 . . My family and I were fortunate to have permission to leave Saigon under the evacuation plan of the United States Government . . .

"My friend, Mac LeDoux had exactly two hours in which to locate Albert. In that two hours, I, too, had to decide whether I would leave Vietnam without Albert in the event that Mac could not locate him. Each movement of the hands on my watch triggered the release of a dull knife forcing its way through my heart. How I wished that time would stand still and the hand on the watch stop their movements. I could not bear to look at my watch. At the same time, I could hardly take my eyes away from it.

"The Tan Son Nhut International Airport was simmering with dismayed and tortured faces of men, women, and children waiting for their turns to be evacuated from the besieged city of Saigon. The air was thick with heat and moisture. People moved frantically, crisscrossing the area weaving their way through the ocean of humans.

"I could hardly believe that my family and I now had a chance to leave Vietnam before the communist take-over. For days and weeks, I had been praying, planning, and working for this escape. For days and weeks, I had been thinking what joy, what excitement, what ecstasy it would be when I found a way of escape for my family and me.

"I never dreamed, however, of facing a situation in which I had to decide whether to leave the country without my eldest child or to remain in Vietnam with him. I was with Bich, my wife, and our two children, Theresa and Tony. Theresa was five years old and Tony three. They were too young to know what was going on. They looked perplexed, confused, and fearful.

"For two eternal hours, Bich and I hardly exchanged a word. We could not bear even to look at each other. From time to time our fugitive eyes met before we could turn away. Those moments were unbearable. Just a glance into each other's eyes was enough for us to know the agony, the hope, and the fear each of us was undergoing. We could only hold hands to give each other courage to go through the ordeal. I hoped and prayed that my friend and colleague, Mac LeDoux, would be successful in getting Albert. I knew that within two hours I had to decide whether or not to leave without my eldest son."

Time came for the families to make their way though the security channels to the airport. Duc and Bich made the decision to leave Albert behind. All the families experienced the trauma of leaving close loved ones behind—sons, daughters, grandchildren, brothers, sisters, and grandparents.

Estep arranged to accompany the first families to leave; others were to follow with Mac LeDoux.

After reporting back to Duc and Bich, Mac and Bill went into the DAO processing center at Tan Son Nhut to complete the paperwork for their departure. However, Mac promised to continue his efforts to locate Albert.

Duc continued the description of those last hours in Vietnam: "As we had made our decision to leave Albert behind, Bich and I had time to think of our present needs. Due to what had happened, Bich and I left home that afternoon with just a briefcase and a handbag. I did not have a change of clothes. Bill and I went into the DAO compound to pick up a few shirts, pants, and bed sheets that the departed Americans had left behind. My new wardrobe was packed in a pillowcase. That evening, I knew what it was to be a refugee.

"For our beds, we spread bed sheets on the asphalt. All around us—men, women, and children huddled on the ground beside their luggage. The roaring sound of jet engines went on endlessly. The sky was lit with flares dropped from airplanes and shot up from the ground. The earth beneath us "tremored" by the explosions of bombs and rockets.

"I watched the flares, listened to the noise, felt the tremors, hoping that these would keep me from hearing the turmoil and thunders of my thoughts. But nothing could keep me from the thoughts of my son and the danger and hardship he would have to face. I was certain that my stay would mean certain death for myself, and a lifetime of misery for my family. I had no doubt that my decision to leave with Bich and the two children was a wise choice under the circumstances. However, this rational conclusion could not stop the surging agony of my heart.

"About one a.m., our names were announced on the speakers. After our proper IDs were checked against the manifest, a bus took us to a waiting C-130. The roaring engines of the plane made everybody tense and nervous. Within minutes, more than one hundred people were aboard, huddled on the floor among their luggage.

"The C-130 took off with its side door open. Two Marines stood on both sides of the door each with a flare-gun in hand ready to divert heat-finding missiles away from the plane. As the C-130 spiraled its way from the ground, everyone on the plane seemed to stop breathing. I watched the reactions of the Marines for signs of danger. They fixed their eyes on the ground, moving their heads from one side to the other. When the Marines put their guns into the holsters and closed the door, I knew that we were safe above the sea.

"We arrived at Clark Air Base in the Philippines about four o'clock in the morning and flew to Guam on another plane about two hours later. As we landed on Guam's Anderson Air Force Base about nine a.m. on April 25, there were rows of cots on the concrete floor for those arriving to lie down and rest. Marine personnel handed out cookies, hot drinks, and food. Refugees kept pouring in. Crowds of people were seen everywhere. Most of the refugees ate the cookies and drank the hot drinks but hardly touched the food.

"By noontime, we were told that all available facilities had been filled and tents were being set up for us. By mid-afternoon, we were transported by bus to our tent city. About thirty minutes later, we arrived at a vast area covered with green tents. Bulldozers were still at work. Green mushrooms continued to spring up from the ground. The tents were empty. New arrivals rushed out to take cots to their tents.

"Toward the evening, long lines were formed at the kitchen areas. The lines grew longer and longer every minute. It took hours for the latecomers to get food and water. The American Red Cross and other volunteer agencies worked around the clock distributing soap, toothpaste, and the like. American volunteers of all ages came to help. The adults donated supplies and the children took soap and milk to mothers with small children.

"I was deeply touched by the kindness and generosity of the volunteers. That night, after my family got cots and food, I started working as a volunteer for the Red Cross.

"Buses kept coming in to unload refugees. Volunteers helped the newcomers settle in their tents. Countless people came to the office asking for assistance. In those busy hours of service to others, I temporarily forgot my own pain. At night, as I walked to my tent in the dark, I imagined my son walking at my side. I reached out to touch him only to realize that he was not there. There were times when I approached my tent and heard Bich sobbing; I kept on walking and walking in the night until my legs could no longer carry my weight. I sat down in the dark and listened to my heart groaning.

"Unknown to me, three days after we left Saigon, Albert was located. My relatives got in touch with Mac on April 27 and asked him to send Albert to the United States. That evening Mac took Albert home to send him out with a Vietnamese family who were to leave Vietnam the next day under Mac's sponsorship.

"At 5:50 p.m., April 28, the flight area at Tan Son Nhut was attacked by an air strike. Saigon was put under a twenty-four-hour curfew. The evacuation of Vietnamese came to a complete stop. Thousands of would-be evacuees were stranded at different locations in Saigon. Albert was still in the besieged city.

"Approximately at 8 p.m., the airlift resumed. Two C-130s landed on the air base. Within minutes 360 evacuees were pushed aboard and the planes took off.

"After the successful take off of the two planes, the evacuation machinery in Saigon received orders from Washington to operate at top speed. Within the following twenty-four hours, 10,000 people were to be evacuated on 60 flights of C-130s.

"That evening, April 28, Albert and the Vietnamese family were taken into the Tan Son Nhut Air Base. About 2:30 a.m., April 29, they ate an early breakfast offered by personnel of the Defense Attaché Office. At approximately 3:30 their C-130 took off.

"About four o'clock that morning, rockets and 130mm shells began showering on the air base and the DAO compound. The attack continued into the evening. The fixed-wing airlift came to an end. A helicopter picked up my friend, Mac LeDoux, the next day as the communists marched into Saigon.

"On the first day of May, the heat in Guam became intolerable. The scorching wind was blowing mercilessly against our faces, which were well burnt by the sun. Theresa and Tony were extremely irritated. For hours they had been crying for their big brother. Bich and I told the children that their big brother was visiting with our relatives and could not be with us for a while.

"Suddenly a voice on the speakers requested relatives of Vo Hoang Tan (Albert's legal name) to come to the Red Cross office and pick him up. Bich and I picked up the children and rushed to the office of the American Red Cross. There, before our very eyes, Albert was standing in a corner with a boiled egg in one hand and an apple in another.

"How heavenly it was to hold Albert in my arms, to look into his eyes and to listen to his heartbeats! There was no need to hold up my tears. I let my tears freely mingle with his. Guam became friendly and inviting. The tent became my new palace. That evening Albert lay on a cot between Bich's and mine. We went into our sleep with sweet dreams of a bright future.

"That next morning, I went to work as a man who owned the world. The day passed by so quickly that I hardly realized that it was gone when evening came. After dinner, we went to the beach. I was happy and proud like a businessman on his summer vacation after closing a multi-million-dollar business deal. There were countless large frogs on the beach. We had a great time chasing them around.

"Three days later, we got our clearance to enter the United States. A bus took us to the metal barracks at Anderson Air Base where we got a hot shower for the first time since we left Saigon. The following day, we got aboard a chartered plane on our long trip to California. . . .

"We were more than grateful to be in this land of freedom. The U. S. Marines were efficient and dedicated. They performed their duties with something like a religious devotion. They deserved the deepest gratitude from us refugees . . .

"The assistance coming from volunteer agencies, churches, organizations, and individual Americans was phenomenal.

"Only a nation where generosity and hospitality had long been developed as national characteristics could such assistance be found . . .

"Finally, my ordeal as a refugee was over as we arrived at the Will Rogers Airport in Oklahoma City on May 22, 1975. It was there I came to know the loving care of Ralph Burcham whom I esteemed as a friend and a father . . .

"Albert is a gift given to me not once but twice. I am delighted that he and my other children have the opportunity and the freedom early in life to fully develop themselves. My hope for all my children is that they will actively contribute their part to keep America a safe haven for victims of repression, tyranny, and injustice for generations to come."

God be praised for the deliverance of many of His people before the fall of the Bamboo curtain on another nation. God had answered many, many prayers in the most marvelous way as we learned the exodus story of many Christians, who escaped Vietnam. Yet, many did not get out and we must continually remember them in prayer.

The traumatic experience of our brothers and sisters in Vietnam should challenge every Christian to re-examine the communist threat, the lostness of people without Christ, and work more diligently in proclaiming the Good News throughout the world.

The history of the communist movement should motivate us to greater efforts in evangelism. In 1903, one man with seventeen followers began his attack on the world. His name was Lenin. By 1918, the number had increased to forty thousand, and, with that forty thousand, he gained control of the one hundred sixty million people of Russia. And the movement has gone on and now controls over a third of the world's population with over a billion in China alone. Over and over, I kept turning over in my mind: "With millions of Christians around the world, can we afford to be less zealous for the greatest cause–the bringing of lost souls to the only Savior?

"Major deterrents to communism are freedom and the message of Christ. Christ frees man from slavery to self and passions; communism enslaves the heart, body, mind, and soul of men. Each Christian must decide to become a soldier for Jesus Christ or, by apathy, we will capitulate to this enemy and find ourselves facing persecution and death just like our Vietnamese brethren. I thank and praise God for those delivered from bondage."

In answer to prayer, I received a call from the Red Cross that some of our people had arrived in the Philippines.

For me, it became a waiting game to see which of my Vietnamese friends made it out. I prayed to God that He would use me in helping those fortunate enough to escape the ravages of war. Though this is not what I had planned for the summer of 1975, God in His wisdom provided means for the greatest exodus in modern times by airlifting thousands out of the clutches of communism. God wanted to teach me that it is not about me but about Him.

After the Fall of Vietnam

"The righteous man is rescued from trouble....
(Proverbs 11:7, NIV)

Etched on my memory is April 30, 1975, as the day when the Vietnam I knew and the people I loved and left behind, became enslaved to a form of government so cruel and evil that most Americans cannot comprehend. How many of the people I knew made it out? I felt deeply for those left behind and wondered about their fate.

Also, pain gripped my heart for the service men and women who had given of themselves to free a nation of people from bondage. Among the Christian servicemen I knew, they demonstrated over and over again to be men of faith, who loved their families, were courageous, full of pride for their military service, loyal to the United States, and desirous of making their lives count. Their friendship sustained me during every crisis our mission faced and their support of our efforts aided in our success.

I had a special feeling of empathy for the parents and loved ones of those suffering from lifetime disabilities and for those making the ultimate sacrifice. Some of these men I deeply loved and respected because I knew them personally. I knew their loved ones had to be asking the hard questions: "Why?" "What was accomplished by my spouse, son, or daughter's sacrifice?" "Was it worth it?" Truly, God blessed my life and our mission with Godly service people, who loved and provided mentoring for me with examples of service and sacrifice.

Gradually, we began to hear from the American Red Cross and from air mailed letters that we had people in refugee camps in Guam, in the Philippines, and in Hong Kong. Then most every day our telephone rang from early morning until midnight with Vietnamese seeking our help.

Two of the Vietnamese Christians, Dao Lien (Pien) and Nguyen Thi Bich Thu, who studied at the Four Seas Bible College in Singapore, received deportation orders. To avoid conflict with the new communist regime, the Singapore government gave all Vietnamese citizens 24-hours to leave. What would happen to those two talented young women if they returned to Vietnam? Missionary friends of mine contacted missionaries in Taiwan to see if they could care for these young women. They agreed to take them. But would we be able to reunite them with their families?

We had no way of knowing about the number of refugees who would come to Oklahoma City. But we knew that our Vietnamese brothers and sisters had left behind everything they owned–homes, furniture, clothing, keepsakes; they would have only the luggage they could hand carry.

In addition, we knew they must have been going through an emotional trauma from the years of chaos the war had brought into their lives. There could be no greater heartache than leaving behind friends and loved ones and a familiar culture for an unknown one. The Bamboo Curtain had fallen and most would be forever separated from their loved ones left behind.

The College church made preparations to receive the refugees.

Knowing the hardships facing the refugees, the elders of the College church authorized me to put together a plan for caring for the refugees on their arrival. The job seemed mammoth to me because within twenty-four hours after the fall of Vietnam we could account for up to 100 Christians and family members.

Housing became my first concern. How could we provide housing for 100 or more refugees? Since Oklahoma Christian, where

I taught, happened to be on summer break, Dr. Stafford North, Dean of the college, obtained permission for refugees to be housed in one of the dorms.

Also, the Lions' Club had a health camp nearby. In the past, it had been used as a camp for underprivileged children but they had decided not to operate it that summer. The facilities of the Lions' park included nine good-sized cabins and a large dining hall. I checked with the Lions' Club leadership and they gave me the use of the camp for as long as needed. Immediately I recruited students and church members to clean up the camp buildings. We mowed, cleaned cabins, organized the kitchen, and collected bedding and other necessities.

This would provide temporary housing but what could be done to help them get apartments?

Questions kept popping up in my few hours of sleep at night: How were these refugees going to fit into our American way of life? What could we do to encourage their spiritual growth in Christ? How could we prepare them for getting a job? Who would hire them? How would they get to and from work? What training would they need to get a driver's license since most had never driven a car? How could we improve their ability to speak English? How could we prepare their children for school in our educational system or assist university students for gaining admission to continue their education?

But beyond temporary arrangements, how could we move these families into a permanent situation so they could get on with their lives? As we explored this question, we decided to make an appeal to get congregations to adopt a family. I sent an article to our brotherhood papers. Also, Maurice Hall, another former missionary, and the Allen Park congregation in Michigan, made a brotherhood appeal for churches to sponsor a family.

The Governor of Oklahoma set up a task force of religious and civic organizations to develop a plan for caring for refugees coming to our State. Because of our past experience in Vietnam, the Governor asked me to serve on this task force. The Governor made available to us various departments of the State of Oklahoma that could be of assistance to us.

We got word that some of our refugees had been transferred from Guam to a base in California and to a base at Fort Chaffee, Arkansas. The Governor flew the task force on a National Guard plane to Fort Chaffee. There we received instructions on the procedures for moving some of these families out of the camp to Oklahoma as soon as they completed their processing.

While at Fort Chaffee, I met with the Nguyen Dan Bao family. When I met the Baos, my heart burst with joy as we hugged each other in silence while the tears freely flowed. Immediately, I offered a prayer of thanksgiving to God for His remarkable deliverance of this family that I loved so much.

Because the Bao family, consisting of seven children, had to go through processing before they could be released, Bao offered to circulate religious materials to those within the camp if I could get materials to him. Immediately, a couple in our congregation, James and Delores Gilliam, who owned a printing company, offered to make reprints of those items we felt would be most helpful including our Bible Correspondence Course; they kept their presses hot for days. The nearest congregation to Fort Chaffee was the Fort Smith Church of Christ who agreed to work with the Baos; they agreed for us to ship them the printed materials; in turn, they would take these out to the Baos. As Bao visited with other Vietnamese refugees, he shared with them the Good News of Jesus Christ and gave them helpful materials to study.

Reuel Lemmons, the editor of the ***Firm Foundation,*** wrote a lead editorial concerning the Vietnamese Christians. He wrote, "South Vietnam has become, more than ever, a sea of suffering humanity. The war has ended but the suffering has not. The tragedy seems to increase day by day. It is too early yet to correctly plan what steps can be taken to minister most effectively to the almost universal need of that people, and more especially to the need of the Christians who are there. During the past decade a number of congregations have been started in South Vietnam and scores of men and women baptized. Some 300 faithful brethren can be counted. For the most part the falling apart of South Vietnam has left their status unclear and extremely hazardous. . . .

"Hundreds of thousands have died in the past twenty years as the Viet Cong spread its reign of terror through the land. What will happen following the surrender none can successfully predict. Now is the time to pray for the Vietnamese brethren. It is possible that God can do for them what armies cannot do–protect them. Pray fervently, often and earnestly for them, remembering that the effectual fervent prayer of a righteous man avails much in its workings.

"It is almost beyond belief that so many faithful brethren have been able to be processed in the evacuation. The day after Saigon fell one group of 19 brethren were located at Clark AFB in the Philippines. Another group of 23 were located in Guam, and were being cared for together in a tent by Bill Estep, a Christian civilian who was in Saigon during the evacuation and helped many to get out. . . .The Red Cross has reported others at other gathering points. Up to 100 Christians have been accounted for in the first 24 hours following surrender, who were among the very first to process. These include most of the leadership of the Saigon church.

"The College church in Oklahoma City, sponsors of Ralph Burcham in Vietnam, have committed themselves to receive and be responsible for these individuals . . . It is planned to keep the group together for several weeks while they become oriented to a new culture and a kind of peace most of them have not known in their lifetimes. Later, plans must be made to absorb them into American society. All this will cost a mint of money, but, after all, such things as this are what Christianity is all about . . .

"Both the Christians who were lucky enough to get out, and the ones left behind are hungry, homeless, penniless, and jobless . . .

"Those who arrive in Oklahoma City, and perhaps else where, will be in a state of shock. They will be among strangers whose language they cannot understand. They will be bewildered and afraid. Misguided efforts of the well intentioned could hinder rather than help. We would suggest that the Oklahoma City church, the church with the most experience in dealing with the Vietnamese, be supported in their direction of the work of making these Christians comfortable, and helping them to adjust to their new culture.

"Christians everywhere should be profoundly thankful that so many of their number have been fortunate enough to escape. This is one tragic emergency in which the church seemed to be there at the right time with the right resources . . . The church has responded with love and money in a most commendable way. And more will be forthcoming."

Lemmons included in his editorial how to contact the College church. From the time this edition of the **Firm Foundation** went out, we started receiving telephone calls and funds and offers to adopt a family came pouring in to the College church.

Because most of the refugees needed help with their English, a lady from a nearby Christian retirement home offered to teach the Laubach system to all planning to conduct language classes; this system had been used to teach English to foreigners. Many of our church members and students at Oklahoma Christian went through this training. These volunteers were ready to teach English as soon as the refugees arrived.

Vietnamese families started arriving at the College church.

Duc and Bich Vo with their three children arrived first. We met them at the airport. Our hearts skipped a beat when we first saw them with Albert, who had been left behind, leading the family. Hugs, kisses, and tears gushed forth as the reporters and photographers tried to get their story. For months, Duc had shared his deepest concerns for his family and the Saigon church. What an answer to prayer to be able to see the impossible unfold before my eyes! The family spent the night with us before moving to the Lion's camp. Then we spent time with them at the shopping mall to get some of the things they desperately needed.

Four days later, the Nguyen Van Khanh family arrived. Again gratitude filled my heart for this family's deliverance. They had experienced so much with Khanh's cancer and successful surgery. By this time, their daughter, Nguyen Thi Bich Thu, who had been deported from Singapore, now lived with the Roy Mullinax family, our missionaries in Taipei, Taiwan; we agreed to try to sponsor her. Emotions were at the breaking point as we welcomed this wonderful family. We took the seven to the Lions' camp.

The next day happened to be our 25th wedding anniversary. We ate at the Lions' camp with the Ducs and the Khanhs and several Oklahoma Christian students who helped everyone to settle in. Later in the evening, the elders and their wives gave us a surprise party. Our Roger and Kathy provided a large cake with punch. This had to be one of our most memorable anniversaries because God had delivered so many of the people we had loved and with whom we had worked. We shared this wonderful occasion with people we thought we might never see again.

The next day we took the Khanh family shopping along with some of Duc's family.

Three days later the Tran Van Can extended family arrived with nine more, which included their son's fiancé and her brother. The Tran family had played such a significant role in our getting our first permanent church building in Saigon. He had guided me through visits with Vietnamese Government officials that allowed us to get legal recognition for the Church of Christ that permitted us to own property and authorizations for operating an international school and an orphanage. As we met, we felt overwhelmed with thanksgiving to God for His wonderful care that had brought us together. We housed the Tran family in a dorm at Oklahoma Christian. Much of the next day we spent in helping them shop for clothing and other necessities.

God had blessed the Tran family with intelligence and multiple talents. Their eldest son, Ngoc, had received his medical degree. Huong had completed her degree in dentistry. Loc had completed his master's degree in physics. The other children were involved in studies in the university. I wanted to find a sponsoring congregation, who would nurture the family and help Ngoc and Huong to get their certification to practice in the United States. The Mayfair congregation in Oklahoma City had offered to adopt a family; because they had several doctors and university professors, I felt they would do a good job in developing the talents of this family.

Then the Nguyen Dan Bao family arrived in Oklahoma City from Fort Chaffee. Seeing them brought back a flood of wonderful memories as I had performed the wedding ceremony for one of their daughters; they had diligently worked in starting a congregation at Bien Hoa and demonstrated their effectiveness in working with children. Bao continued to show his evangelistic spirit by working at Fort Chaffee by distributing Christian literature and Bibles. We placed the Baos with their six children in one of the cabins at the Lions' Club camp. The next day, we took them shopping. Eventually Maurice Hall recommended this family be placed with a congregation in Michigan.

The Nguyen Van Thuongs arrived with fifteen family members, including a grandmother born in 1895. We placed them at the Lions' camp. The Southwest congregation in Oklahoma City offered to take this family and provided two houses next door to each other for them to live. They equipped the houses with furniture and necessities and gave them a station wagon.

The Luongs came with twelve family members; this very talented family had the reputation for creating and making stuffed animals; the Village church adopted this family; they provided two houses next to each other. The Luongs made me a stuffed lion, which served as a symbol of the Lions' Camp, where they began their new life in America.

The Huynh Van Mungs came with five family members. Eventually, we got a job for Mr. Mung with an ice cream manufacturing plant. The day I took him for an interview, the personnel manager took us on a tour of the plant. When we walked into the large freezer, Mung had never experienced such cold. Mung said, "I couldn't work here, I'd die!" The manager assured Mung he would be working in the part of the plant, which they kept at 60 degrees. He told Mung he could wear long johns.

By now the hot weather had settled in so I got him long johns and told him he could put them on at the plant. The first day at his work, Gladys got a telephone call from an OC student who worked at the plant. He said, "Mrs. Burcham, you will not believe this but the little Vietnamese man is running around the plant in his long johns."

To which Gladys replied, "Tell him to put his other clothes on over his long johns."

To which the exasperated student said: "How can I; I don't speak Vietnamese!"

Gladys responded with "Well, demonstrate what he is to do." Even though this gave us a chuckle, it did give all of us a better understanding of what all these refugees had to be experiencing in one way or another as they acclimated themselves to a new culture.

Then more and more Vietnamese began coming in larger numbers from singles to small families.

Providing food for all of them became a major undertaking. Rice could be purchased in 100-pound sacks at a Japanese food store; also, we could buy other oriental foods there, such as dried fish and soy sauce. Several volunteers helped us in buying groceries. The Vietnamese prepared their food in the large kitchen at the Lions' camp. The OC dorm being nearby allowed those living there to walk.

The Pillsbury Company started sending us various kinds of mixes to aid these families. We were amazed at the generosity of Pillsbury because this first shipment weighed 370 pounds. It consisted of mixes of various sorts; in all, we received about 1200 pounds. Since the Vietnamese had no familiarity with cake, cookie, or muffin mixes, Gladys took three ladies at a time to our kitchen for baking lessons. After the lesson, each lady proudly took her baked products back to the Lions' camp for all to enjoy.

To keep the refugees from getting bored, we immediately started English and Bible classes along with sessions on how to shop and live in America. We made an assessment of the level of English for each person. We assigned private tutors to each one. Dr. Vickie McElroy, a reading expert, taught the group songs; also, she used flash cards with pictures to help them expand their vocabulary and to learn correct pronunciation. For the adults and older children, Dr. Darrel Alexander taught linguistics; this class proved to be one of the best classes for university students in helping them become more proficient in English.

Members of the College church worked as a terrific team. Faye Baird, one of our church members, organized a group of ladies to make quilts for each of these families. Laverne Southerland spent hours recording funds received and acknowledging every donor with a personal letter.

Church members and college students spent time with them in teaching American customs and culture. Members invited them into their homes and took them sightseeing.

At first, we asked for volunteers to provide driver education. They practiced on the Oklahoma Christian parking lot. Safety of everyone became an issue; therefore, I arranged with Central State University to give them instruction in their driver education program.

When the Roy Mullinax family received Thu from Singapore, she lived with them for a time. Accompanying Thu from Singapore is Dao Lien, known as Pien. Also, the Mullinax family aided Pien's brother and sister, Dao Nam and Dao Thuc My (May). Pien had a sponsor in the States; therefore, we offered to sponsor Nam and May; however, they decided to stay in Taiwan and attend college there because their brother living in Hong Kong provided some financial help. Mullinax praised the faithfulness of Nam and May; later they came and attended Oklahoma Christian.

At the request of the Khanh family, we sent sponsorship papers for Thu. Since she could not come under the refugee program, we sent money to buy her plane ticket to the U. S.

I had received several letters in the Vietnamese language, Bao began helping me with translations. One of these came from Sister Nguyen Thi Sam; she and five of her children had escaped Vietnam by boat and now lived in the Dodwell's Ridge Refugee Camp in Hong Kong. She did not know if any other family members made it out. However, before the fall of Saigon, she had given each of them my name and address and asked them to contact me if they made it out.

Sam felt a deep concern for her husband, Nguyen Tuyen. Since he served as a high ranking police officer in Saigon, Sam knew that he probably faced imprisonment and punishment under the new communist regime. During the week in which the communists took over Saigon, Sam's family tried to board ships headed out to sea; she felt deep concern in case the others did not make it out. Fearful that her letters had not been received, she sent an airmail letter every two or three days.

In Sam's letter, she included information about each family member that included his or her date of birth, their birthplace, and their Vietnamese ID number. As Bao translated the information for me, he said: "Two of her children, Vic and Tom, are already in Oklahoma City." Since Bao knew the family, I called and talked to Sam's son, Vic. I asked him: "Do you know Mrs. Nguyen Thi Sam?"

To which, he replied: "That's my mother. Do you know anything about her?"

When I told him that she made it to Hong Kong, Vic became quiet and I could hear the sobs of joy over the phone. I told Vic that five of his brothers and sisters lived with his mother in Hong Kong and that we planned to sponsor his family and help them get to the United States.

By now, the State Department had set up a locator service. I sent the names of Sam's family and asked for help in locating each one.

In an airmail letter to Sam, I told her what had been done and gave her the address of Vic and Tom, who stayed with a relative. I assured her that we would sponsor her family in their resettlement.

Immediately Sam replied: "We received your letter; this is the most important letter you sent for us. We are very happy and grateful you will help us. We don't have anyone familiar with us in the U. S. A." Then Sam quoted Jeremiah 33:3 in her letter: "Call to me and I will answer you and tell you great and unsearchable things you do not know." She went on to say, "When we were without hope and miserable, God opened for us a way and guides us to safety. We pray that God will be with you as you preach the Good News of Christ for every creature . . .

"We stay here in the camp with not enough food and physical things. But in our Spiritual life we have the opportunity to read the Bible every day and pray. Our Spiritual life has peace and strength . . . At last, we send a greeting to all brethren in His Church." Signed Nguyen Thi Sam

In response to brotherhood articles and Lemmons' editorial, offers for adopting a family came in from many churches. When I reviewed the offers, I felt the Broken Arrow Church of Christ in Broken Arrow, Oklahoma, made an offer that fit Sam and her family. They had an empty parsonage where the family could live and the congregation offered to furnish it. Also, they needed someone to clean and care for their church building. Many of their church members offered to provide for their necessities, teach English classes to the family, and assist them in adjusting to the public schools. I contacted them about adopting the Nguyen Thi Sam family.

Through the State Department's locator service and the Red Cross, we located all of Sam's family, except for one son, who did not escape. Her husband, Tuyen, lived in a refugee camp in Guam. During the week when Saigon fell, the family went out by heavily laden refugee boats–five different ways with none knowing if the remainder had successfully made their escape. Philip told me so many people got on his boat that its captain paid extra to a tugboat owner to pull the ship out of the harbor.

Nguyen Thuyen, the husband and father, became the next of Sam's family to arrive. We picked up his two sons living in Oklahoma City and the Broken Arrow church came for them to begin their new life in Broken Arrow.

It took us almost six months to get the family re-united. On Thanksgiving Day, 1975, the College church had a homecoming celebration for those who had escaped and were making their adjustments to their new life in the States. During this celebration, Nguyen Tuyen put on Christ in baptism. (Note. In Appendix B is the story of the other son and his family who came to the States 15 years after the fall.)

God blessed these families in their resettlement.

My goal was to get each family and individual in their own apartment by the middle of August. Since I would be teaching at Oklahoma Christian and classes would soon start, I needed to vacate the OC dorm and Lions' camp. All of the school-age children and the university students needed to be located so they could begin classes on schedule. I knew this to be a challenge but God blessed us with the resources to make this happen.

College church members immersed themselves in the resettlement efforts. They helped locate jobs and took the Vietnamese to those jobs until they could legally drive and get their own transportation; they helped find apartments or rental houses and showered these families with furniture and the necessities for setting up their own households.

Churches across America adopted Vietnamese families and stayed with them in their early adjustments to their new homeland.

Adjustments or transitions are never easy!

The distinct four seasons in Oklahoma caused many Vietnamese to eventually move to more moderate climates. Having been accustomed to a summer climate the year around, many had problems with our cold winters and hot summers. Also, job and educational opportunities caused many to relocate.

Through this experience I praised God and thought: "Because of the trauma of leaving their homeland behind them, I feel a sense of pride for the many who are making tremendous contributions to American society." Among those we sponsored, there are very successful businessmen and women, doctors, dentists, pharmacists, educators, engineers, information specialists, and church workers.

"I get the greatest satisfaction from the many who are rearing their children to love and serve Christ. But I could not forget those left behind in Vietnam? Did God forget them?"

Overcoming Tragedies with Triumphs—

"Making the Best of Trying Circumstances"

"The Lord is a refuge for the oppressed, a stronghold in times of trouble. (Psalms 9:9)" "The righteous man is rescued from trouble. . . .

(Proverbs 11:8a)"

What happened to the Saigon Church and those who did not make it out?

When Vietnam fell, I agonized over those who did not make it out. I felt distressed to think that God blessed only those who made it out safely. However, I discovered God's providence continued to work in lives left behind. I wondered and prayed for Nguyen Dang Minh who did not make it out.

This young man and I developed a close relationship through many shared experiences. Because of my inability with the Vietnamese language, I had to depend on interpreters and translators to help in my work when English could not be used. This made communication awkward at times.

Several small orphanages had been started. The different churches sponsoring these orphanages worked independently of my work. One of those congregations decided to combine some of their orphanages into a larger facility. This meant the family, who had housed some of these children, was no longer needed as house parents. Being the eldest in our mission, this family blamed me for losing their income. As a result, they asked to meet with some of our Christian brothers to discuss this decision. This family employed an interpreter. I asked an interpreter to assist me.

At the meeting, I explained that I had nothing to do with those changes and those concerned should communicate with the representative of the congregation, who made this decision. The conversation became heated. The interpreter representing the house parents made a statement in both English and Vietnamese. He said, "Please excuse me; I will not interpret for you because of your attitude." Then he walked out of the room. I followed and introduced myself to Nguyen Dang Ming; we exchanged information and addresses.

Ming made such a positive impression on me that I arranged to go to his home the next day. Ming spoke fluent English and served in the Vietnamese military as a translator. In addition, he studied at the university. This talented young man loved God and desired to follow Christ in every aspect of life.

He became one of my translators. Our friendship grew as we spent much time in discussing the Scriptures, life in Vietnam, the military situation, and life in general. Once I asked, "What do you see as the future for Vietnam?"

Ming's reply stunned me, "The future of Vietnam depends entirely on U. S. policy."

At that time I felt that, if this were the case, then Vietnam would enjoy a good future. As events developed, I came to realize how right Ming had been and how wrong I was about the future of Vietnam.

After we returned home from our first stint in Vietnam, the Vietnamese military sent Ming to the United States for additional training. While in the States, he came to visit us.

Kathy and Roger thought they should introduce Ming to some of the finer aspects of American life. They excitedly took him to an amusement park for a ride on a roller coaster. We watched them being strapped into their seats. Ming had a puzzled look on his face. Then off they went making all of the loops and dips.

When they got off the ride, Ming's puzzlement had changed to disbelief. As he approached Gladys and myself, he said, "What is the purpose of that!"

We all had a good laugh. Then I thought, Ming raised a good philosophical point. So often we go through the motions of life and never ask, "What is the purpose of whatever we are doing?"

Ming's desire to serve Christ and live the Christian life permeated his conversation and his dreams. Ming translated some of the most valuable Christian literature used in our mission.

After the fall of Vietnam in 1975, I continued to wonder what happened to him. Then I heard from a former teacher of Ming's living in Ho Chi Ming City, formerly Saigon. In my response to his teacher, I asked her to give our special greetings to Ming and his family and I requested his mailing address. When I received Ming's address, I wrote him a letter. As a result, I heard from Ming.

He wrote, "My wife and I were deeply moved as we read your letter together. Thank you so much, especially when we learned that we have still been in your prayers for so long and during such eventful times as the past ten years."

After asking about each family member, he kept the focus on my work and life. "Are you still teaching at Oklahoma Christian? How about your life serving the Lord, and how is the Church of Christ growing in Oklahoma?"

Then he raised the great longing in his heart: "Oh, how much I long for the freedom to worship and serve the Lord that you enjoy in the States?"

For months, I worried about the Christians and whatever happened to our church building. Ming brought me up to date with the shocking news about the Christians I worked with and the church building that I helped raise the funds to buy. "The Church of Christ at Suong Nguyet Anh has been closed and the property confiscated . . ."

Ming shared about his life under communism. He said, "I think you would now like to know what happened to my family and myself since we last met in Saigon in 1973 when we had our firstborn. Now we have three children–two daughters and one son. After the fall of Saigon government, I started a life of compulsory labor in various concentration camps, all of which kept me in jungles, leaving behind a jobless wife and two minor children of one and two years old. But surprisingly enough, we survived."

I've often wondered how one could survive under such conditions–harsh treatment, slave labor, unable to communicate with family, and without the support of Christian friends. His answer provided insight on how Scripture could help one who lived under the severest kinds of stress.

"All along the five years in the jungles, Psalm 118:17 kept shining in my mind: 'I shall not die, but live, and declare the works of the Lord.' Hunger, dangers, accidents, sickness, and 'divers of temptations' came to me as well as to my wife and children, but the Lord delivered us from all.

"We spiritually grew much more during the years of trouble than during those of peace. We came to know God more personally and experienced His goodness more richly."

Being robbed of some of the best years of his life with his family, only a Christian could look at this experience with a positive outlook. "Mr. and Mrs. Burcham, we never, never regret those years of suffering since we recognized how much God has trained us and taught us and showed us His boundless love and mercy.

"Since 1964, when I personally accepted Jesus, my greatest desire of wholly dedicating my life to serve Him has always been burning in my heart. Many times I attempted to go to a Theological Seminary but failed. I knew I needed training, but God has chosen to train me in His own way and not in the way I much desired.

"Seven years in the Army followed by five years in concentration camps, I was released in 1980. Eight months after my release my mother died of cancer. Oh, God's mercy was so great that He gave me the opportunity to be near, to comfort and care for my dear mother in her last months. Despite all the pain she suffered, she was much pleased to be going to be with the Lord.

"Now, the Theological Seminary in Nha Trang is closed and confiscated, and I have never had a day trained in such an institute. Yet, God gives me opportunities to share my faith among many groups of Christians. Little by little, I learned to serve in His special plan for me. However, I believe that preaching the Gospel is the greatest task of all, and I know I need more training. I hope some day the Lord will give me the chance to study His words systematically and efficiently to get ready for a new phase of my life."

Ming's brother worked for Bank of America in Saigon and the bank helped their employees to leave Vietnam before the fall. Some years later, he sponsored Ming and his family to come to the United States. Ming is fulfilling the Psalm that kept him alive during his years in concentration camps; he did not die and is now declaring the works of the Lord in radio messages in Vietnamese that are being broadcast by short-wave radio into his beloved homeland.

God's love and mercy abound even in the greatest struggles of life. The power of God's Word to sustain one undergoing the greatest struggles of life remains amazing. God be praised for the life of Nguyen Dang Ming, who looked to God for strength during his darkest hours, days, and months! The good news is that God delivered him from all of his troubles.

What I learned from my Vietnam mission experience?

Though the Vietnam War provided the background for all of our mission work, God used this to patiently teach me some of the critical lessons of life. The greatest lesson learned had to be a complete dependence on God through His Word and prayer. Maurice and Marie Hall put into my psyche that "God will provide." Over and over again we could see God working behind the scenes.

"Patience" is not a cultural quality of most Americans, certainly not mine; however, I came to appreciate this quality in Asians, particularly after reading Rudyard Kipling's poem: "It is not good for the Christian's health to hustle the Asian brown."

More than ever, I am convinced that the most significant war being waged is a spiritual battle for the souls of men. God is at work in His world to win souls to Himself.

But the enemy in this battle is Satan who is trying to convince every soul that "self" is our god. Therefore, selfishness reigns supreme. This could be seen as I walked down Saigon's Tu Do Street filled with bars and massage parlors. There some of the most attractive women in the world invited passers by in for a drink or to their massage parlor. How easy it is for young men to be drawn in for companionship at the bar or for sexual fulfillment only to find temporary gratification leaves one empty, guilty, and searching for real happiness.

But I witnessed first hand how American servicemen found real fulfillment by giving their lives to a higher cause. As I taught and baptized servicemen, they provided overwhelming evidence of the power of Jesus Christ in winning the battle for one's heart and soul.

Over and over again I saw servicemen use their time in Vietnam for constructive purposes. I am thankful for the vision of servicemen who first started the Churches of Christ in Vietnam. Servicemen became my mentor in mission work. In the beginning of our work, I do not think I could have survived without the advice and counsel of Captain Jim Hopkins. When I despaired over the loss of money for our radio work, Jim Reynolds came to my rescue by giving me Kipling's poem; and the teachers at the school, who lived on a subsistence salary, made up my loss.

When overwhelmed with work needing to be done or seemed impossible to accomplish, servicemen came to my rescue by keeping my typewriter hot from morning till night; thanks are inadequate for men like Paul Cook and Ralph Nichols. Personal encouragement came from Johnny Everett, Gary Simpson, and Fred Hall–our guardian angels during the Tet Offensive, and a host of others. Civilians working in Vietnam also provided tremendous support, such as Dennis Rush, Bob Fairless, and Fred Givens. Servicemen provided security information; thanks to Fred Givens, Johnny Everett, Jim Reynolds, Gary Simpson, and many others.

It is amazing how God used Maurice and Marie Hall in bringing together 13 very talented teachers and the rest of our mission team, who gave themselves fully to teaching in the American-Vietnamese International School. They influenced children from 13 nations by their teaching and by their example of a life in Christ. Many formed friendships and taught the Vietnamese the Gospel; Judy Colvin set the example for the teachers by the conversion of her five best friends. The teachers' loving friendship and their consistent encouragement helped me weather some of my greatest struggles. I will be forever grateful for Dick DiNucci who, after becoming a Christian, decided to resign his commission in the military and later join our mission team to teach in the Christian school. DiNucci's expertise with the Vietnamese language served our mission well.

Dennis Rush opened my heart to the plight of the orphans living on the street. To make an orphanage possible for these children, the Village Church of Christ in Oklahoma City accepted the challenge and made it a reality. However, it had to be the persistence of Ken Hobson, who obtained the support of the Village congregation and touched the hearts of many churches with the needs of these children. God used Jim Casey in reaching the proper Vietnamese officials for gaining authorization to operate an orphanage. However, from the orphans themselves I learned so much about the power of love to change the hopeless situation of boys and girls into the possibilities of a life in Christ.

In my opinion, no greater work in Vietnam approached what the servicemen at Cat Lai accomplished. They amazed me as they gave their time and resources, built an orphanage, provided health and dental care, and devoted their time and talents in the lives of orphaned boys and girls.

All over South Vietnam the servicemen invested their time and resources in reaching out to the lost, in providing medical care, in the building of schools, and by providing necessities for the "down and out." I will be forever grateful to Dr. Lanny Hunter, who served as a military doctor. He took a Montagnard boy, Y-Kim, taught him English, but, more important, taught him the gospel. Then Y-Kim worked with the Wycliff translators on the book of Mark in his native language of Rahde; eventually he prepared himself to be a more effective preacher in studies at the Philippine Bible College.

Those servicemen, who came for advice or counsel and made the supreme sacrifice, provided me with the greatest example of love for Jesus Christ and loyalty to their families and their beloved United States. I hold in highest esteem Captain Robert N. Bradley, Dan M. Dennis, William (Bill) Hall, and William E. Jerkins–all made that supreme sacrifice.

In addition, I appreciate more than ever those service men and women, who endure lifetime handicaps from war injuries. There must be a special crown for their caregivers, like Edna, the wife of Kenneth Reppart, who received brain damage. Edna will always be my hero because of the loving care she gave to Ken. From the early period after Ken's injuries, Edna coached him into reality and stayed by him during rehabilitation. After their marriage, Edna spent long days and nights helping Ken regain normalcy of life.

Tran Van Can continues to inspire me!

Time does not permit me to reflect on the accomplishments of all the Vietnamese sponsored by the College church, but I must hold up Tran Van Can, who befriended me in Vietnam, who helped me get into important government offices during our labors there, who provided advice and counsel, and who loved and encouraged me.

Words cannot express my appreciation for the friendship and faithfulness of Tran Van Can. Shortly after arriving in the United States, he got a job as counselor for refugees with the Oklahoma City Public Schools. In the evenings, he started translating religious materials for future mission work in Vietnam. He has written very valuable books in his native language. In addition, he has recorded over 800 sermons in Vietnamese that are broadcast daily by short wave into Vietnam. Born on August 19, 1914, he continues (in 2007) to work on his computer or record sermons most every day. When he learns of someone going to a place where Vietnamese resettled–many in foreign countries, he sends materials to be used by the missionary in reaching out to his people. No one has ever been more dedicated in evangelizing a lost world. I bask in the love and loyalty of this dedicated friend.

Of all the Vietnamese who escaped before the fall of Saigon, I will ever be thankful that my life crossed the path of Tran Van Can and that God allowed him safe passage to the United States.

God does move in mysterious ways that are beyond our comprehension!

Life is full of surprises! Beyond my wildest dreams, I could not imagine that a farm boy from southwest Oklahoma would have the opportunity to reach out with the good news of Christ to the people of war-torn Vietnam.

Our amazing Vietnam experience became possible by young people at Oklahoma Christian who dreamed of reaching a lost world for Jesus Christ. During their World Mission Workshop in 1963, God moved my heart for the plight of the lost of Vietnam. Truly, God led us to the Vietnam mission by missionaries at the workshop, Maurice and Marie Hall; through their loving nurture, encouragement, and recruitment, we answered the call. After arriving in Vietnam, I felt overwhelmed when they were recalled and I felt so inadequate to have a small part in carrying on the task. But Hall's final advice before leaving Vietnam that "God will provide" sustained me and opened to me a bigger view of how God does provide.

Oftentimes I felt left dangling out over a cliff with no visible rescue. Since I wanted to spend my time in reaching the lost, I resented the time and energy expended in keeping harmony within our team. But, as I immersed my life into the lives of the Vietnamese and American service men and women and our Christian teachers, I came to realize that God used them in calling me back to His purposes.

From our experiences, we witnessed over and over again how God, through His Word and His people, touched hearts and changed lives. When I reached the pit of despair, God brought someone into my life to help me keep my focus on His mission.

There is a great battle for the minds of men. Those who learn to trust in God and give their lives to Jesus Christ find a rich fulfillment for which every person yearns. Truly, God desires a relationship with every person in every nation around the world. His love and mercy reaches out and touches lives for eternity. But God relies on weak human messengers to proclaim the message of Jesus Christ as Savior and Lord. I am Exhibit A of how God is the one who empowers those messengers. Just as Jesus selected fishermen and tax collectors, not the religious establishment, to be Apostles, so God continues to empower men and women of faith in all walks of life to be His messengers today.

The hearts of men and women are the real treasure worth more than all the gold and diamonds in the world. My feeble efforts were bathed in prayer. God answered those prayers, not according to my desires, but according to His eternal purpose. I wanted passionately to return to Vietnam in 1975. I had made special plans; trained four talented young men; raised the funds; got all the shots, and the Vietnamese Christians had developed a strategy for reaching the lost. But God said "No" to those plans.

My heart sank as the northern provinces in South Vietnam started to fall. When the Vietnamese Christians asked me to help them escape, I felt this to be beyond anything possible from my limited perspective. My family and I had experienced the turmoil that war brings during our days in Saigon during the Tet Offensive. We experienced the goodness of God during our deliverance from the ravages of war. But how is it possible to help scores of my Vietnamese friends to experience deliverance? I had no political power and limited financial resources.

But God provided Bill Estep and Mac LeDoux, who were serving in Vietnam and had the courage to help many escape, even at the risk of their own lives. Estep and LeDoux will always be my heroes. God be praised for the greatest exodus of people in modern times. My prayers and those of many others had been answered in a most powerful way. Though I had planned to return to Vietnam with four young men to preach and teach, God had other plans and delivered the Vietnamese to our door.

Not many foreign missionaries ever have the opportunity to help most of an entire congregation relocate to America.

Members of the College Church of Christ, now Memorial Road Church of Christ, opened their hearts and became servants to those traumatized by the fall of their beloved country. To God belongs the praise for raising up such a congregation.

God's amazing grace and mercy became so visible in this great exodus and the resettlement of many of His followers to the land of freedom and opportunity. Yet, God continues to work in the lives of those left in Vietnam after the fall. I came to realize, it is during our toughest times, that we forge the richest friendships. Our relationship to God is forged into a deeper faith as He leads us through the fiery furnace of difficulties, struggles, and trials.

Yes, we experienced many challenges and tragedies but the victories and triumphs far outweigh the difficulties and struggles of life. It is God who empowers our feeble efforts; it is God who gives the victories. It is God who saves through His Son Jesus Christ. It is God who turns tragedies into triumphs. To God belong the praise and glory for any triumph. And the ultimate triumph is Eternal Life.

Appendix A

Tribute to a Missionary Wife–
Gladys Burcham, by Ona Belknap

A Christian home is a mere taste of "heaven on earth." As the members of the family fulfill their God-given roles, the fruit of the home will shine forth with the spirit of Christ into the darkness of hearts without God.

God has clearly defined the role of each member of the family. How influential a Christian home will be depends upon the ability of each member to understand his or her place and responsibilities in the home and the desire of each member to be totally committed to Christ and His will.

The happy home of Christians will find the husband leading, the wife assisting, and the children obeying both parents. (See Ephesians 5 and 6) Each role is important and each must be fulfilled if there is to be harmony and happiness in the home. The sanctity of the home must be carefully guarded. Every Christian must be alert to the dangers that are eroding family life in America.

Often foreign missionaries gain insights that give needed perspective into the problems facing Christians on the American scene. The experiences and impressions of a missionary serving abroad can be helpful to every Christian woman to gain insights into those qualities that make for a happy home. In the description of God's ideal woman in Proverbs 31, we see that she was a dedicated homemaker but all of her relationships were permeated by devotion to God. With this in mind, I would like to present Mrs. Gladys Burcham, who is serving with her husband in war-torn Vietnam.

When asked, "What was the major influence that prompted our going to Vietnam?" Gladys replied, "Ralph. It was his decision. Though I did not understand fully, I determined long ago to be his helper in serving Christ wherever he chose to serve. God has led us to Vietnam. Though our Christian metal has been tested to the 'inth' degree, there is no question but that God has been with us every day."

Gladys has a good understanding of the role of the Christian woman and tries diligently to live by Bible principles. Before leaving for Vietnam, Gladys taught a class for college women on this important subject. Her experiences in Vietnam have given her many new examples that she will use in lectures when returning to the States. Her guide is "She will comfort, encourage, and do him (her husband) only good as long as there is life within her. (Proverbs 31:12, AMP)"

When the Burchams made the decision to serve in Vietnam, many questioned their wisdom in leaving their home in Oklahoma City, their work at the College Church and at Oklahoma Christian, and their influence with hundreds of children in the summers at Camp Rock Creek, a Christian camp near Norman. It was soon evident that their influence was not ended when hundreds of friends gathered at the airport in Oklahoma City to see them off. Campers, counselors, students, and Christian friends have kept in constant contact with them during their first year in Vietnam. The Mayfair congregation in Oklahoma City had a special day of prayer on their behalf and the ladies in Mrs. Helen Wright's class have sent Gladys letters every week. Ladies from 12th and Drexel and the College Church have encouraged them regularly. Gladys once said, "With so many people praying for us, how can we fail in our service to God!"

Their example has provided courage for many. It is so easy to let material things possess us and Gladys has shown that it is possible to leave the conveniences of a comfortable home when service for God demands because the Burchams left the airport with only the things in their suitcases. The only items shipped were four boxes of books.

In arriving in Vietnam, the first order of business was to locate a house. "The Maurice Halls," writes Gladys, "were so helpful. If it had not been for them, I would have been hopelessly lost. Marie Hall spent days driving me around looking and bargaining for a place to stay. She was most helpful to the 13 missionaries who arrived with us. Marie had given herself unselfishly and had worked diligently for many weeks accumulating dishes, linens, and small appliances in order that everyone might set up housekeeping immediately.

"Because of impure water in Vietnam, there were many adjustments to make. Drinking water had to be boiled daily and filtered. Since there are no help-your-self laundries, and we do not have a washing machine, it was necessary to wash everything by hand just as women have had to do for centuries. Our home does not have hot water–cold showers are the order of the day. The electric power is frequently off because of shortages and our kerosene bill one month almost equaled the electric bill."

The Burchams have always shared their home with others. In their first year of married life, they had a foster girl, a German. Since that time, they have had three foster boys and one college student to live in their home for extended periods of time. Their home was always open to college students and their parents. This hospitality has continued in Vietnam. A Montagnard boy lived with them for several months. Their home is always open to servicemen, who come frequently–some almost daily; some of the men come just to visit, some for counseling, or some come just to get away from military routine for a while. Often men come out of the battlefields of Vietnam for a brief refresher. Gladys writes "our most trying moments have been the tragic news of a casualty of a serviceman who had been in our home just a short time before." The wife of one of these casualties wrote: "I want to thank you both for the pleasant day you gave to my husband. You were the only Christians he was to meet the four and half months he was there. He sent us two pictures of you and your home."

"She tastes and sees that her gain from work (with and for God) is good; her lamp goes not out; but it burns on continually through the night (of trouble, privation or sorrow, warning away fear, doubt and distrust. (Proverbs 31:18, AMP)"

Gladys enjoys cooking and the servicemen enjoy her pastries. One week she baked two recipes of cookies, six-dozen doughnuts, a large chocolate cake, a cherry pie, and two-dozen cupcakes. Every Wednesday afternoon she bakes several dozen cinnamon rolls that the servicemen and missionaries enjoy after the Wednesday evening service at the Saigon Church of Christ. It is rare indeed for them not to have guests at their table. "She looks well to how things go in her household, and the bread of idleness she will not eat. (Proverbs 31:27, AMP)"

Gladys packs a lot into every day. After breakfast and family devotions each morning, Roger and Kathy accompany her to school, where she teaches from 7:45 until 12:10. Her fourth and fifth graders love and appreciate daily Bible stories and singing. "Her children rise up and call her blessed; and her husband boasts of and praises her. (Proverbs 31:28, AMP)"

Some of the prominent people of Vietnam have children in her classes, including children of the Consul General of India, Military Attaché of Korea, Military Attaché of the Philippines, the Managers of Banks of Korea, Japan, and China, leading businessmen, and the Publisher and Editor of the Saigon Daily News–the leading English newspaper published in Vietnam.

At least two afternoons each week finds Gladys at the Saigon Church teaching Bibles classes. She has private Bible study sessions at home on Saturday mornings and Sunday afternoons.

Weekday afternoons and evenings are devoted to help Ralph keep up with the large volume of mail they receive. Clothing items for the orphans must be acknowledged and processed. A frequent highlight is a visit to the orphanage sponsored by the Village Church of Christ in Oklahoma City. She bakes cookies for the children or takes candy or gum sent from the States. In describing the children's day cele-brated recently at the orphanage, she writes: "We were invited out to our orphanage for lunch and to see the children. We had a real feast and Roger and Kathy had a toy that had been sent from the States for each of the kids. Of course, we had moon cake–everyone has moon cake on Children's Day, which is a national holiday of Vietnam.

Getting to cut it honored me. On top of the moon cake is a friendly dragon and Satan. The cake is a symbol of peace, but I wonder how many moon cakes it will take." The needs of Vietnamese orphaned children are great and Gladys has a real compassion and desire to help them. "She opens her hand to the poor; yes, she reaches out her filled hands to the needy (whether in body, mind, or spirit). (Proverbs 31:20, AMP)"

One of their friends from the College Church wrote: "We talked about all of you Burchams in Ladies' Class yesterday and used you as an example of how one Christian can inspire another to good works by her own commitment to Christ." It is hoped that these experiences of one committed to Christ will be an encouragement to every woman to strive a little harder to live up to the ideals of God's pattern that our homes may be truly Christ-centered.

"A capable, intelligent and virtuous woman, who is he who can find her? She is far more precious than jewels, and her value is far above rubies or pearls . . . Charm and grace are deceptive, and beauty is vain (because it is not lasting), but a woman who reverently and worshipfully fears the Lord, she shall be praised! (Proverbs 31:10,30, AMP)"

Appendix B

Sam's family experiences a surprise 15 years after the fall of Vietnam.

I am so very proud of the adjustments so many have made since coming to the United States after the fall of Vietnam. Time does not permit an update on all the families and individuals. But here is an example of one family who has been so faithful to the church.

Nguyen Thi Sam, who first made her escape to Hong Kong with five of her children; her family made their escape five different ways; none knew whether or not the others made it out. But through the State Department and the American Red Cross we were able to locate all but one son who did not escape. Eventually, we were able to sponsor her entire family with the Broken Arrow Church of Christ in Broken Arrow, Oklahoma. In an article in the **Broken Arrow Scout**, Roberta Parker wrote an article about a wonderful happening in the life of Sam's family when their son, who was left behind in Saigon, rejoined them. It is entitled *"Nguyens of Vietnam join family here."*

"Laughter, tears, and catching up on years of news until the wee hours of the morning–that's the scene in the home of Tuyen and Sam Nguyen for the past couple of weeks.

"Their eldest son has come home–home to America, home to Oklahoma, home to Broken Arrow–a land, state, and city he had never seen before and had held little hope of ever seeing!

"Giao Nguyen arrived at Tulsa International on June 14 (1990) and for the first time introduced his family to his parents and brothers and sisters.

"Since the Tuyen Nguyens escaped Vietnam 15 years ago during its fall to communism, their son has married and is the father of six children.

"In addition to hearing the news of the old country, the Nguyens are getting to know their daughter-in-law and their grandchildren.

"Nguyen Tuyen was a high ranking police officer in his home city at the time of the communist take-over. As a wanted man by the new regime, he knew that his escape must be swift.

"Afterwards he learned that communist soldiers with heavy military equipment came to his home to arrest him. Then, recently he found out that those of similar rank are just now being released from work camps deep in the jungle where the communists imprisoned them . . . and some aren't returning!

"During the take-over week, Tuyen, his wife and eight of their children went out to sea in heavily laden boats–in five different ways with none of the five groups knowing if the remainder had successfully made escape.

"Meanwhile in the United States, Ralph Burcham of Oklahoma Christian and a former missionary in Vietnam, had found a way to help several families escape, ones he had worked with in the country . . .

"Tuyen Nguyen, on Guam, read his wife's name on a paper and knew she was out of Vietnam.

"'That is a great little family,' says Burcham. 'They have good work ethics, are extremely intelligent, are very independent, and never want to impose.

"'It took about six months to get the family together and it was one of the most moving stories. On this end we could just imagine their feelings from the letters we were getting.'

"Burcham placed the many families he was serving with Churches of Christ across the country.

"The Nguyen family was picked up by the Broken Arrow Church of Christ 'almost as soon as the father landed in Oklahoma City,' says Burcham.

"Tuyen was united with his two sons in Oklahoma City and the three of them moved to Broken Arrow.

"Eventually Sam and the other children arrived. The Nguyens and six of their children were established in Broken Arrow while the two older sons remained in the Oklahoma City area...

"The six children who stayed in Broken Arrow learned to speak English; all graduated from the Broken Arrow High School and all earned college degrees...

"Andrea (Thinh) is a graduate of Oklahoma Christian and taught math in Moore before moving to California with her new husband recently. Vic holds an electrical engineering degree from OU and recently resigned a position in Oklahoma City to help his parents during his brother's move here.

"Philip, after completing his bachelor's at Oklahoma Christian, completed his doctorate at OU in chemical engineering and is employed at Halliburton Oil in Duncan.

"Tom completed high school in 1981 and served as student council president in Broken Arrow. He has a degree in computer science from Oklahoma Christian and did graduate work at OU."

When several major oil companies decided to negotiate for drilling rights off the Vietnam coast, Philip was selected to be the interpreter for the delegation. When he returned to Vietnam, he found it difficult to recognize once familiar sights.

More than their educational accomplishments, Nguyen Thi Sam is so grateful that all her children are faithful to Christ and are finding ways of serving Him. Sam will always be one of my heroes. She demonstrated her faith in the many struggles and trials she faced as Vietnam fell. Her diligence, her persistence, and her prayers God answered by delivering her family to the shores of freedom in the United States. May God continue to bless this family!

Appendix C

YOU are invited to walk the path that leads to Eternal Life[1] by Ralph Burcham

The Search for God

Man is constantly searching for meaning to life. In this search, he often turns to religion. He desires to know more about the supernatural. Is there a God? Can man know God? How does God reveal Himself to man? Where did man come from? What is the purpose of man's existence? What will happen to man after death? Is it possible for man to have eternal life?

---

[1]Note. This is the introduction to the Bible which our mission team placed in each copy given away since most recipients were totally unfamiliar with God's Word. On the cover page a free Bible Correspondence Course and literature were offered and included the location and mailing address of the church.

There is a void in the life of every man that demands fulfillment. Many seek this fulfillment in riches, in entertainment, in education, in drugs and alcohol, in following the pleasures of this life, or in the worship of man-made idols. Yet, many find these to be empty; and man is left with nothing to give meaning to his life.

The crucial issue basic to true religion is God, and whether or not we can possess knowledge of the true and living God. Yet, God has made Himself known to man through both general and special revelation.

The God of General Revelation

God is seen in the world He has created. "For since the creation of the world God's invisible qualities–his eternal power and divine nature–have been clearly seen, being understood from what has been made, so that men are without excuse." (Romans 1:20, NIV) "The heavens declare the glory of God; the skies proclaim the work of his hands. (Psalm 19:1, NIV)"

What characteristics of God do we see in His works? First, creation testifies that God is intelligent. Infinite variety and beauty speak of a wise intelligence. Then, the universe declares that its maker is a Being of power. And it shouts aloud of His glory.

The God of Special Revelation

Our knowledge of God would be inadequate if He had revealed Himself only through nature. However, the true and living God has made Himself known to man in a special way in history, in the Incarnation of Jesus Christ, in His revealed Word, and in His Son. God has promised that those who come to Him through His Son will have eternal life. (See John 17:3) God reveals Himself and His will for man in the Bible. The Bible teaches that God is triune: Father, Son and Holy Spirit. (See Matthew 28:19; II Corinthians 13:14) Not that there are three Gods, but three persons and one God. This is an important doctrine in the teachings of the Bible.

The God of the Bible is a God of metaphysical attributes. He is omniscient, knowing all; He is omnipresent, being everywhere.

346

(See Psalm 139; Jeremiah 23:24; Psalm 33:19) He is omnipotent, all-powerful. (See Matthew 19:26)

The God of the Bible is a just and righteous God. (See Romans 3:26) His law must be respected; the majesty of His government must be upheld. He holds men guilty in His sight who trample His law under their feet. (See Exodus 34:7)

Yet, the God of the Bible is a God of mercy. He desires man to repent of his evil ways and turn back to Him. He is just only when He has to be; he is always merciful when He can be. (See Exodus 34:7) He is only a God of severity toward those who reject Him, but also a God of goodness toward those who are obedient and have a contrite heart. (See Romans 11:22)

Also, the God of the Bible is a God of love. "For God so loved the world that he gave his one and only Son, that whoever believes in him shall not perish but have eternal life." (John 3:16, NIV) "Whoever does not love does not know God, because God is love." (I John 4:8, NIV) "How great is the love the Father has lavished on us, that we should be called children of God." (I John 3:1, NIV) God loves the world, yes, but he loves you as an individual. Jesus would have died for you if you had been the only sinner.

Man's Search for God Ends with the Bible

How grateful we should be for the true and living God. ". . . Holy and awesome is his name." (Psalm 111:9b, NIV) "Oh, the depth of the riches of the wisdom and knowledge of God! How unsearchable his judgments, and his paths beyond tracing out!" (Romans 11:33, NIV)

How thankful we should be that God has revealed Himself and that He has not left Himself without witness. (See Acts 14:17) We stand amazed as we see His power and wisdom reflected in the works of His hand. But how much more thankful we should be that He has revealed Himself in His Son and in His Word. It is through God's Word–the Bible –and His Son that we actually get acquainted with God, who is our Father and Creator. (See John 20:30,31)

Since we know God is just and righteous, we fear Him with reverence and awe. Because He is merciful, we rejoice. Because

He is love, we love Him. When we come to know God through His revealed Word and His Son, we are confident that He does all things well and that whatever He does is right. (See Genesis 18:25)

Another great evidence for the existence of God is the man whose life has been changed through the acceptance of Christ. God is the spiritual Father of those who accept His Son and follow His Word. Those who believe in Him and who know Him in the forgiveness of sins can testify that He is the greatest source of strength and victory that one can have in this life.

The God of the Bible Desires a Relationship with You

You are invited to walk the path that leads to eternal life. Eternal life is in Jesus Christ. (See I John 5:11,12) This Bible is presented to you because it has the power to change your life as you come to a fuller understanding of God, of His will for your life, of Jesus and His death on the cross for your sins, and of eternal life that is available in the resurrected Christ.

As you begin your study of the Bible, notice that it is divided into two parts: The Old Testament and the New Testament. The Old Testament begins with Genesis; the New Testament begins with Matthew. We are living in the New Testament period; yet, the Old Testament is most useful to aid us in our learning of God's dealings with man, to see the prophecies and their fulfillment, and to give us counsel or warnings. (See Romans 15:4; I Corinthians 10:11; II Timothy 3:16,17)

To begin your study of the Bible, here is an outline of key passages that will give you a basic "Framework of Christianity." It is suggested that you read and meditate on each Scripture. These Scriptures are easily located by using the Table of Contents. The name of the Book of the Bible will be given first; the number following the name of the Book is the chapter; the numbers after the chapter will be the verses.

May God bless your efforts as you begin your search for eternal life, which is available only to those who accept the Son of God and who follow in the path given in the Bible! "A crown of life" is promised to those who are faithful to Him until death. (See Revelation 2:10)

Introduction to the Bible[1]

God—What does the Bible tell us about God?

"In the beginning God . . ." begins the Bible as it reveals to us the Being who created the universe and all that is in it. God is the creator of all life. (Genesis 1 and 2) God is all-powerful, all-wise, and ever present. God is love. (I John 4:16-21) The most important thing we can learn about God is that He loves us and expresses this love in many ways. God is also righteous, which means that He can do no evil.

God is a personal God; that is, He is concerned about us as individuals and is able to give us individual love and attention. He would be near us. He would know us and love us as a father loves a child. He would have us know and love Him as intimately as children love their fathers. Truly, God created us for a purpose. (Acts 17:24-31)

Other attributes of God: He is holy, which means that He can do no evil. (I Peter 1:15-16) God is just, which means His judgments are fair and he shows no favoritism. He will render to every person according to one's deeds. (Romans 2:2,6,11) God is merciful, that means He desires to show mercy to those who have sinned against Him. (Romans 11:32)

---

[1]Note. This section contains *"A Framework of Christianity."* It answers the question: *"What must I do to be saved?"* It includes an outline of the basics of Christian faith that every person needs to hear.

God's Word—How do we get to know God?

To know God is the essence of religion. God has revealed Himself to us through the inspired pages of the Bible. (II Timothy 3:16,17; John 8:31,32; Hebrews 1:1-2)

Man—Why do we exist?

In the beginning God made us in His own image and breathed into us the breath of life, and we became a living soul. (Genesis 1:26-27; 2:7)

God loves us and desires a relationship with us. (I John l:1-5; 4:7-21) God created us free moral agents with the ability to make choices; however, the purpose for which we were created was to honor or glorify God. We could, therefore, find true happiness only to the degree that one was able to honor or glorify God. We could, therefore, find true happiness only to the degree that we are able to honor God in our life. We are at our best when we love and serve God.

Sin—What is sin? (Romans 1:18, 21-25a)

Each one is accountable to God and His judgment is according to truth. (Romans 14:12; 2:6-11) This relationship of love between God and His children was destroyed by something the Bible calls "sin." What is this "sin" which has separated us from God and brought despair and sorrow to both us and to God? Sin is defined in the context of the nature and personality of God. Sin is ungodliness. To be like God is to be godly. To be unlike God is to be ungodly. This may be illustrated simply: God is love; therefore God loves us. If we love each other, we are like God. If we hate each other, we are unlike God. Our hate is sin.

We must understand sin in this context and not be content to know merely that sin is "transgression of the law." The reason for the law is to reveal God, His nature and personality, His will for us. Thus breaking the law of God is wrong because it indicates we have fallen short of God's nature and personality. "For all have sinned and come short of the glory of God." (Romans 3:23) Sin is neither arbitrary nor illogical.

To sin is declared wrong because it is to be different from God. It brings the consequence of death because God and sin cannot co-exist and the sinner is thus separated from God as darkness must flee when light comes. We are created to live with and be sustained by God. When we are separated from God who is the source of life, we will die.

Sin entered the world by human choice; consequently, when any person sins, we separate ourselves from our Creator. (Romans 5:12) When we turn our back on God, God has no choice but to give us up. When we leave God out of our lives, sin becomes the ruling force and leads us into all kinds of evil and immorality. (Romans 1:24-32) Sin is the great chasm erected by us that separates us from our God. (Isaiah 59:2) When we sin, we do not possess the power within ourselves to return to God. We find ourselves in a helpless, hopeless state crying for a deliverer. Paul expressed this hopelessness with a declaration of despair: "What a wretched man I am! Who shall rescue me from this body of death?" (Romans 7:24)

In describing the former life of the Ephesians before becoming Christians, the Bible clearly pictures the life controlled by sin. (Ephesians 2:1-3)

Where does sin originate? The Scriptures show that sin originates in one's heart. (James 1:13-15) In the book of Galatians, we see the fruit of the sin-filled life. (Galatians 5:19-21)

Guilt—Who has sinned?

At sometime in life, every person becomes a sinner. Paul declares, "There is none righteous, no not one" and "all have sinned and come short of the glory of God." (Romans 3:9,10,23)

Penalty for Sin—Condemnation—What are the consequences of sin? (Isaiah 59:1-2; Romans 6:23)

God's justice demands that every one be punished for one's own sin. From the beginning, God's decree has been "the soul that sins, it shall die." (Ezekiel 18:4,20) "But every one shall die for his own sin . . ." (Jeremiah 31:30) In the letter to the Romans, Paul pictures the condemnation that comes to those who do evil. (Romans 1:18-32) Also, Paul reaffirms this condemnation of sinful people: "For the wages of sin is death." (Romans 6:23)

"Sin came into the world through one man, and his sin brought death with it. As a result, death spread to the whole human race, because all men sinned." (Romans 5:12, TEV)

Everyone needs to understand that we have sinned against God and that we are unable to cope with the "power" of sin apart from divine help. Only when we realize we are guilty of sin and under the just condemnation of God are we capable of understanding and appreciating the sacrifice made in order that we might be reconciled to God. Without Christ in our lives, we are groping in spiritual darkness and there is no hope of eternal life.

Christ's Sacrifice—The Meaning of the Atonement—Who is Christ? What is Christ like? What did Christ's death accomplish?

The problem of every human being then is to find a way back to God. We are unable to provide the way because we are powerless by sin. We are unworthy, helpless, lost. Since sin is the inevitable captor of the soul, every person is under the penalty of death. Justice demands death for the sinner, but God's love for us expresses itself in His mercy and grace that provide the Savior as a substitute for our death. Jesus Christ becomes the Savior.

Jesus existed as "The Word" from the beginning. He became flesh so that we could have a Savior. (John 1:1-3, 14) It was necessary that the Savior be both human and divine. As a human being He could understand temptation and human weakness and thus be a merciful and sympathetic high priest—and He could die in our place. As a divine being of infinite worth, His death could take care of the sins of the world. The cross is the atonement—the remedy for sin—the basis on which God can justly forgive the guilty sinner and set us free. (Romans 3:21-26) The cross is the product of the love and mercy of God; God's love and mercy are not based on any merit we possess.

What Christ's death accomplished for us is pointed out in many Scriptures. Isaiah remarkably foretold about seven centuries before Christ that Jesus would bear the punishment for our sins in order that we might be healed. (Isaiah 53:5-12)

The sacrifices offered under the Law of Moses were a faint outline of the perfect sacrifice Christ would make, but "the blood of bulls and goats can never take away sin." (Hebrews 10:4, TEV) The description of the blood sacrifices offered under the Law helps us to understand what Christ accomplished for us when He gave His blood. (Leviticus 17:11, RSV) Since the life of the flesh is in the blood, Christ gave His life when He shed His blood. He gave His life that we might have life. (See Hebrews 10:9,10,12) God's judgment against sin has been satisfied as Christ paid the penalty God's justice requires. Jesus Himself said: "This is my blood, which seals God's covenant, my blood poured out for many for the forgiveness of sins." (Matthew 26:28, TEV)

In one of the most loved passages of the Bible, John parallels Christ's death on the cross with the brazen serpent erected by Moses. When the children of Israel left Egypt and were in the wilderness, the people soon forgot the marvelous things God had done for them; they rebelled against God. God sent a plague of serpents; when they were bitten, they died. God instructed Moses to place the brazen serpent in the center of the camp. When an Israelite was bitten, he could look upon the serpent and be healed. (Numbers 21:5-9) Just so, sinful persons can look upon the lifted up Christ and receive healing. (John 3:14-17)

God's loving gift to us is His Son. Christ came to seek and save the lost. The sinless Christ took upon Himself our sins. (II Corinthians 5:15,17,18,21)

The only way we can receive spiritual healing is by accepting God's Son as "Christ himself carried our sins on his body to the cross, so that we might die to sin and live for righteousness. By his wounds you have been healed." (I Peter 2:24, TEV) It is through Christ that we are brought into a right relationship with God. (I Peter 3:18)

Truly Christ came to earth in human flesh and conquered the devil, sin, and death in the atonement made for our sins. (Hebrews 2:9,14-18) Because He suffered the temptations common to all, Jesus is able to plead our case before God. (Hebrews 4:15) "Salvation is to be found through him alone; for there is no one else in all the world, whose name God has given to men, by whom we can be saved." (Acts 4:12, TEV; also, see John 1:12,13; 12:32; 14:6)

Jesus saves then is Gospel—Good News or Glad Tidings. The total fact of Christ—His life, death, burial, resurrection, ascension, and mediation—is God's only saving resource.

The fact, the reality of the crucified, resurrected Savior is the drawing power to bring us to God. Each person needs to kneel at the cross and prayerfully declare, "Behold the Lamb of God, that takes away the sin of the world." (John 1:29)

Grace/Mercy—What is grace? What does God's grace mean to the sinner?

God's grace and mercy are based upon the atonement of Christ. Yes, the Good News of Christ portrays salvation as the gift God bestows upon us. The most precious of all gifts is based upon the sole merits of the sacrifice of His sinless Son on the cross; thus salvation is extended to us according to God's loving grace, or unmerited favor. God's righteous Judgment against sin has been met at the cross. (Romans 3:26; also, see Ephesians 2:4,5,8,9; Titus 3:3-7; Romans 5:21; John 3:16; Hebrews 2:9)

Faith—What is faith? How does one develop faith?

What is the proper response of the sinner to the cross? How can one appropriate the blessings made possible through the cross? What we must do to claim the Savior is not arbitrary or illogical. Our response is logically based on the nature of grace and the atonement. What response does the Savior call forth? He calls for faith or trust. Biblical faith or trust is the principle of depending on someone else to do what one cannot do for oneself. This is the principle by which we appropriate the Savior. It is naturally expressed in turning from sin and becoming one with the Savior in a new birth that is spiritual in nature.

This trust or faith comes as a natural result of having heard the Good News that Christ has offered up His life for our sins. (Romans 10:17) God is able to extend His loving grace because Christ has paid the price in full on the cross for the wages of our sins. (Romans 6:23) Since salvation is depicted in the gospel as the gift of God's loving grace through the merits of Christ, we cannot earn or deserve it, but only accept or receive it through faith. (Romans 4:25; 5:1,2)

Faith includes complete reliance and dependence—belief and trust—in Christ's power to save. Faith involves many responses. All of these responses we make in accepting the gift of salvation relate to Christ and Him crucified.

a. Repentance. What is it? Why is it necessary? God does not want anyone to perish but He wants everyone to turn away from sin. (II Peter 3:9) It is sin that separates us from God. Since all sin is committed against God, we must turn away from sin and look in faith to Jesus Christ. (Acts 2:38; 20:21; also, see Luke 24:45-47)

b. Confession. What is it? Why is it necessary? Confession must also reflect one's faith in Jesus Christ as a sin offering. The Christian confession is faith spoken—

a verbal expression from the heart of our belief and trust in Jesus power to save. (Romans 10:8-10)

When we have heard the Good News that "Christ bore his sins on the cross," a faith is produced in the Savior that demands public acknowledgment. When Christ is confessed before others, He has promised to confess us before the Father. (Matthew 10:32)

c. Baptism. What is it? What does it picture? Baptism is a spiritual expression of faith—an outward act that shows trust and reliance upon Jesus Christ for salvation. The sixth chapter of Romans shows that the sinner comes to the cross and dies. We die to a life of sin that is demonstrated by being buried in a watery grave. When we go down into the grave of baptism, the person is acting out one's repentance. The believer is showing to the world that he or she has died to sin. (Romans 6:3-11)

In baptism, as the embodiment of faith and repentance, union with Christ is affirmed—thus allowing a spiritual birth; for here the Christian is conceived. One is raised to a new life with Christ for the believer has put Him on. (Galatians 3:26,27) From the moment one has been brought into union with Christ, the believer has been reconciled to God and belongs to Jesus Christ. The world no longer has control over the Christian because we have been crucified to the world, have become free from the power of sin, and now belong to the Savior. The baptized believer is a new creation; the old person is dead and all is become new. (II Corinthians 5:17)

To the one who has accepted Christ by repentance and baptism, sin has no further claim on us for the penalty for sin has been paid; and its account completely settled through the merits of Christ.

Now the redeemed person has help in living the Christian life because the Spirit of Christ is living in our soul giving strength to live for the redeemer. (Acts 2:38; Romans 8:26,27)

The Holy Spirit aids the Christian by constantly representing us before God.

It is made quite clear in the following Scriptures that Christ is received by the sinner by faith embodied by repentance and baptism in order to receive the forgiveness of sins. (Acts 2:36-38; Colossians 2:12-14)

The Gospel reveals the wonderful truth that salvation is in Christ, by God's grace, through our faith. When we are convinced through the testimony of the Holy Spirit in the inspired, divine word that we are lost in sin and that the resurrected, living, reigning Son of God has all power to save through His blood shed on the cross, the sinner reaches out in trust, submissive faith. This faith is expressed in genuine repentance of sins and heart motivated baptism to accept and receive God's gift of salvation; we surrender our life without reservation to Christ. In thus relying on divine power, we reject any notion that we have the merit to deserve or earn salvation. There is no room for pride or boasting on our part. The believer has received salvation as the unmerited, undeserved gift of God, and we glory solely in the divine source of so great a gift. (Galatians 6:14)

Being Right with God—Justification—What does justification mean? Who has a right standing with God?

Death to sin is the only way anyone can be justified. Forgiveness comes as a result of our death to—and separation from—sin. The only reason we can escape the condemnation of sin is through the forgiveness, which is accomplished through a sharing in the death of Christ. When we are baptized, Christ's death effects the forgiveness of sin and justification and completes our separation from sin as Christ gives strength to live for Him.

When giving our life to Christ in trusting, obedient faith, we are then placed in a right relationship with God. We have been justified by the blood of Christ.

In Romans, Paul declares that fellowship with God is made possible through an acceptance of Jesus Christ. (Romans 5:1,2,6,8-11)

Living for God—Sanctification—What does God expect of His followers? What help does God provide through the Holy Spirit? How do we become a part of Christ's church? What is the significance of the church?

Not only does the gospel reveal Jesus Christ as the power of God to save from sin, but it also represents Him as the power to keep us saved. Christ sustains the Christian's life in His kingdom. The Gospel portrays the Christian life as the substitution of the Christ-life for the self-life, the Christ-will for the self-will, so that Christ's power becomes the Christian's power for fruitful, victorious living. (Galatians 2:20, 5:22-25; Romans 6:22; 8:1; 12:1,2; I John 3:22-24)

One of the best descriptions of the high ethical character God expects of His children can be found in the twelfth chapter of Romans.

The Church. God provides for our support needs in keeping us saved through Christ's church. Christ shed His blood for the church (Acts 20:28) and is the head of the church (Colossians 1:18). The church provides fellowship for those called out from sin to serve the living God. (Hebrews 10:23-25) This fellowship provides weekly worship, including singing, praying, partaking of the Lord's Supper in memory of Christ's death for our sins, giving, and learning more about God's word and His will for our lives. The church is essential in keeping us saved, in growing in service, and in reaching out to the lost.

The Goal of Living for God—Eternal Life—Glorification—What does the future hold for the Christian?

How wonderful it is to know that we can be victorious over death through the power of Jesus Christ! God has promised a wonderful victory if we commit our life to the care and keeping of God's beloved Son: "Your real life is Christ, and when he appears, then you too will appear with him and share in his glory!" (Colossians 3:4, TEV) The glories of Heaven are promised to those who are faithful to the Savior. (Romans 6:23; I Corinthians 15:50-58; I Thessalonians 4:13-18; Revelation 2:10; 21:3,4)

What about YOU?

Have you grasped the basic meaning of the cross, emotionally as well as intellectually? Can you say, "Christ died for me, personally, to deliver me from my sins and to bring me to God?" Do you have the power that only Christ can give for a life of sacrificial giving and loving, a life of devotion and service?

Have you accepted Christ, the sin offering? Have you accepted the gift of God's grace by coming to the cross? Do you believe in Jesus with a full trust for salvation? Have you repented of sins? Have you confessed before men your belief in Christ as the Son of God and your personal Savior? Have you been baptized into Christ for the remission of your sins? If you have done these things, you possess a message that our lost world needs to hear. You can help God fulfill His desire for all to be saved and to come to a knowledge of the truth.

The basic question that confronts each person is "Have I accepted the Christ?" For only in Christ can one have the hope of eternal life. "This, then, is the witness: God has given us eternal life, and this life is ours in his Son. Whoever has the Son has this life; whoever does not have the Son of God does not have life." (I John 5:11,12, TEV)

Printed in the United States
112949LV00005B/103-135/A